The **Dark Side** of the **Crescent Moon**

The **Dark Side** of the **Crescent Moon**

The Islamization of Europe and Its Impact on American/Russian Relations

Georgy Gounev

With a new epilogue by the author

Transaction Publishers

New Brunswick (U.S.A.) and London (U.K.)

Library of Congress Catalog Number: 2014009853
ISBN: 978–1-4128–5406–1
Printed in the United States of America

Library of Congress Cataloging-in-Publication Data

Gounev, Georgy.
    The dark side of the crescent moon: the Islamization of Europe and its impact on American/Russian relations / Georgy Gounev.
        pages cm
    ISBN 978–1-4128–5406–1
    1. Islamic countries—Relations—Europe. 2. Europe—Relations—Islamic countries. 3. Islam and world politics. 4. United States—Relations—Russia. 5. Russia—Relations—United States. 6. Islam—21st century. I. Title.
    DS35.74.E85G68 2015
    305.6'97094—dc23

                                                    2014009853

To Hristina, with deep gratitude for her constant support throughout the years.

Contents

Acknowledgments

This book would not have been published without all the support of my close friend and associate Pat English, who, in addition to her outstanding editing and research services, made possible my traveling to conduct interviews throughout Europe. In recognition of the magnitude of Ms. English's contribution, I dedicate this book to her.

This book is dedicated as well to the memory of Mona Mahmudnizhad, an Iranian woman who was brutally tortured. On June 18, 1983, she was hanged, together with nine other women who shared her Baha'i faith, in Adelabad prison, located in the city of Shiraz. The appeal for clemency by the president of the United States, Ronald Reagan, was ignored by the Islamo-totalitarians. At the time of her execution, Mona was just eighteen.

Dr. Milcho Lalkov was a chair of the Department of Balkan Studies at the University of Sofia, Bulgaria, and a close friend of mine. He saw the mortal danger for the civilization emanating from radical Islam much earlier than me. His untimely death was a heavy loss for Bulgarian science and culture. The book is also dedicated to the memory of Deniza Grozeva.

Acknowledgments

This book would not have been published without all the support of my close friend and associate Pat English, who, in addition to her outstanding editing and research services, made possible my traveling to conduct interviews throughout Europe. In recognition of the magnitude of Ms. English's contribution, I dedicate this book to her.

This book is dedicated as well to the memory of Mona Mahmudnizhad, an Iranian woman who was brutally tortured. On June 18, 1983, she was hanged, together with nine other women who shared her Baha'i faith, in Adelabad prison, located in the city of Shiraz. The appeal for clemency by the president of the United States, Ronald Reagan, was ignored by the Islamo-totalitarians. At the time of her execution, Mona was just eighteen.

Dr. Milcho Lalkov was a chair of the Department of Balkan Studies at the University of Sofia, Bulgaria, and a close friend of mine. He saw the mortal danger for the civilization emanating from radical Islam much earlier than me. His untimely death was a heavy loss for Bulgarian science and culture. The book is also dedicated to the memory of Deniza Grozeva.

Introduction

The Sunset of the Cold War and the Dawn of Radical Islam

There are two major challenges that historians and the political observers are encountering. The first one displays the lack of ability of the scholars and politicians to trace the birth and the first steps of some new and extremely important social and political trends. It would be enough to recall the fact that the world missed the first signs of the future triumphs of totalitarianism in its right-wing and left-wing versions. The second equally important failure of those who by trade are supposed to trace at least some of the main dimensions of the future dangers threatening mankind involves the lack of ability to predict either the beginning of the important trends or their end.

As far as the strategy that contributed to the end of communism is concerned, it is obvious that President Reagan realized the combined impact of the two factors as far back as 1982. It would be reasonable to assume that he saw his main task as far as the Afghan War was concerned was to provide all-out American support for the forces of resistance fighting the Soviet invaders. What President Reagan did not know and could not have suspected, together with the rest of the world, was that, as a matter of fact, the United States was rendering support to its future worst enemy.

Radical Islam matured in Afghanistan, but it was not born there. There is some confusion involving the very term "radical Islam." To start, the adherents of the extremist ideology would point out that there is no such phenomenon. According to them, there is one and only one true Islam, the purity of which they must defend.

It could be argued that a very important component of the ideology of radical Islam has emerged in the speeches and writings of Sayyid Abul Ala Maududi, who was one of the leading religious thinkers contributing to the Muslim revival on the territory of Colonial India.[1]

1

The main premise of Maududi's powerful message that had a tremendous impact over the minds of later generations of Islamic jihadists was his loud and clear proclamation that what mattered to him was not the national liberation of the Muslim countries and nations from the European colonial control. All that mattered to Maududi was the creation of Islamic states that strictly followed each of the requirements of the earliest period of Islamic history. The creation of such states will be only the first phase leading to the second one, the establishment of a Muslim domination over non-Muslim parts of the world. The justification for this ambitious goal has been Maududi's firm conviction that Islam is the only religion that acts in keeping with God's will, and, consequently, the elimination of all other "wrong" belief systems would be an action supported by God.

The fact that the entire Arab-Muslim world had been colonized by the theocratic Ottoman Empire, which was the only great Muslim (but not Arab) power, brought about a feeling of humiliation and hostility among the Arabs. At the same time, however, from an Arab-Muslim prospective, the dissolution of the Ottoman Empire in the aftermath of World War I meant that the Muslim world had been completely eliminated from any kind of participation in the global political process. It could be argued as well that the failure of the Muslim world to perform the process of modernization under European domination brought about the emergence of a religious-based attempt to establish a global Muslim identity designed to provide Muslims with the feeling of pride and belonging. Later, this concept was enriched with the formulation of a new goal that aimed to establish a model Muslim state much larger than the territories conquered by early Islam in the seventh and eighth centuries. According to contemporary Islamic extremist leaders and their followers, the Islamic theocratic state should include the entire continent of Europe.

The first phase in the development of radical Islam was connected with the creation in 1928 of an organization called the Muslim Brotherhood. Its founder was a religious thinker and charismatic leader by the name of Hassan al-Banna.[2] Al-Banna was born in 1906 in the small Egyptian city of Mahmudiyya into a family of an imam who graduated from the prestigious Al-Azhar University in Cairo. The boy developed an unusually early interest in religion and politics. He was twelve years old when he joined an Islamist order, and at thirteen he took part in an anti-British demonstration. He was only twenty-two when he created the Muslim Brotherhood. The incredible organizational and political talents of Hassan al-Banna brought about a stunning and completely unexpected development: on the eve of the outbreak of World War II, the membership of the Muslim Brotherhood reached half a million devotees.[3] The influence of the organization extended well beyond the borders of Egypt when the Brotherhood found followers in Syria, British Palestine, and Transjordan.

No author or scholar has failed to mention the Islamic fanaticism that marks the ideology of the Muslim Brotherhood. What remains far less understood is the startling similarity between the modern political Islam and the main concepts of German Nazism. In short, according to the program of the Brotherhood, the entire educational system of the country was to be put under the direct supervision of the Muslim clergy by subjugating the schools to the mosques. Very importantly, all political parties and organizations in Egypt were supposed to be banned as well.

The defeat of Nazi Germany brought about confusion within the ranks of the Muslim Brotherhood. Its influence started shrinking, and a real crisis erupted in the aftermath of the assassination of al-Banna, who died in 1948 from the bullets of government agents. Given the powerful surge of the secular socialist and nationalist appeal of an organization named the Young Officers, led by Colonel Gamal Abdel Nasser, many contemporaries reached the conclusion that the time of the Egyptian version of radical Islam had gone. They were very wrong.

It turned out that the ideas of the organization and the charisma of the slain leader had a much deeper impact over the hearts and minds of the new Muslim generation than the opinions expressed during the period of the long rule of Nasser. There is another interesting phenomenon: the times of the nationalistic, secular, socialist, and authoritarian model introduced by President Nasser are gone forever, while the Muslim Brotherhood's ideas that seemed to only fit the requirements of an extremist sect are flourishing today all over the world in a very dangerous way.

If we look for the main predecessor of the contemporary radical Islamists, undoubtedly this is a man who, at least at first glance, did not look like someone able to inspire the present-day jihadists. The name of this man was Sayyid Qutb, and his life was marked with bitterness, loneliness, suffering, and torture before his execution in 1966.

Nothing during the early periods of Sayyid Qutb's life suggested that one day he would become the main ideologue of the most extreme form of political Islam. At first glance, he was the most unlikely candidate to influence the minds of thousands of young men and women to the degree of transforming them into fanatical and suicidal murderers. The young Sayyid wanted to be a teacher, and in the pursuit of his dream, he became one. At this point in his life, although he was a deeply religious Muslim, he had a lot of respect for European civilization and technology, and he even liked America.

The deepest change in Qutb's life took place in the immediate aftermath of his three-year-long stay in the United States, between 1948 and 1951. The length of the stay had been determined by Qutb's status as one of the best educators ever employed by the Egyptian Ministry of Education. Already on American soil, Sayyid Qutb remained indifferent to the appeal of the multiparty system, uncensored press, and freedom of speech, or by the ability of the American political system to offer the coexistence of different national and religious groups living side-by-side in peace. All he saw in the United States was open and greedy materialism, drinking and alcoholism, and sinful (according to him) relationships between men and women.

Given the time frame and the specifics of the American period of his life, which was marked by the institutionalized racism of the pre–civil rights movement of the South, one would assume that a visitor coming from a semicolonial country would have expressed a lot of compassion for the victims of discrimination and segregation. Well, Qutb's record in this respect was more complicated. On one hand, the Egyptian visitor to the American South was shocked and outraged when he and a group of Egyptian students were denied access to a movie theater because the owner assumed they were black locals. When the students explained that they were Egyptian, he apologized and invited them to enjoy the movie.[4] Upon Qutb's insistence, the students rejected the offer. On the other hand, however, judging by his description of jazz music, Qutb obviously shared some of the most common racist stereotypes about black people: "The jazz music was created by Negroes to satisfy their love of noise and to wet their sexual desires."[5]

Having reached the conclusion that Western civilization is primitive, materialistic, hedonistic, and soulless, Qutb elevated his philosophical concept to the next level: human society should not be ruled by men, but by a theocratic leadership strictly following "God's will." The practical implementation of such a worldview means that the return to the values and the political-judicial system of early Islam offers not only the ultimate solution to the problems of the Muslim community but to the problems of the entire world as well.

Upon his return to Egypt, the bitter educator joined the Muslim Brotherhood and quickly became its most popular ideologist. Qutb paid the price for his beliefs when the organization clashed with the secularist and authoritarian regime of Nasser. Following an assassination attempt on the life of the dictator in 1954, Sayyid was arrested, tortured, and detained in horrifying conditions for several years. Very soon his fragile health was completely undermined, and the warden had him reassigned to the prison hospital. This move enabled Sayyid Qutb to complete his writings that currently serve as a jihadist bible. It was in the prison hospital where the indomitable detainee wrote his most famous book, *Milestones*.[6]

The main premise of *Milestones* is the deep conviction of its author that, for all practical purposes, in the middle of the twentieth century Islam was "extinct," the Muslim countries and societies were dominated by foreign powers, and the people were exploited and unhappy. The reason for this pitiful state of affairs, according to Sayyid Qutb, was because Muslims were calling themselves by this name but had abandoned the road to truth shown to them by the founder of their religion, and they did not follow the laws given to them by God: the sharia laws.

To make his point clear, Qutb invented a special term, *Jahiliyyah*, to describe the world that existed before Islam, which was, of course, a dark and pitiful place, according to the fanatical thinker. Qutb used the same term to describe the Muslims who, according to him, are Muslims in name only and who, by committing even the slightest deviation from any requirement or rule of Islam, have committed an act of deadly sin. Another very important component of Qutb's concept is his belief that there is an irreconcilable contradiction within Islam, which he believed propagated only one strictly defined political and judicial system. The following excerpt explains quite well Qutb's views: "Jahiliyyah, to whatever period it belongs, represents a deviation from the worship of the one and only Allah and the way of life prescribed by Allah. It derives its system, laws, regulations, habits, standards and values from a source other than Allah. . . . Islam cannot accept any mixing with Jahiliyyah. Either Islam will remain, or Jahiliyyah; no mixed situation is possible."[7]

In Sayyid Qutb's interpretation, the true Muslim should only follow God's will. The continuation of the logic behind this concept means that the Muslims should not recognize any form of secular authority that does not fit the religious requirements according to the political and judicial structures established back in the seventh century by Prophet Mohammed.

In Qutb's view, the awakening of Muslims to his powerful appeal for a return to the norms and values of early Islam would automatically remove all problems, and their lives would be filled with joy and satisfaction. There are two main components of Sayyid Qutb's views that are very important to the understanding of the ideology of the contemporary jihadists and radical Islamists. The first one is his absolute certitude that Islam is the only belief system whose God has a monopoly over the truth. Consequently, every other belief system and every other lifestyle are incompatible with Islam and, for this reason, are wrong.

Sayyid Qutb's thoughts explain in the clearest possible way the reasons why present-day radical Islamists are so ungrateful for everything Europe is offering them and, at the same time, so indifferent to European culture and laws. If we look at Europe through the lens of radical Islam as propagated by Sayyid Qutb, we see that there is no reason for any gratitude. It is the Europeans who must be grateful that representatives of the only true faith are giving them the chance to see its light. They are blind to this light but must one day convert to it because this is God's will. The only choice the Europeans will be offered is the way of acceptance of the right faith. In other words, the conversion will be performed the soft way or the hard way.

As far as European complaints about the lack of interest on the part of so many young Muslims toward all aspects of their culture, Qutb made it abundantly clear that every dimension of cultural, political, and social activity that is not inspired by the Muslim faith is not only worthless but outright harmful. He believed that the representatives of the other religions were engaged in conspiracies and evil deeds against Islam and the Muslims, and for this reason there could not be any option for peace and understanding with them. In Qutb's view, the Jews were particularly dangerous because they were engaged in a global conspiracy to concentrate the entire financial wealth of the world in their hands.

After being released in 1964 as a result of the intervention of the Iraqi president, Abdul Salam Aref, Qutb was rearrested in August of 1965. Later he was accused of participation in the Muslim Brotherhood's antigovernment conspiracy, and, together with five other leaders of the Brotherhood, he received the death sentence, which was carried out in August of 1966. Sayyid Qutb died bravely, after rejecting Colonel Nasser's offer to give up his ideas. In return, the crafty president of Egypt had contemplated offering his influential enemy some important position in his administration.[8]

It would be interesting to follow the events that took place after Qutb's execution from the prospective of the jihadist trends that developed within the framework of the Sunni and Shia branches of the Muslim religion. As far as the political expression of the Sunni version of radical Islam was concerned, although based upon the tenets of Wahhabism, born in the present-day territory of Saudi Arabia, it was Egypt that became the place where the ideas of jihadism received their current shape.

The first unexpected, surprising, and extremely powerful outbreak of the radical Islamist volcano did not take place in an Arab country. It was on January 30, 1979, when, arguably, the largest crowd ever assembled throughout human history extended the warmest possible welcome to a person who shared the visions and ideas of the executed Egyptian radical Islamist. Ayatollah Ruhollah Khomeini proclaimed the emergence of an Islamic republic that would be ruled in keeping with all the requirements of early Islam, and the crowd went berserk. In their defense, it must be pointed out that the people were applauding their dreams, not the realities of the theocratic totalitarian regime that they were about to encounter once the era of the enthusiastic greetings were over.

Too many authors and scholars tend to see the thirty-year regime ruling Iran as a structure born out of a religious and moral opposition to the dictatorial and oppressive regime of the shah. This explanation fits the politically correct image of the cleansing nature and power of the revolution. Its only fault is that it is not correct. Inside Iran, the Islamic control eliminated all forms and degrees of political and intellectual freedom that had existed under the shah. In the area of foreign policy, the regime was following the basic purpose of radical Islam, which was nothing less than the establishment of a global Muslim domination. What many commentators forget or ignore about Islamic Iran is that the spread of radical Islam and the support of every organization created by the Muslim opponents of Israel, and ipso facto of the United States, has been a constant feature of the foreign policy of Khomeini's regime.[9]

Strangely enough, the next major contributors to the emergence of an ideologically motivated, superbly armed, and well-trained military force inspired by the tenets of radical Islam were the main protagonists of the Cold War era: the United States of America and the Soviet Union. The large, poor, and underdeveloped country of Afghanistan became the site of the last Soviet-American confrontation and the birthplace of the new, world-threatening edition of radical Islam.

The Soviet invasion and occupation of Afghanistan was determined by three factors. The first was the Kremlin's intent to render support to the pro-Soviet regime established by the People's Democratic Party of Afghanistan (PDPA) in April of 1978. This regime was established in the aftermath of a coup d'état that ended with the murder of Prime Minister Mohammad Daoud Khan, along with the members of his family. In a way, PDPA was the first modern political party of Afghanistan. Its members were inspired by moderate to radical left-wing ideas that gradually moved it closer and closer to the official ideology of the Soviet Union. As a result, Moscow became the ally and protector of what has been a bit prematurely and solemnly called the "Afghan Revolution."

As a matter of fact, the PDPA could have claimed that its activities were directed toward agrarian reform, the elimination of feudal structures, and the end of the barbaric treatment and isolation of the women and could be described as an attempt to modernize Afghanistan. This aspect of the party's program made it popular among the young generation of educated Afghans. On the other hand, the secular ideology of the PDPA and its attempt to impose the power of the central government over the clannish and tribal countryside sparked a spontaneous and quickly growing resistance that finally threatened the very existence of the pro-Soviet regime. This situation was deeply aggravated by the division along ethnic and personal lines within the PDPA between the adherents of two factions led by Babrak Karmal and Hafisula Amin. Consequently, the first reason for the Soviet intervention was the salvation of this regime.

The second important Soviet concern was the effect of the Iranian revolution on the hearts and minds of the residents of the Central Asian "republics" of the Soviet Union who shared the religion, and in the case of Tajikistan even the language, of Iran. The growing Islam-inspired resistance to the pro-Soviet Afghan regime was adding a very dangerous dimension to an already existing threat.

The third impulse was a defensive one: Moscow was deeply worried by the increased presence of the American Navy around Iranian shores in connection with the growing conflict between the United States and Islamic Iran. Obviously, from Leonid Brezhnev's point of view, the establishment of direct Soviet control over the unstable Afghanistan was the best possible remedy against all those problems. This concept proved to be not just wrong but in many ways deadly for the very existence of the Soviet Union.

Every attempt to analyze American involvement in the Afghan War has to start at its beginning. Logic suggests that the United States' role in the conflict was determined by the Soviet invasion. One of the American experts even pointed out the time when the fateful decision was made—two weeks *after* the Soviet invasion.[10] This logic, at least theoretically, looks spotless: the American assistance to the mujahideen represented a response to the Soviet invasion. However, the truth about the American actions during that dramatic year of 1979 is very different.

Nineteen years later, the former national security adviser to President Carter, Zbigniew Brzezinski, gave an interview with the prestigious French magazine *Le Nouvel Observateur*. In the very beginning of the interview, Brzezinski made an important statement:

> According to the official version of history, the CIA aid to the Mujahedeen began during 1980, that is to say, after the Soviet army invaded Afghanistan—24 Dec. 1979. But the reality, secretly guarded until now, is completely different: Indeed, it was July 3, 1979, that President Carter signed the first directive for secret aid to the opponents of the pro-Soviet regime in Kabul. And that very day, I wrote a note to the president in which I explained to him that in my opinion this aid was going to induce a Soviet military intervention.[11]

Further in the interview, Brzezinski made clear that he did not regret the secret involvement of the United States in the Afghan War. He justified this by stating that because of the secret (at least in the beginning) American involvement, the Soviets were tempted to invade Afghanistan, which in the long run contributed to a large degree to the breakup of the Soviet Union.

One of Brzezinski's answers deserves to be quoted verbatim. In response to the question "Do you regret having supported the Islamic fundamentalists, and given them arms and advice to future terrorists?" Brzezinski responded, "What is most important to the history of the world—the Taliban or the collapse of the Soviet Empire—some stirred-up Moslems or the liberation of Central Europe and the end of the Cold War?"

> [Question] But it has been said and repeated: Islamic fundamentalism represents a world menace today.
>
> [Brzezinski] Nonsense. It is said that the West had a global policy in regard to Islam. That is stupid. There isn't a global Islam. Look at Islam in a rational manner and without demagoguery or emotion. It is the leading religion of the world with 1.5 billion followers. But what

9

is there in common among Saudi Arabian fundamentalism, moderate Morocco, Pakistan militarism, Egyptian pro-Western or Central Asian secularism? Nothing more than unites the Christian countries.[12]

Brzezinski's answers not only display an attitude bordering on arrogance that is typical of someone who is convinced that, on one hand, he knows everything and, on the other, that he is always right.

As a matter of fact, in this interview, the prominent scholar and diplomat was wrong on both points he was trying to make. First, the adherents of radical Islam are much more dangerous enemies of the United States than the absurd Warsaw Pact alliance consisting of the Soviet satellites and the superpower that deprived them of their freedom and independence. It is true that the Soviet Union was a military superpower that possessed a huge arsenal of deadly weapons. At the same time, however, the communist system was extremely unpopular with the majority of the people it dominated. During the last two or three decades of communism, even the majority of the members of the Communist Party had lost their faith in the system. That is why the system, which generations of Russians and Eastern Europeans believed in, crumbled so quickly.

On the other hand, radical Islam's strength is not connected with the possession of any of the attributes of the superpower's state organization. As a matter of fact, except for Iran and the Taliban-dominated Afghanistan at the end of the 1990s, radical Islam does not have a state organization. This makes its appeal and influence even more dangerous because the hatred- and fanaticism-filled Islamist message crosses every border with incredible speed. Most importantly, its propaganda is making a huge impact on large sections of the populations of all countries mentioned by Brzezinski as examples of diverse political systems.

The second mistake of the prominent politician and scholar is his equation of the politics of some governments in the Muslim world with the attitude and politics of their citizens. According to Dr. Brzezinski's thesis, states such as Saudi Arabia and Morocco are pro-Western because of the politics of their governments. At the same time, however, many citizens of those two countries are among the most devoted followers of the tenets of radical Islam. The ethnic composition of the suicidal and murderous team that shed the blood of 3,000 American citizens on 9/11 provides enough support for this argument.

Turning back to Afghanistan, it was on October 4, 1979, during a visit to East Germany, when in the course of a conversation with the

East German dictator Erich Honecker, Leonid Brezhnev gave the following assessment of the events in Afghanistan:

> The situation in the country has improved. . . . In some provinces, however, military encounters continue with hordes of rebels who receive direct and indirect support from Pakistan and direct support from the USA and from China. In addition, there are tensions within the Afghan leadership. . . . Frankly; we are not pleased by all of Amin's methods and actions. He is power-driven. In the past he repeatedly revealed disproportionate harshness. But with regard to his basic political platform, he has decidedly confirmed to the course of further development of the revolution, of furthering cooperation with the Soviet Union and other countries of the socialist community.[13]

Finally, against the advice of numerous Soviet experts on Afghanistan and the intelligence officers familiar with the region, on the very eve of the 1980 New Year, Brezhnev gave the green light to an all-out Soviet invasion of Afghanistan. The very first act of the invaders was to murder the man who allegedly "invited" them to invade his country—President Hafisula Amin. A Soviet military radio station pretending to be Radio Kabul, but actually beaming from Uzbekistan, lied to the world that President Amin had been executed by Afghan military personnel.[14] The change of guard in Kabul was performed with the unification of the PDPA, which had been bitterly divided along ethnic and personal lines in two wings led by Hafisula Amin and Babrak Karmal. Consequently, the Soviet leadership solved the problem by murdering Amin while bringing Karmal all the way from distant Prague where Amin had sent him as an ambassador.

The beginning of the military intervention in Afghanistan probably created the wrong impression among the Soviet leadership that the smooth start of the operation contained the promise for its successful ending as well. Against too many Western perceptions, the strictly military dimension of the Soviet invasion of Afghanistan had a limited objective that was supposed to be performed by a moderate fighting force for a limited period of time. The strategic goals of the Kremlin were the establishment of firm control over the capital city and a changing of the guard in Kabul to the point of making it functional and effective. The important additional Soviet objectives were related to the extensive training of the armed forces of the ruling regime in Kabul and the control over the communications between the Soviet border and the Afghan capital city.

In the Kremlin's view, this kind of military arrangement was supposed to provide the background for intense political activity by

Karmal's government aimed at winning the allegiance of at least some part of the Afghan population that would allow the regime to function in a less hostile environment. Those expectations were not about to be met. The situation continued to deteriorate because of the substantial increase of the spontaneous guerilla movement in the rural areas as a result of the emergence of six major resistance organizations whose support grew on a daily basis.

The outcome of the American presidential election in 1980 brought to power the administration of Ronald Reagan. The new leader quickly found out that the only geographical and political area of continuity with the policy of his predecessor was Soviet-occupied Afghanistan. Using the Afghan connection of the Pakistani intelligence service, all necessary arrangements were made to enable the different branches of American intelligence to establish contacts and make the necessary evaluations of the nature, size, and needs of the enemies of the Soviet occupation of the country. The CIA developed a special program (code named Cyclone) that was generously financed and strictly executed by the Reagan administration.[15]

Once the problem of establishing reliable contacts with the Afghan resistance was resolved, a very important dimension of the operation became the activity of the CIA Special Activities Division. This involved the training of the Afghani guerilla forces by American paramilitary experts. Following this period, a powerful stream of weaponry and supplies started reaching the detachments of the insurgents operating in the uncontrollable mountainous areas of Afghanistan. As early as November of 1982, a document prepared by the Defense Intelligence Agency (DIA) of the United States pointed out that

> All six major resistance groups appear to have adequate supplies of modern assault weapons and ammunition but still lack the heavier weaponry needed to turn the military situation in their favor. . . . The rugged terrain, limited manpower thus far available to Soviet/Afghan commanders, hostility of the local populace and the resourcefulness of the resistance argue against a successful effort to permanently close the passes.[16]

The gradually expanding American support for the Afghan guerilla movement escalated dramatically in the aftermath of CIA director William Casey's secret visit to the training camps established by his agency on Pakistani territory near the Afghan border.[17] Casey's Pakistani hosts were stunned when they heard that the high-level

American guest had a much more ambitious agenda than the expansion of homegrown resistance against the Soviet occupation of Afghanistan. What the stunned Pakistani listeners heard was Casey's idea to smuggle anti-Soviet propaganda materials through Afghanistan to the Muslim-populated Central Asian republics of the Soviet Union. Very soon, thousands of copies of the Koran and books depicting Soviet crimes against Islam committed during different periods were on their way to Soviet Central Asia.

Gradually, however, the attention of the American planners shifted entirely toward the support of the guerilla side of the Afghan battlefield. It could be successfully argued that the US backing of the mujahideen warriors occupied a central place in American foreign policy. As a matter of fact, the barely concealed US participation in the Afghan War quickly became the main content of the Reagan doctrine, the purpose of which was all-out American assistance to every enemy of the Soviet Union.

The entire enormous stream of weaponry, munitions, and every other possible brand of material assistance, plus the military training of the mujahideen, was reaching its destination through the services of the Pakistani Inter-Services Intelligence (ISI). The ISI was the Pakistani agency in charge of coordination of the transportation and distribution of the material and military support to the Afghan resistance arriving from the United States, Great Britain, Saudi Arabia, and China. During the period 1978 to 1992, the ISI trained over 100,000 insurgents. For the entire duration of the war, the assessments about material assistance received by the mujahideen vary between $3 billion and $20 billion.[18]

The Soviet military intervention in Afghanistan brought about very important consequences to which almost no one paid attention at the time. The dramatic conflict ravaging Afghanistan gave birth to a quick expansion of radical Islam—the ideology of the numerous volunteers from the Arab countries that flocked into Afghanistan to take part in the fight against the "infidel" occupiers of the Muslim country.

It would be an almost next-to-impossible task to determine who produced the first spark that started the Afghan-related outbreak of radical Islam and when and how. Beyond any doubt, however, there were two main factors that brought the Arab volunteers to Afghanistan.[19] The first manifested itself in the activities of the ISI. Some of the highest-ranking Pakistani recruiters had an additional agenda that for some reason evaded the attention of their American financiers. General Hameed Gul, for instance, who was the head of ISI for a while, left the following description of the ideology and the role of the Arab volunteers ready to fight the Soviet invaders of Afghanistan: "We are fighting a Jihad and this is the first Islamic International brigade in the modern era. The Communists have their international brigades, the West has NATO, why can't the Muslims unite and form a common front?"[20]

The Pakistani journalist Ahmed Rashid, who is one of the most knowledgeable experts on Afghanistan because of his numerous visits to the country over a long period of time, provides the following description of the emergence of the jihadist version of radical Islam:

> The United States was the main provider of arms to the Mujahedeen in the 1980s and then just walked away from the situation once the Soviets had completed their exit from Afghanistan in 1989. The whole issue of terrorism and the pressure of foreign mercenaries in Afghanistan is a result of American and Pakistani encouragement of radical Muslims in the 1980s to come to Afghanistan from all over the world and fight a jihad.[21]

It would be a mistake, however, to assume that the activities of the CIA and the ISI were the only reason for the emergence of the "Afghan Arabs" on the battlefields of Afghanistan. A very important role in recruiting young Arabs for a war effort designed to promote the cause of radical Islam was played by a fanatical, educated, and extremely influential Sunni Islamic scholar by the name of Abdullah Yusuf Azzam.[22]

Abdullah Yusuf Azzam was born in 1941 in the vicinity of the city of Jenin, which at that time was a part of the British Mandate of Palestine. Following his college years and a short teaching career in a small Jordanian village, Azzam joined the Sharia College of the University of Damascus, where he obtained his university degree in sharia. In the aftermath of the June War of 1967, Azzam joined the massive Palestinian exodus from the Israeli-occupied West Bank of the Jordan River and became involved with the Palestinian branch of the Muslim Brotherhood: the Palestine Liberation Organization (PLO).

Azzam took some part in PLO-sponsored anti-Israeli activities, but because he was a deeply religious person, he was disappointed by the Marxist and Soviet influence over the PLO. At this time, Azzam was already dreaming about an Islamist alternative to the secular strategy of the Palestinian movement.

An already bitter young man left Jordan to continue his education at the famous Al-Azhar University in Cairo. It was here where Azzam became acquainted with the ideas of Sayyid Qutb and where he met some of Qutb's followers, including the future al-Qaeda number two,

Dr. Ayman al-Zawahiri.[23] Azzam adopted some of the main ideas of Sayyid Qutb, primarily the one about the necessity to remove secular governments from power to create a theocratic Islamic state.

Upon obtaining his doctorate from Al-Azhar University, Abdullah Yusuf Azzam returned to Jordan, but his university career there had been terminated because of his extremist views. There was only one place for him to go, Saudi Arabia, where he took a teaching position at King Abdul Aziz University in Jeddah. At the same time, Osama bin Laden was one of the students, and this is probably where the two met for the first time.

The fundamentalist revolt that culminated in the seizure of the Grand Mosque of Mecca in November of 1979, somewhat inevitably, produced a climate of increased repression, and given the extremist views of Azzam, he had to leave the hospitable shores of Saudi Arabia. It was in Pakistan that he heard the news about the Soviet military intervention in Afghanistan.

The first reaction of Abdullah Yusuf Azzam to the shocking news was to issue a religious proclamation (fatwa) that pointed out the similarities between the Israeli occupation of the Palestinian land and the Soviet occupation of Afghanistan. According to Azzam, in both cases the primary responsibility of all Muslims in the world must be to unleash war against the occupiers of the Muslim lands and to kill as many of them as possible.

In the following months, Azzam unleashed a strenuous campaign directed at the recruitment of Muslim volunteers for the Afghan War and for their accommodations in the areas of Pakistan that bordered Afghanistan. The center of this activity became the city of Peshawar, located ten miles from the border. It was there where Osama bin Laden arrived after the end of his studies in Jeddah. The young Saudi multimillionaire provided the financing that allowed the expansion of the shelters and training camps for the volunteers. The scope of the activities of Azzam and their range increased with the expansion of the participation of the Muslim volunteers in the anti-Soviet guerilla movement on Afghan soil.

For clarification, many authors indiscriminately use the term "Afghan Arabs" as a term encompassing all foreign subjects that fought the Soviet Army together with the Afghan mujahideen. Because of Sheikh Azzam's organizational genius, his organization managed to recruit 16,000 to 20,000 volunteers from twenty countries, without counting the presence of Bosnians and Chechens.[24] The fact that the Arabs were the majority among the foreign guerillas does not provide any reason for the dismissal of the non-Arab component.

Sheikh Azzam divided his efforts between visits to guerilla detachments and negotiations with their leaders and traveling throughout the Middle East, Europe, and the United States, where he looked for volunteers and new sources of material or financial support. He lived long enough to see the withdrawal of the Soviet troops from Afghanistan, but he was murdered in 1989, at the end of the victorious period for the radical Islamists.

It is obvious that too many issues involving the birth of the jihadist version of radical Islam on Afghan soil are still waiting to be clarified. What is abundantly clear even now, however, is that there were American policymakers who, in their desire to inflict as much damage to the main enemy of the free world as possible, enabled the emergence of the jihadist version of radical Islam. With American financial and material assistance, the radical fanatics from the entire Muslim world were transported to the battlefields of Afghanistan after being trained and armed on Pakistani soil. There is a question often asked to justify the US support for the jihadists: wasn't it a moral duty for America to render assistance to the freedom fighters of Afghanistan? A logical follow-up question would be this: was it possible for the American politicians or intelligence officers to check the belief system of every mujahideen before deciding whether to train and arm him?

Obviously the correct answer is a negative one. This should be the third, and the last, question: given the already mentioned extenuating circumstances, what precisely is the mistake of the US politicians who unconditionally supported the armed resistance directed against the Soviet invaders? The plain truth is that back in 1989, both countries, Afghanistan and Pakistan, completely disappeared from the radar of official Washington in the immediate aftermath of the Soviet withdrawal from Afghanistan. It was a time when Washington did not care at all about the outcome of the last stage of the Afghan War that ended with a victory for the Taliban, which further reinforced the already existing bond between the jihadists.

We are not blessed with the knowledge that future historians will say about the current events. As far as the emergence of the radical Islamist threat, however, one of their conclusions is clearly visible even today; undoubtedly they will point out that in their desire to inflict as much harm as possible to its main adversary at the time, the American policymakers brought to life another enemy, which in many ways is far more dangerous than the one that had been defeated on the battlefields of Afghanistan.

Notes

1. About the life, times, and writings of Mawdidi, see R. Bonney, *Jihad: From Qur'an to Bin Laden* (Hampshire: Palgrave Macmillan, 2004).
2. See more about Hassan al-Banna in Trevor Stanley, "Hassan al-Banna: Founder of the Muslim Brotherhood, Ikwan al-Muslimum," *Perspectives on World History and Current Events*, 2005, www.pwhce.org/banna.html.
3. Hassan al-Banna, "Why Do the Muslims Fight?" in *Jihad in Modern Islamic Thought a Collection*, ed. Sheikh Abdullah Bin Muhammad Bin Humaid, www.majalla.org.
4. "Sayyid Qutb," *Wikipedia*, http://en.wikipedia.org/wiki/ Sayyid_Qutb.
5. Sayyid Qutb, *Milestones* (The Mother Mosque Foundation, 1981).
6. Sayyid Qutb, "The Right to Judge," http://islamworld.net/docs/justice.html.
7. Quoted from a brochure published in Bulgarian, most probably in the early 1980s, and distributed among the foreign students from the Muslim countries.
8. See the details in Robin Wright, *Sacred Age* (New York: Tough Stone, 2001), 35–40.
9. Alan J. Kuperman, "The Stinger Missile and US Intervention in Afghanistan," *Political Science Quarterly* 114, no 2 (June 1999).
10. Zbigniew Brzezinski, interview in *Le Nouvel Observateur* (January 15–21, 1998), 76, www.kersplebedeb.com/mystuff/s11/brzezinski.html.
11. Ibid.
12. The National Security Archive, "Afghanistan: Lessons from the Last War: The Soviet Experience in Afghanistan: Russian Documents and Memoirs," ed. Svetlana Savranskaya, October 9, 2001. "Document 5: Minutes of Conversation of General Secretary Brezhnev with Erich Honecker, October 4, 1979," www.gwu.edu/-nsarchive/NSAEBB/NSAEBB57/us.html.
13. Alexander Lyakhovskiy, "Inside the Soviet Invasion of Afghanistan and the Seizure of Kabul, December 1979," *Cold War International History Project: Working Paper #51* (Woodrow Wilson International Center for Scholars, January 2007).
14. Peter Schweitzer, *Victory: The Reagan Administration's Secret Strategy That Hastened the Collapse of the Soviet Union,* (New York: Atlantic Monthly Press, 1994).
15. Defense Intelligence Agency, Directorate for Research, "Subject: Afghan Resistance," November 5, 1982, http://www2.gwu.edu/⊠nsarchiv/NSAEBB/NSAEBB57/us3.pdf.
16. Steve Coll, "Anatomy of a Victory: CIA's Covert Afghan War," *Washington Post*, July 19, 1992.
17. Steve Coll, *The Secret History of the CIA, Afghanistan and Bin Laden, from the Soviet Invasion to September 10, 2001* (London: Penguin Books, 2004); Digital National Security Archive, "Afghanistan: The Making of US Policy, 1973–1990," http://nsarchive.chadwyck.com/afessayh.htm.
18. Coll, *The Secret History of the CIA, Afghanistan and Bin Laden, from the Soviet Invasion to September 10, 2001.*
19. Ahmed Rashid, interview in *Atlantic Monthly*, August 10, 2000, www.theatlantic.com/unbound/interviews/ba2000–08–09.html.

20. Ibid.
21. Ibid.
22. Chris Shellentrop, "Abdullah Azzam—The Godfather of Jihad," *Slate*, April 16, 2002, http://slate.msn.com/id/2064385.
23. Ibid.
24. Ibid.

1

The United States, the Soviet Union, and the Muslim World during World War II

Let's make this abundantly clear from the very beginning: the impression created by many American books and movies that World War II was fought and won mainly on the battlefields of Normandy and the Pacific is wrong. It was the Soviet Army that played the decisive role in the defeat of Nazi Germany during the war and made an important contribution to the Allied victory over Japan. At the same time, according to the most accomplished Soviet military leader, Marshall Zhukov, without American assistance within the framework of the Lend-Lease program, the victory of the Soviet Army would have been impossible.[1]

Unlike the situation in Russia, where the memories of the war still touch some raw nerves even after sixty-five years, except for the thinning group of veterans who fought the common enemy in the Pacific and Europe and professional historians, very few people in the United States care about the legacy of WWII. As far as the young generation of America is concerned, the history of the dramatic global conflict is as unknown to them as the historical background of the Greco-Persian Wars fought millenniums ago.

The answer to the question why the legacy of WWII is such an emotional issue in Russia and such a nonissue in the United States is simple: the Soviet Union lost 27 million people during the war, while the American losses were in the neighborhood of 300,000. There is something else though; ever since the times of Joseph Stalin, the official Soviet policy with regard to the legacy of the war has always been to keep the deep wound open. This practice was temporarily abandoned in the aftermath of the breakup of the Soviet Union, but it was recently renewed.

The celebration of every anniversary of WWII in Russia has two dimensions. The first one is the formal celebration of the Soviet victory that runs with the smoothness of a huge and carefully prepared military operation. It manifests itself in military parades proudly shown to the entire world and endless, repetitive articles, speeches, radio and TV broadcasts, and a lot of ceremonies around the monuments of the fallen defenders of the country.

Besides the official celebrations marked by the inevitable bureaucratic deadness, the anniversaries also have a deeply touching human dimension. Victory Day, May 9, is when the few remaining veterans get together to pay tribute to the countless multitudes of their fallen fellow warriors. At the end of those reunions, without paying any attention to the respectful looks of passersby, the veterans trade powerful hugs, knowing that this meeting could well be their last.

As for the locations of the veterans' meetings, they range from the foggy and often snow-covered northern port of Murmansk all the way to the balmy Mediterranean at Tel-Aviv. The people of Israel look with bewilderment at the small groups of white-haired people who proudly display the Soviet-era decorations earned on the deadly Eastern Front. These are the Jewish veterans of the Soviet Army who found their home in Israel and for whom May 9 is precisely as meaningful as it is for the participants in the reunions on Russian soil.

Remembering one of the best examples of ancient Rome's wisdom, stipulating that "to understand doesn't mean to justify," let's try to understand the attitude of the Russian leadership toward the history of WWII. There is absolutely no way to reconcile the artificially created positive image of the totalitarian Soviet Union with the historical truth.[2] There are Russian politicians who are not able to acknowledge that for thirty endless years their country was ruled by an individual who happened to be a fellow dictator and a former partner of Adolph Hitler. As if this part of the truth is not enough, another aspect of their dilemma is that Joseph Stalin managed to murder a much larger number of human beings than the Nazi Führer. A very important fact that is not well known is the Stalinist attempt to conceal the truth about Soviet politics before the Nazi aggression.

August 23, 1939—The History of an Extremely Dangerous Flirt

Maybe the most damaging piece of information for the contemporary Russian admirers of Joseph Stalin was provided by Joachim von Ribbentrop, the Nazi minister of foreign affairs, who in 1939 was twice honored as a guest of the Soviet dictator. Living in the shadow of the Nuremberg gallows, Ribbentrop made Stalin's expectations abundantly clear: "When I came to Moscow in 1939, Marshall Stalin didn't discuss with me the opportunities for a peaceful solution of the German-Polish conflict. . . . He was eager to make sure that if he doesn't get half of Poland and the Baltic countries. . . . I should immediately fly back to Germany."[3] The Soviet connection to the outbreak of WWII, however, has a long and complex history that climaxed in the successful Nazi-Soviet negotiations during the night of August 23–24, 1939.[4]

Before addressing the consequences of those negotiations, however, it would be quite interesting to briefly explore an alternative behavior of Joseph Stalin during that memorable August night in 1939. The question is what would have been the correct Soviet strategy during the negotiations with the Nazi foreign minister if, indeed, Joseph Stalin's goal had been the prevention of Nazi aggression, as some contemporary Russian politicians and historians are claiming.

The examination of this issue would lead the potential researcher to *only two* possibilities open to the Soviet dictator. The first one would have involved an outright rejection of the "peace initiative" of Adolph Hitler. The Soviet leader could have told the Nazi Führer's envoy, "Look, Mr. Ribbentrop, my government has only one purpose at this moment, and it is to prevent war. The way we see the situation is that Poland is not about to attack you, but rather Germany is preparing to attack Poland. Such action could provoke a British and French reaction that will transform your invasion of Poland into a global war threatening my country as well. We are in no position to tell you what to do, but if you attack Poland, you are on your own. As far as the Soviet Union is concerned, it will drastically escalate its preparation for every eventuality."

Had Joseph Stalin said those words to the Nazi foreign minister, at least as far as the fall of 1939 was concerned, the outbreak of WWII could have been prevented. Even an adventurer such as Adolph Hitler would have thought twice before attacking Poland with the probable involvement of Great Britain and France in the conflict while also facing an unpredictable Joseph Stalin in the east, who had just rejected his offer.

The second option the Soviet dictator had at his disposal would have required a combination of two important considerations. Under this scenario, besides preventing German aggression, it would have been possible for the Soviet Union to take advantage of the German invasion of Poland to occupy the eastern part of the country. Then Germany would have taken from Poland an area only large enough to provide a solid territorial continuity between Germany proper and the city of

Danzig (the formal reason for Hitler's aggression), while the Soviet Union would incorporate the eastern areas of the country. As a result of such an arrangement, Poland would have suffered a serious loss of both sovereignty and territory, but although substantially weakened, the country would have continued its uncertain existence by separating totalitarian giants full of mistrust for each other.

Such strategy would have provided bloodless gains for the Soviet Union, while at the same time it would have denied the dictators of Nazi Germany and the Soviet Union the opportunity to jump at each other's throats by not offering a common border between their countries. Those were the *only* two options open to Joseph Stalin that could have enabled him to effectively block the road for future Nazi aggression against the Soviet Union.

It is time to move from the area of what could have happened to the field of what actually happened. To put it bluntly, Hitler needed the war to achieve his dream of world domination. Joseph Stalin also needed that war. He was planning to sit on the fence while Nazi Germany and the Western democracies entered the war after the German attack on Poland. Then, remembering what happened at the end of WWI, the Soviet dictator hoped that "a revolutionary situation" would emerge that offered limitless opportunities for Soviet intervention at the most appropriate moment. In other words, what happened in Moscow in August of 1939 was nothing less than an act of coordination of a joint Nazi-Soviet strategy designed to kindle a fire that would burn the world for the next six, seemingly endless, years under the name of WWII.

However, what Joseph Stalin was unable to grasp was that by establishing a common border with Nazi Germany he had created a deadly danger for his own country. The most carefully hidden piece of truth about the Nazi-Soviet deal reached during the night of August 23–24, 1939, was that with the signing of the nefarious document, Joseph Stalin bears precisely the same amount of responsibility for the outbreak of WWII as his new friend, Adolph Hitler.[5]

One of the most important historical facts with regard to the early stages of the Nazi-Soviet relations was the Soviet contribution to the German military effort. The main components of this contribution manifested in the transformation of the northern Soviet ports (primarily Murmansk) into bases that catered to the needs of the German sea operations against Great Britain, the endless supply of raw materials that enabled the German conquest of Western Europe, and the placing of the huge Soviet propaganda machine at the service of the Nazi partners.[6]

One particularly odd event from the point of view of Stalinist historians is that the fuel for the German bombers that devastated London and wiped out Coventry was produced from Soviet oil. There was also an array of shocking joint activities conducted in Poland by them People's Commissariat of Internal affairs (NKVD) and the Gestapo. A rather obnoxious Nazi-Soviet mini-deal took place when Joseph Stalin handed a large group of German communists (political refugees in the Soviet Union) to the Gestapo. An even uglier adventure had been the shameful (and unsuccessful) Soviet aggression against tiny Finland, "given" to Joseph Stalin by his generous new ally, Adolph Hitler.

Meanwhile the clock of history mercilessly counted down each hour Joseph Stalin allegedly needed "to buy" from Adolph Hitler to prepare the defense of his country. When the Nazi Führer made his decision to invade the Soviet Union, the country was still completely unprepared for the incredible might and intensity of the upcoming assault. It was Joseph Stalin who bore the crushing burden of responsibility for the complete strategic surprise achieved by the enemy. The dictator had been completely deaf and blind to every sign of the approaching avalanche. His confusion reached its climax on the eve of the German invasion. Tempted to strike first, but not daring to assume the risk of such an attack, Joseph Stalin postponed the choice between offense and defense and failed to prepare his army for either of those strategies.

President Roosevelt's War

Franklin Delano Roosevelt and Adolph Hitler came to power in the same year, 1933—Hitler in January and Roosevelt in March. It was as early as April of that same year when, during a conversation with the ambassador of France, FDR quietly and in a matter-of-fact statement called Adolph Hitler "a mad man."[7] This episode never received proper attention and provides every reason for the conclusion that President Roosevelt was among a very limited number of politicians who grasped the very nature and magnitude of the threat created by Adolph Hitler. Six and a half years later, when the Nazi assault on Poland marked the beginning of WWII, CommentPresident Roosevelt saw with absolute clarity the danger emanating from the Nazi quest for global domination. At the same time however in the eyes of the public opinion of the country, it was just a distant conflict from the flames of which USA should be kept away.

Unlike the case of Joseph Stalin, the German invasion of the Soviet Union was one of the best bits of news President Roosevelt received for the duration of the war. He understood that the fate of the conflict would be determined on the Eastern Front, and with this consideration in mind, FDR decided to organize an unprecedented flow of material and military assistance to the Soviet Union. A month after the start of the German-Soviet War, Harry Hopkins, who was possibly the only individual who had the unconditional trust of the president, was negotiating in the Kremlin with Joseph Stalin.[8]

Because of his acting talents, Joseph Stalin managed to conceal from his erstwhile guest the calamity that had befallen the Soviet Union and to convince him of his best feelings with regard to President Roosevelt. Hopkins's report prompted the long string of telegrams FDR kept sending for years in which he begged the dictator to agree to a personal meeting.[9] There can be little doubt that the president had other important considerations involving the highly desirable Soviet participation in the war against Japan once the battle for Europe was over. To achieve this goal, Roosevelt was ready to grant American recognition of the "Soviet right" to dominate Eastern Europe.

Throughout the war years, the Roosevelt administration committed military and strategic gaffes that had far-reaching consequences. There can be little doubt that executing a large-scale landing operation on the French coastline was impossible in 1942. However, according to exhaustive British research, it would have been absolutely possible for an American and British landing force to launch the Normandy invasion a year earlier.[10] There would have been very important positive consequences from the earlier conduct of such an operation. It would have shortened the war and saved a great many human lives, including many thousands of Jewish lives because one of the conveniently forgotten facts of WWII history is that 1944 was the bloodiest year of the Holocaust. An earlier launch of the cross-channel invasion would have prevented the spread of bitterness among the Soviet population, who grew to share the opinion of their rulers that the Western Allies were dragging their feet while the Soviet Union was bleeding white.

The Mufti's War

As far as the Muslim world was concerned, WWII had a different impact on various regions and countries, and both the challenge and response were delivered along secular lines. The attitude of the residents of this world toward the belligerents also differed in many important ways. If we start with the easternmost extensions of the Muslim world, Dutch East Indies, (present-day Indonesia) and the Muslim part of the

Philippines, the reaction to the Japanese occupation and the resistance against it was delivered entirely along secular and nationalistic lines.

The situation in Northern Africa and the Middle East, however, was completely different. Given that in the aftermath of the WWI the Arab world and Iran were divided into French and British zones of influence and domination, the precipitous rise of Nazi Germany from the ruins of defeat, humiliation, and crisis caused a corresponding rise in German popularity.

There were three dimensions of the Nazi ideas that received a warm reception throughout the Arab world and Iran. The first one was the escalating conflict of Nazi Germany with France and Great Britain, who were considered oppressors by the majority of the population of the area. On the other hand, the crisis of the Western democracy during the Great Depression and the successful management of the economy by the totalitarian regime of Adolph Hitler produced an additional reason for the popularity of Nazi Germany. There was also the fierce anti-Semitism of the Führer that generated a lot of enthusiasm for the Nazi regime in the Arab world in general and in British Palestine in particular.

The situation in the area became very volatile after the end of WWI. With irresponsible promises made to the representatives of both components of the population of Palestine, the British politicians transformed the area into a ticking time bomb. In all fairness to them, as early as the mid-1930s, they openly admitted their mishandling of the Palestinian situation:

> In order to obtain Arab support in the War, the British Government promised the Sheriff of Mecca in 1915 that in the event of an Allied victory, the greater part of the Arab provinces of the Turkish Empire would become independent. The Arabs understood that Palestine would be included in their sphere of influence. In order to obtain the support of the Jewish community however, in 1917 the British Government issued the Balfour Declaration.
>
> The Jews understood that, if the experiment of establishing a Jewish National Home succeeded and a sufficient number of Jews went to Palestine, the National Home might develop in course of time into a Jewish State.[11]

The dynamics and the legacy of the conflict that to a certain degree inevitably broke out in Palestine between WWI and WWII have always been (and still are) objects of diametrically opposed interpretations. Undoubtedly, the escalation of the conflict between both communities involved the growing anti-Semitism among the Arab majority of Palestine propagated by the incendiary speeches of the Mufti of Jerusalem, Haj Amin al-Husseini. The growing Nazi influence over Arab nationalism and the leading role of the Mufti as a main propagandist of anti-Semitism throughout the Muslim world was a crucial factor during the entire period between 1921, when al-Husseini became the Mufti of Jerusalem, to 1948, when he lost the position.

According to a well-known expert on the problems of the Middle East, Matthias Kuntzel,

> The main achievement of Al-Husseini, the Mufti of Jerusalem, was to combine the Jew-hatred of ancient Islam with modern anti-Semitism into a new and persuasive rhetoric. I discovered a speech he gave in 1937 with the title, "Jewry and Islam." Here, he mixed modern anti-Semitism with the stories of very early Islam going back and forth from the 7th and the 20th centuries, and connecting both kinds of Jew-hatred. This was something new.[12]

Following his success in organizing large-scale anti-Jewish riots in Palestine during the 1930s, after the outbreak of the war, the Mufti established himself in Berlin. Adolph Hitler considered him such an important asset that even at the height of the battle for Moscow he found time on November 28, 1941, for a long conversation with the Arab cleric. The record of the conversation contains some interesting moments such as the following:

> 1. The Fuehrer stated that the fight will continue until the last traces of the Jewish-Communist-European hegemony have been obliterated. 2. In the course of this fight the German army would—at a time that cannot be specified but in any case in the clearly foreseeable future—reach the northern exit of Caucasus. 3. As soon as this breakthrough was made the Fuehrer would offer the world his final assurance that the hour for the liberation of the Arabs had struck. Thereafter, Germany's only remaining objective in the region would be limited to the annihilation of the Jews living under British protection in Arab lands.[13]

The years of the German exile turned out to be the busiest period of the indomitable cleric's life. Part of the Mufti's activities were connected with the organization of a very effective radio program beamed by Radio Berlin all over the Middle East. The popularity of those programs was immense. The future leader of the Iranian Revolution and the founder of the theocratic regime ruling Iran today, Ayatollah

Khomeini, remembered how in the company of some friends he listened on a regular basis to the broadcasts. Radio propaganda also became actively involved in a large-scale recruitment effort designed to bring Muslim volunteers into the SS detachments of the German Army.

The Mufti had been instrumental in the creation of two SS divisions entirely composed of Muslim residents of Albania and Bosnia. The divisions, Hanjar and Skenderbeg, took part in the German campaigns against the communist partisans and in the repressions against the civil population suspected of assisting the guerillas. The wartime activities of the Mufti and his role are well researched and documented.[14]

What should be mentioned in this connection is that the intensity of al-Husseini's anti-Semitism and the scope of his contribution to the Nazi war effort produced an emotional impact on most of the researchers and authors, which is easily explainable but does not make good history. For instance, the Mufti is credited with developments he did not have anything to do with. This trend appeared in the very beginning of the historiography devoted to the life and deeds of the Mufti marked by the appearance of a book written by a talented, competent, and prolific writer by the name of Joseph B. Schechtman titled *The Mufti and the Führer*, published in 1965 while the Mufti was still alive. Case in point, according to Schechtman, the fact that the Muslim population of the North Caucasus greeted the German troops as liberators was because of the Mufti's propaganda.[15] This claim, repeated by many authors and lecturers, is wrong. As a matter of fact, back in 1942, no one in Chechnya or Ingushetia had even heard of the Mufti. Let's not forget that as early as the last week of June 1941 all privately owned radios in the Soviet Union were confiscated by the authorities and only returned to their owners after the end of the war.

The Germans were greeted as liberators by the Chechens and Ingushes in the Caucasus and by the Tartars in the area of the Crimea Peninsula not because of the propaganda abilities of the Mufti of Jerusalem but because of the repressive politics of the Stalinist regime. Throughout the 1920s and 1930s, the communist government conducted a clearly defined antireligious assault on the Muslim religion as much as it did on the Christians. Consequently, during the war it collected the fruits of its own policies.

At the same time, however, it was true that the German command did not spare any effort to create a separate SS detachment composed of former Soviet prisoners of war with Muslim backgrounds. It was only the defeat of Nazi Germany that terminated the activities of the Mufti on German soil. In 1945, al-Husseini did not think about the extermination of the Jewish community of Palestine, but, rather, how to save his own life. During the spring of 1945, there were only two places on earth that offered a safe haven to Nazi criminals: South America and the Middle East. Naturally, the Mufti preferred to go to the area where he was born and still popular.

For the Israeli and Jewish biographers of the Mufti and for the majority of the experts on the Middle East in general, it is beyond any doubt that during the wartime period the top Arab cleric of the British mandated Palestine contributed in a very substantial way to the propaganda and military dimensions of the Nazi war effort. The magnitude of the Mufti's contribution to the Nazi cause has been denied by Norman Finkelstein. An author of Jewish descent whose family was affected by Nazi persecutions of the Jews, Finkelstein raises the following argument: "If the Mufti was such a pronounced war criminal, then why didn't the Israeli intelligence make him face justice the same way Eichmann faced it? All the more that for some time the Mufti was living openly in Lebanon?"[16]

What Finkelstein ignores is that maybe there were Israeli considerations not to increase the incredibly high tension in the Middle East by kidnapping someone who was very popular throughout the Arab world. Outside the area of the Middle East, the Mufti wartime actions in the early postwar period provoked a Yugoslav political and judicial démarche against him because of his role in the formation of the SS divisions in Bosnia and Kosovo. At the same time, there is no convincing proof that the Mufti traveled to any of the Nazi death camps to observe the practical implementation of the Holocaust.

What would the Palestinians think of all those issues? Given the fact that throughout my teaching career I had many Palestinian students, perhaps the best way for me to present the opposite point of view would be to make use of their collective opinion. Their studies were in the areas of history and journalism, and, more importantly, all of them were deeply interested in history and politics. With no exception, all of them firmly and sincerely believed that it was the Jewish and later the Israeli side to blame for the emergence and development of the Israeli-Palestinian conflict.

One of those students (the smartest and the most aggressive among them) added the argument that before the increased Jewish immigration to Palestine and the "Jewish grab" of the Palestinian land, there was no anti-Semitism in Palestine whatsoever. Encouraged by my silence, he slightly raised his voice while he asked me how I would have felt if a large-scale Turkish immigration had swept Bulgaria because the country was part of the Ottoman Empire for five centuries. He was also interested in what my attitude would have been with regard to Israel if I had been born in Palestine instead of Bulgaria. My answer was sincere: Yes, I would oppose a second edition of a Turkish invasion of Bulgaria based on "historic" arguments. Had I been a Palestinian, I told them, I would have been among the opponents of the Israeli occupation of the West Bank and Gaza.

The students (already collectively!) continued to drill me in search of my answer to what would have been my attitude had I been born in a Palestinian family that had lost its home during the war of 1948. The answer was not as difficult as they were assuming. On the one hand, I reminded them about the thousands of Jews living in the Arab countries who in 1948 were deprived of their homes. On the other hand, I pointed out that had I been a Palestinian whose family roots were located in the present-day territory of Israel, I would not have wasted my time with pipe dreams about the destruction of the Jewish state. I would rather have been involved in the activities aimed at the establishment of a Palestinian state. It was this statement that ended our conversation.

In a follow-up meeting, which I had frankly not expected to take place, I asked my Palestinian students what they thought about the connection between Arab anti-Semitism, as exemplified by the Mufti of Jerusalem, and the Mufti's wartime activities on German soil. The discussion about the legacy of the Mufti led us nowhere. The reason was the Holocaust. My argument that any leader who not only got involved in ferocious anti-Semitic propaganda in the middle of an ongoing genocide but who also recruited volunteers for the murderous SS detachments deserves severe condemnation just hung in the air.

To put it bluntly, there was no reaction whatsoever on the part of my listeners. The explanation for this lack of reaction is simultaneously both sad and simple: The Holocaust is a nonissue for the Arab world. As a matter of fact, the majority of Arabs are divided between the opinions that the Holocaust never took place or that it was Jewish propaganda that had been blown way out of proportion. Even more, by and large, the sympathies of the Arab world for Nazi Germany survived the war.

An extremely gifted Algerian writer by the name of Boualem Sansal, who lives in France and whose books are forbidden by the government of his native country, based the subject of his last novel, *The German Village*, on a set of real events.[17] About twenty-five years ago, while traveling across the Setif region of Algeria, Sansal found himself in a small town that definitely looked out of place when compared to the traditional surrounding areas.

The locals proudly explained to the intrigued writer that their city had benefited enormously from the generosity of one of the heroes of the Algerian War for Independence, who had contributed so much to the prosperity of the city. There is a small additional detail: the ruler of the city was a former SS officer and military adviser to the Egyptian Army who had been sent by Nasser to help the Algerian rebels against the French colonialists. He was a national hero of Algeria who had acquired Algerian citizenship and converted to Islam.

In one of his interviews, the writer shared an interesting observation: "I sensed that my interlocutors felt real admiration when they talked about the man's Nazi past. This didn't surprise me: the Hitler salute has always had its partisans in Algeria, like in many Arab and Muslim countries—and undoubtedly even more."[18]

Some Important Consequences of World War II for the Muslim World

One of the last acts of wartime British and American diplomacy took place in March of 1945 when on their way back from the notorious Yalta Conference, President Roosevelt and Prime Minister Churchill met King Saud.[19] Roosevelt met the Saudi ruler aboard the USS *Augusta*, anchored at the entrance of the Suez Canal, while the prime minister of Great Britain saw King Saud at one of the nearby hotels. Given the fabulous oil wealth of the Desert Kingdom, there was an obvious economic consideration for the leaders of two victorious powers of WWII to meet the little-known Saudi monarch. In addition to that, however, there was a very important consideration guiding Roosevelt and Churchill during the negotiations. They hoped to enlist the support of the respected custodian of the sacred cities of Mecca and Medina for the creation of a Jewish state in the territory of British-mandated Palestine.

The leaders motivated their concern with the cruel Nazi destruction of the European Jewish community and the necessity to provide a national home for the Jewish people. The king was very hostile to the idea, and he countered those suggestions with the argument that if the Germans had murdered the majority of the European Jews, then the Jewish national home should be created on German territory.[20] There was another component of the WWII legacy as far as the Muslim world was concerned, which unfortunately has been completely forgotten or ignored by the historians. What we are talking about is the fact that because of the efforts of the Mufti of Jerusalem, for the first time since the formal dissolution of the Islamic caliphate in 1924 by the creator of modern Turkey, Kemal Ataturk, Muslims from different countries had fought together within the ranks of an army inspired by totalitarian, antidemocratic and a ferociously anti-Semitic ideology.

Notes

1. For more details, see the outstanding work of the Russian scholar B. V. Sokolov, "The Role of the Lend-Lease in the Soviet Military Effort 1941–1945," http://:lib.ru/sokolov1/04/html.

2. For a detailed analysis of the current rehabilitation of Joseph Stalin, see Nina Khrushcheva. "Rehabilitating Stalin," www.worldpolicy.org/journal/articles/wpj05–2/khrushcheva.pdf.

3. I. Pavlova, "Search for the Truth about the Eve of the Second World War," an article from the anthology of articles devoted to the analysis of the concepts of Victor Suvorov in www.tapirr/ruhtml.

4. "Memorandum of the Conversation Held on the Night of August 23 to 24 between the Reich Minister and the Chairman of the Council of People's Commissars Molotov," *Nazi-Soviet Relations 1939–1941*, Documents from the Archives of the German Foreign Office, ed. Raymond James Sontag and James Stewart Bedie, Department of State, 1948, 72–76.

5. See the document containing Joseph Stalin's considerations on the eve of WWII that was discovered by the Russian historian T. Bushueva after the fall of communism: "Centr Hranenia Istoriko-Dokumentalnikh Kolekzii Osobi Archiv SSSR," f 7 Op 1, D 1223, published in the magazine *Novi Mir*, December 1994, Moscow, 230–237.

6. Igor Bunich, *The Tempest: The Bloody Games Played by the Dictators* (Moscow: Veche Publishing House, 2000), http://militera.lib.ru/research-bunich1/index.html.

7. Thomas R. Maddox, *The Years of Estrangement: The American Relations with the Soviet Union, 1933–1941* (Tallahassee, FL: Tallahassee University Press, 1980), 14.

8. See the record of the conversation between Joseph Stalin and Harry Hopkins in the Foreign Relations of the United States (FRUS), vol. 1 (Washington DC: Government Printing Office, 1941), 798–801.

9. *My Dear Mr Stalin: The Complete Correspondence between Franklin D. Roosevelt and Joseph V. Stalin,* edited with commentary by Susan Butler (New Haven, CT: Yale University Press, 2005).

10. John Grigg, *The Victory That Never Was* (London: Hill and Wang, 1980).

11. Series of League of Nations Publications VI. A. Mandates 1937.VI A.5 Palestine. Royal Commission on Palestine Report, www.mideastweb.org/peelmaps.htm.

12. Matthias Kuntzel, interview in *Democratiya*, no. 13, May 25, 2008, www.matthiaskuentzel.de.

13. "Hitler and the Mufti" (November 28, 1941), http://jewishvirtuallibraryre-source/Holocaust/hitq2.html.

14. Lukasz Hirsowicz, *The Third Reich and the Arab East*, (Toronto: Routledge and Kegan Paul, 1966); Philip Matar, "The Mufti of Jerusalem and the Politics of Palestine," *Middle East Journal* 42 (Spring 1988); E. A. Green, "Arabs and Nazis—Can It Be True?" *Midstream* (October 1994).

15. Joseph B. Schechtman, *The Mufti and the Fuehrer: The Rise and Fall of Haj el Amin, Thomas Yoseloff* (New York, 1965), p46.

16. Norman G. Finkelstein, *The Holocaust Industry* (London: Verso, 2003).

17. "A Thin Line Separating Islamism from Nazism?" An interview with Boualem Sensal, *Sunlit Uplands*, June 2008, www.sunlituplands.org/2008/06/thin-line-separating-islamism-from.html.

18. Ibid.

19. For the meetings of King Saud with Churchill and Roosevelt, see http://cambridge-forecast.wordpress.com/2009/01/13/fdr-meeting-with-saudi-king-ibn-saud.

20. Ibid.

2

The United States, the Soviet Union, and the Muslim World during the Cold War

As a matter of fact, it was George Orwell whose writer's and journalistic genius in addition to his knowledge of totalitarianism enabled him to introduce the unusual term "Cold War."[1] In Orwell's words,

> We may be heading not for a general breakdown but for an epoch as horribly stable as the slave empires of antiquity. James Burnham's theory had been much discussed, but few people had yet considered its ideological implications—that is the kind of world-view, the kind of beliefs, and the social structure that would probably prevail in a state which was at once unconquerable and in a permanent state of "Cold War" with its neighbors.[2]

This part of George Orwell's article contains two of the main features of the phenomenon that were destined to be covered by the term "Cold War." The first feature was the unexpected stability of the postwar system of international relations that Orwell predicted. The reality born out of the equilibrium of fear created by the introduction of a monstrous weapon able to deny the right to live even to the still unborn generations looked frightening to Orwell for a different reason. The author was afraid of the possibility of a tyranny lasting forever provided that war was not an option for its destruction. It was the postwar Soviet Union that in the eyes of Orwell was the unconquerable tyranny that had been deliberately kept by its rulers in a state of isolation and permanent "Cold War" with free countries.

Both the Soviet and American interpretations of the conflict missed an important point. Instead of providing a clear and convincing answer to the questions of who started a global conflict destined to replace the one that just had ended and why, most of its interpretations are based on the ideological preferences of those who made it. By the way, the so-called revisionist interpretations of the Cold War that emerged under the form of a left-wing reaction to the legacy of the Vietnam War are indistinguishable from the official Stalinist propaganda clichés about the Soviet-American conflict.

The Road to the Cold War

Going to the real events instead of their biased interpretations, we will see that the first important American decision maker who had to face the enormous postwar Soviet challenge was the president of the United States, Harry S. Truman. The Soviet-era totalitarian specula-tions about him were that it was Truman who started the Cold War by breaking the pattern of the harmonious American-Soviet relations that had existed under Roosevelt. The same thesis has not only been repeated and supported by American revisionist historians, but it has been transferred even in the post-Soviet era.[3]

James Carroll, for instance, in an article published as late as 2002, continues to claim that "Roosevelt's inclination to pursue cooperation with Moscow was replaced by Truman's apparent hunger for con-frontation."[4] What were his reasons for such a categorical conclusion? Mr. Carroll provides the following explanation: "On April 23, 1945, the new President met in Washington with Soviet Foreign Minister Molotov. The Russian had requested the meeting hoping to avoid 'differences of interpretation and possible complications' that would not have arisen if Roosevelt lived."[5] It was Molotov, however, who made the following statement: "What does the 'Cold War' mean? We were simply on the offensive. They became angry at us, of course, but we had to consolidate what we conquered."[6]

The most important consideration of Joseph Stalin for breaking his alliance with the democratic West was connected with the internal stability of his regime. Millions of Soviet citizens spent years beyond the borders of the Soviet Union, and even the countries ravaged by the war looked like a slice of paradise compared to the incredible misery of prewar Stalinist Russia. That is why countless numbers of Soviet citizens were murdered or traded Hitler's concentration camps for Stalin's as soon as the Stalinists got hold of them. The lasting global peace dreamed about so intensely by FDR would have represented a deadly threat to the Soviet totalitarian system, which needed an enemy and permanent isolation to survive. It was that particular need of the system and its creator that made the Cold War unavoidable.

There is a very important argument that for some reason has been constantly overlooked or ignored that should be brought to the attention of those American historians who succumbed to the temptations of BAFS, or "Blame America First Syndrome." As a matter of fact, this argument is extremely simple: if Joseph Stalin had acted in keeping with the provisions of the Yalta agreements, humankind most definitely would have been spared the saga of the Cold War. In other words, if the Soviet-occupied countries of Eastern Europe had received the same opportunity to determine their political future that had been offered by the American and the British military authorities to the voters of France, Italy, and Belgium, for instance, there would have been no tension between the East and the West and, consequently, no Soviet-American conflict.

The most important foreign policy factor for the outbreak of the Cold War was Joseph Stalin's view that the countries occupied by the Red Army were a legitimate Soviet acquisition. In addition, the dictator was contemplating an additional expansion of his sphere of influence at the expense of the sovereignty and the independence of Greece, Turkey, and Iran.

As early as the spring of 1945, even before the ink of Joseph Stalin's signature of the Yalta documents had dried, Dr. Georgy M. Dimitrov, the leader of the most popular Bulgarian political party, the Bulgarian Agrarian Union, was placed under house arrest. This "measure" was an obvious prelude to his murder.[7] The indomitable leader, however, was successful in making an unbelievably brave and risky escape. His secretary, a twenty-three-year-old woman, was arrested and forced to "admit" that Dr. Dimitrov had been involved in spying activities. The girl refused to sign the carefully prepared statement and was tortured to death in such a barbaric way that her ordeal attracted the attention of the British prime minister, Winston Churchill.[8] Meanwhile, the Department of State instructed the American envoy to Bulgaria, Maynard B. Barns, not to offer any protection to Dr. Dimitrov. Barns disobeyed the cowardly order and accepted the Agrarian leader into his personal residence, thus saving his life.[9]

It was also as early as 1945 when the Soviet Union made public its territorial pretensions toward Turkey.[10] The forcible establishment of totalitarian and pro-Soviet regimes in Bulgaria and Romania had been launched as early the fall of 1944. At the same time, the Communist parties of Western Europe, particularly strong in France and Italy during the first postwar years, had been ordered to adopt a strategy designed to increase their influence by organizing coalitions with the other parties on the left.[11]

From the very beginning of his presidency, while dealing with Joseph Stalin, President Truman was facing a completely different person from the nice and kind Uncle Joe who had been so dear to the heart of FDR. The Soviet challenge was growing and expanding: Central Europe, the Balkans, Turkey, Iran, and so on.

As a matter of fact, the strategy of the American side of the Cold War had been determined by the concepts developed by one single individual. His name was George Kennan—an American diplomat with rich firsthand experience with the Soviet Union. Facing the growing tension in the relationship between the former allies, on February 22, 1946, Kennan, who was stationed in Moscow at the time, sent a document that was unprecedented in American diplomatic history called "The Long Telegram."[12] A year later he provided details of the telegram in an article printed in the July 1947 issue of *Foreign Affairs*.[13] The main concept of this unusually long document could be explained with one single statement: facing a world divided between the spheres of influence of the United States and the Soviet Union, the best thing America could do would be to keep out of the Soviet-dominated areas while not allowing Soviet interference in the American zone of influence.

During the early period of the Cold War, it was Greece that had become the main battlefield between the superpowers. In 1946, the country was engulfed in a full-scale civil war. It was this conflict that gave birth to the Truman Doctrine, the main content of which was the readiness to provide military and economic aid to Greece to enable its government to win the brutal conflict ravaging the country.

At the same time, however, there was a rather "delicate" dimension of the Balkan strategy of the United States that for a variety of reasons remained outside the attention of the scholars. The situation in Bulgaria, the northern neighbor of Greece, represented a complete reverse of the problem the West was facing in Greece. Regardless of the communist dictatorship and the presence of a large Soviet occupational force, the Bulgarian Agrarian Union, under the inspirational leadership of Nikola Petkov, had been transformed into one of the most powerful and well-organized anticommunist political parties in Eastern Europe.

George Kennan had thought that the withdrawal of the Soviet troops from Bulgaria would eliminate the danger of a direct clash between the superpowers in the Balkans. It was abundantly clear, however, that Joseph Stalin would not remove his forces from Bulgaria before the elimination of the oppositional party commanding the support of 80 percent of the population. Having considered both interrelated events, the withdrawal of the Soviet troops from Bulgaria and the inevitable destruction of the Agrarian Union, Washington decided that the positive impact of the first one outweighed the negative consequences of the second one.

On February 5, 1947, however, Maynard B. Barnes sent the following memorandum to the Department of State: "Evidently Eastern Europe emerges as an area destined to be the Achilles heel of the Soviet Union and with this reason in mind, my recommendation is to do everything we could possibly do in this area in order to support the hopes and the morals of the truly democratic elements of Eastern Europe."[14]

Given that the concept expressed by Barnes was in stark contradiction with Kennan's containment design, he received the much unexpected and highly undesirable assignment as the US ambassador to Jordan. Barnes understood that this offer represented a nicer way to remove him from Bulgaria at a crucial time in the country's history and rejected the new position. In keeping with his predictions, the beginning of the withdrawal of the Soviet occupational troops from Bulgaria triggered the destruction of the country's democratic opposition.[15]

The Bulgarian Agrarian Union had been banned, and its active members were sent to the prisons and concentration camps. Its inspirational leader, Nikola Petkov, was arrested and brutally tortured. The passionate appeal of Barnes, who had requested to be sent to Bulgaria to try to save Petkov's life, had been coldly rejected by the State Department, and the execution by hanging took place on September 23, 1947.[16]

The most disturbing aspect of the sad and tragic Balkan saga was that, even from a purely practical point of view, the American abandonment of the Bulgarian democratic forces was not necessary. What must have been perfectly clear even sixty years ago was that Joseph Stalin could not have afforded to unleash a kind of "part-time" war in Greece that involved the direct participation of the Soviet troops stationed in Bulgaria. Consequently, the Balkan games with Moscow initiated by Kennan and dutifully played by the Department of State did not yield any positive results for the United States. At the time when Joseph Stalin continued to maintain the fire of the Greek civil war with the assistance of his Bulgarian, Albanian, and Yugoslavian cronies (before his break with Tito), the American diplomacy did not react to the massacre of the democratic and popular anticommunist opposition in Bulgaria, and the country sank for decades into totalitarian mud.

Beyond the slightest doubt, a long list of crimes and deficiencies could have been attached to the actions of the Soviet policymakers throughout the years of the Cold War, except for one: the Soviets never abandoned the people and causes that were serving their interests and purposes, which, unfortunately, could not be said about the American policymakers.

President Eisenhower, for instance, was so concerned about "the legitimate friendly environment" of the Soviet Union that he did not even object to the Soviet military intervention in Hungary in November of 1956. Nikita Khrushchev, however, did not even blink when he ordered the installment of the Soviet missiles in Cuba, where the deadly devices were greeted with totalitarian hospitality by Caudillo Castro. Regardless of the huge military and technological superiority of the United States, the Soviet leader gambled and won. Almost half a century later, the Castro brothers are still around, although withered like Komodo dragons.

A fact that should not be forgotten is that the main reason for the breakup of the Soviet Union was the complete neglect of even the most basic requirements of the economy. Otherwise, the Soviet Union was winning the Cold War. The difference between both rivals was that Moscow had a strategy that had been followed consistently at all levels. At the same time, all the United States was doing was to improvise ad hoc tactical responses to the powerful and permanent Soviet strategic challenge.

The Muslim World during the Cold War

The reaction to the end of WWII in the Middle East was completely different from the thoughts and emotions of the Europeans whose continent had been ravaged for years by the hurricane of death and destruction. Except for the battles of the North African campaign that took place primarily in the unpopulated desert areas of Libya, Tunisia, and Egypt, the Arab world was not affected by the whirlwind of war. This fact does not mean that the population of the region, or rather the majority of it, was indifferent to the outcome of the global conflict. To put it mildly, the antifascist atmosphere prevailing in Europe that in many ways influenced the political process of the continent did not exist in the Middle East. One of the American Office of Strategic Services (OSS) reports from June 1945 contains an interesting description of the mood in the Arab world with regard to the upcoming trials of the main Nazi war criminals. The conclusion of the American intelligence officers was that there was a strong opposition against the very idea of bringing them to justice.[17]

As a result, many Nazi war criminals found refuge not in South America, which has so often been described as the only and ultimate Nazi hideaway in an array of books and movies, but in the much friendlier countries of the Middle East, with Egypt and Syria being the friendliest. The reasons behind the shocking hospitality were in both cases ideologically motivated, and in the Syrian case military as well. As it turned out, many Nazi refugees were used in the capacity of commanding officers of the Syrian Army during the Arab attempt to prevent the creation of the State of Israel. The Nazi participation in the war was so prominent that, in April 1948, the Israeli command stipulated that "European Nazis should be delivered to the British military authorities."[18]

Speaking of the southbound Nazi criminals, after a short detention by the French authorities, the Mufti of Jerusalem was released, and in the spring of 1946, he made his triumphant return to the Middle East. A report of the OSS office in Cairo, dated June 1, 1946, quotes the statement of the founder of the Muslim Brotherhood, Hassan-al-Banna, in connection with the return of Amin al Husseini, for whom the Mufti was

> a hero who challenged an Empire and fought Zionism, with the help of Hitler and Germany. Germany and Hitler are gone, but Amin al Husseini will continue the struggle. . . . There must be a divine purpose behind the preservation of the life of this man, namely the defeat of Zionism. Amin! March on! God is with you! We are behind you! We are willing to sacrifice our necks for the cause. To death! Forward March.[19]

Evidently the Mufti had followed this advice because, during the period of 1946 to 1948, he became the main architect of an all-Arab coalition designed to prevent the creation of a Jewish state in the territory of Palestine. The story and the legacy of the Israeli War for Independence, as it is known in Israel, or "Nakbah," the Catastrophe, if we use the Palestinian term, represents a hotly disputed subject among the experts on history and politics of the Middle East.

Meanwhile, every step toward expanding cooperation between the United States and Israel was adding a new dose of anti-Americanism into the Arab world. Conversely, the anti-Semitic wave that seized the Soviet Union during the last years of Joseph Stalin's dictatorship and the establishment of a close relationship between the Soviet Union and Nasser's Egypt in the mid-1950s greatly improved the image of the Soviet Union throughout the Arab world.

When one starts reminiscing today over the global strategy of the superpowers and the Cold War they waged with such intensity for such a long time, inevitably, Orianna Falachi's million-dollar question comes to haunt us. What the remarkable Italian journalist and author did not understand was how did she, together with the rest of the world, manage to miss the first signs of the present-day jihadist assault on the rest of the world?

The same question asked by Orianna Falachi applies to the American and the Soviet leaders during the long years of the Cold War. For the average residents of the Soviet Union, the United States, and Europe, the Muslim world did not constitute any particular interest. The same attitude was marking the decision-making process and the strategy of the main protagonists of the Cold War. Even when the permanent confrontation of the Cold War was affecting a Muslim country, the religious factor marking the tradition or politics of this country was never examined. Orianna Falachi was right: the non-Muslim world was so bitterly divided that no one paid any attention to the Islam-related developments in the Muslim countries.

Still later, Brezhnev was opposing what he perceived as American aggression in Southeast Asia, while in Washington the policymakers of the Johnson and Nixon administration were firmly convinced that the establishment of communist North Vietnamese domination over South Vietnam would trigger a domino effect throughout most of Asia. As far as Afghanistan was concerned, neither Moscow nor Washington was able to predict or to act accordingly with regard to the danger of radical Islam.

In the Middle East, the Soviet bet was on Arab nationalism, which in its capacity as an ideology was secular, anticapitalist, anti-American, and socialist and served perfectly well the needs of the Soviet strategy in the area. The fact that the authoritarian, dictatorial, and nationalistic regimes that made their appearance on the political scene of the Middle East used to regard the local Communist parties as instruments of foreign influence did not bother Moscow at all. The Soviet leadership was coming into the power play in the Middle East by its generous offers of financial and military assistance, which were gratefully accepted by the Arab autocratic rulers who were anticommunists, but what mattered to the Soviet Union was that their attitudes were much more anti-American rather than anti-Soviet.

The Western reaction to the Soviet-supported secular and socialist branch of Arab nationalism expressed itself in a way that today could be looked at with a large amount of bitter irony. The policy followed by the United States and Great Britain in the Middle East during the Cold War era in the long-term turned out to be deadly from the point of view of Western civilization. The problem was that in their fear of losing the fight for the future of the Middle East, the American and British policymakers had extended their support to the reactionary forces of Islamism, whom they had wrongly considered as the best possible antidote against the challenges of their pro-Soviet secular foes.[20]

It was Great Britain that first got involved in the conflict with the secular and nationalistic forces of the region as early as the beginning of the 1950s. The British confrontation with Iran erupted in 1952 when Iran nationalized the Anglo-Iranian company, and Egypt nationalized the Suez Canal. Because of the presence of the Soviet factor and out of solidarity with its most reliable ally, the United States got involved in the British conflict with the secular, nationalistic, and socialist regimes of the Middle East. The intelligence agencies of both countries started working together to bring down the democratically elected government of Prime Minister Mossadegh in Iran. Even worse, as far as the situation in Egypt was concerned, the same agencies started looking for allies in their desire to unsettle the regime of President Nasser. Unfortunately, they found such allies in the face of the Muslim Brotherhood. From both the American and British prospective, the religion-based opposition in Egypt was the best instrument to bring down Nasser and the best possible barrier to the expansion of Soviet influence throughout the Middle East.

The policy based on this approach logically led Washington and London to the establishment of a close relationship with Saudi Arabia, which, of course, similar to its status today, was the most conservative state in the Arab world. From a British perspective, it was the coup d'état performed by the secular left-wing military against the ruling imam in Yemen that forged a real alliance between Great Britain and the Desert Kingdom. The fact that the new Yemeni regime received substantial Egyptian and indirect Soviet military and material support prompted a joint British-Saudi effort designed to help the Yemeni royalists waging guerilla warfare against the new rulers of the country. The conflict gradually escalated to the point where thousands of Egyptian soldiers fought on the side of the republicans, while the royalists received substantial military assistance from Great Britain.[21]

Crown Prince, later King, Faisal of Saudi Arabia decided to take advantage of the British and American support to undertake an initiative that greatly enhanced the advancement of the cause of radical Islam throughout the world. In 1962, under the tutelage of Crown Prince Faisal, an international Islamic conference took place in Mecca, which ended with the creation of an organization called the International Muslim League. Given that the league was put under the control of the high-level Wahhabi clergy, the organization sent missionaries to many countries, and they took advantage of the generous support of numerous Saudi religious foundations.

With this financial support, the league built mosques and religious schools to propagate Wahhabism. A very important factor for the quick spread of the ideas of political Islam was the Saudi use of the members of the Muslim Brotherhood who had been accepted as political refugees by the government of Saudi Arabia.[22] Many of them became actively involved in the activities of the league, and with Saudi financial support, some of the missionaries established themselves in Western Europe where they created all the necessary conditions for the massive brainwashing of the quickly growing number of Muslim immigrants arriving on the shores of the Old Continent.

Besides the American-British-Saudi axis that opposed secular Arab nationalism, the American and British policymakers initiated the Baghdad Pact. The organization was binding together Turkey, Iran, Iraq, and Great Britain against the background of powerful American support in case of any appearance of the Soviet-inspired threat. This kind of protection of the Western interests in the oil-rich region did not last for long though because of the elimination of the Iraqi membership in the Baghdad Pact.

Up to July 14, 1958, the Iraqi people had had every reason to look with optimism toward the future. Free of the conflicts and many of the problems plaguing the rest of the region, the pro-Western government of the country, under the nominal control of King Faysal (not to be confused with King Faisal of Saudi Arabia), in a quiet but effective way was leading the country toward economic prosperity while creating the ground for the emergence of a democratic political system. An Iraqi expatriate doctor expressed with a lot of sadness the opinion that pre-Baathist Iraq was combining the best features of the political systems of the main rivals of the Cold War era. According to him, every educated resident of Iraq in the early 1950s had the right and the opportunity to create his own business, just like everywhere else in the Western world. At the same time, however, the subjects of King Faysal were enjoying the benefits of free health care and education at a much higher level than in the communist countries. In addition to this almost idyllic situation, the secular Iraqi structure was offering equal opportunities to career-minded Iraqis without regard to their ethnic belonging or religious orientation. The Shia, the Sunni and the Kurds were represented in the government institutions of old Iraq.

Unlike the case with Iran and its clashes with the British-Iranian oil company, and similarly to the case with Saudi Arabia, in 1952 the Iraqi government was successful in reaching a fair agreement with the foreign developers of the Iraqi oil deposits by splitting the profits with them in an equitable manner. As a result, the Iraqi government was able to devote substantial financial resources to the development of infrastructure, education, and health-related services. This peaceful reality that was providing all the necessary conditions for progress and modernization ended on July 14, 1958, when a group of Iraqi officers, influenced by Nasser's nationalist and socialist ideology, organized and performed a successful coup d'état. King Faysal and the members of his family were murdered. The democratic trend in the Iraqi development was terminated, and for many future decades, the population of Iraq led an uncertain existence under increasingly cruel dictatorships.

Embroiled in their global conflict, the leaders of the rivaling super-powers were surprised by the rapid development of a huge crisis in the Middle East that culminated in the Six Day War of June 1967. No other event since the end of WWI has changed the map, the relationships, and the rivalries in the area so dramatically as the War of 1967. As a rule, the analysis of numerous scholars and authors who tried to describe the dramatic confrontation and its aftermath tended to concentrate on the territorial changes that marked the map of the Middle East after the war and their impact over the politics of the belligerents. Very few of them, however, managed to grasp the most important consequence of the Six Day War—that the Israeli victory had inflicted a mortal blow upon the secular and socialist version of Arab nationalism.

One of the best representatives of this minority is the Israeli American historian and diplomat Michael B. Oren, who wrote one of the most compelling histories of the war.[23] In an interview printed as an appendix to his remarkable book, Michael Oren made the following observation:

> Of great political changes brought by the 1967 war, few were as traumatic and as momentous as the collapse of Nasserism. . . . Egypt's

defeat opened the door to new and compelling ideologies in the Middle East. Palestinian nationalism rose to the fore, and the PLO under the leadership of Yasser Arafat became a dominant force in Arab politics. More influential still was the rise of Islamic extremism, which also sought to unify the Arab world, albeit as part of a global Islamic nation, on the basis of a common Muslim identity.[24]

The massive change of heart that took place within the hearts and minds of the residents of the Arab world was determined primarily by the outcome of the wars that ravaged the area in 1948, 1956, and 1967. The crushing defeat suffered by the Arab countries inflicted an extremely painful blow upon the self-esteem of the Arab world. It was the same event that marked the end of the socialist and secularist brands of Arab nationalism. The living symbol of both trends, Gamal Abdel Nasser, never recovered from the humiliating defeat that brought about his premature death in 1970, at the early age of 52. It could be argued that the death of the founder of the Arab version of secular socialism was followed by the defeat of his ideas as well. The radical Islamic dream propagated by the severely persecuted, banned, and seemingly smashed by the merciless Nasserist repression Muslim Brotherhood suddenly became popular again. The questions that were tormenting the minds of many Egyptians were at the same time simple, logical, and very painful: What was wrong with the Arab countries? What was the reason for the multiple defeats, each one larger and more humiliating than the preceding one?

Maybe the road chosen by Nasser had been a wrong one. Maybe the radical Islamists were right after all in their claim that the Arabs were successful and victorious only when they followed all the requirements of their religion. Evidently, the affirmative answer to the last question has been provided by a number of individuals large enough to breathe new winds into the sails of the ship of radical Islam. Embroiled in the rhetoric and conflicts of the Cold War that stretched into five decades, the world missed an extremely important episode demonstrating just how successful the radical Islamists were in implanting the seeds of a future confrontation that would be much more dangerous than the American-Soviet rivalry.

The episode in question took place in 1982, but the details became known much later. On November 7, 2001, while the ruins of the Twin Towers were still smoldering, with prompting by the FBI, the Swiss police raided a luxurious villa in the outskirts of Lugano. The owner of the villa, Youssef Nada, was the president of Al-Taqwa Bank in

Lugano and de facto the main financial expert of the international Muslim Brotherhood movement. The most interesting finding of the raid though was not the evidence of the financial transactions that the FBI was after, but rather a fourteen-page document written in Arabic.[25] The translation and the analysis of the unusual finding revealed that the document represented a memorandum created a quarter of century earlier on the eve of a secret meeting of leading members of the Muslim Brotherhood (already well-established on European soil) created in the aftermath of a meeting of radical Islamists that took place in 1982. The memorandum outlined the strategy that has to be implemented by radical Islamist organizations to achieve complete global domination. The explanation provided by the dubious villa's owner was that the document had been composed by some "Muslim researchers." It would be curious to see the results of the research.

The author of the memorandum made clear that the purpose of the document was to outline the best ways for the followers of radical Islam to make possible "the establishment of an Islamic government on earth." It is also worthwhile to take a look at some of the recommendations offered by the author:

- Avoiding open alliances with known terrorist organizations and individuals in order to maintain the appearance of "moderation."
- Infiltrating and taking over existing organizations to realign them toward the Muslim organizations Brotherhood's collective goals.
- Using deception to mask the intended goals of Islamist actions, as long as it doesn't conflict with Sharia law.
- Establishing financial networks to fund the work of conversion of the West, including the support of full-time administrators and workers.
- Cultivating an Islamist intellectual community, including the establishment of think tanks and advocacy groups, and publishing academic studies, to legitimize Islamist positions and to chronicle the history of (the) Islamist movement.
- Developing a comprehensive hundred-year plan to advance Islamist ideology throughout the world.
- Instituting alliances with Western "progressive" organizations that share similar goals.
- Inflaming violence and keeping Muslims living in the West "in a Jihad frame of mind."
- Adopting the total liberation of Palestine from Israel and the creation of an Islamic state as a keystone in the plan for global Islamic domination.
- Instigating a constant campaign to incite hatred by Muslims against the Jews and rejecting any discussions of conciliation or coexistence with them.

- Linking the terrorist activities in Palestine with the global terror movement.
- Collecting sufficient funds to indefinitely perpetuate and support jihad around the world.[26]

Even a superficial glance at the contents of this document would convince every reader to what extent the advancement of the agenda of radical Islam throughout the world had been performed in full keeping with the main points of the ambitious plan forgotten somewhere in the interior of the luxurious villa in the vicinity of the Swiss city of Lugano. The only question that the document left unanswered was who precisely will lead, coordinate, and advance the realization of the Islamist agenda.

Notes

1. George Orwell, "You and the Atomic Bomb," *Tribune*, London, October 19, 1945, http://orwell.ru/library/articles/ABomb/english/e_abomb.
2. Ibid.
3. Gar Alperovitz, *Atomic Diplomacy: Hiroshima and Potsdam: The Use of the Atomic Bomb and the American Confrontation with Soviet Power* (Pluto Press, London, 1966); William Appleman Williams, *The Tragedy of the American Diplomacy* (New York: W.W. Norton, 1972).
4. James Carroll, "A Buildup in Search of an Enemy," *Boston Globe*, Boston, February 3, 2002.
5. Ibid.
6. Felix Chuev, *One Hundred Forty Conversations with Molotov* (Moscow: Moscovskii Rabochii, 1990), 86.
7. Charles Moser, *Dimitroff of Bulgaria* (Ottawa, IL: Carolyn Press, 1979).
8. Ibid., 72.
9. Ibid.
10. "Soviet Cold War Perceptions of Turkey and Greece (Looking out the CC of the CPSU Headquarters: Information and Appraisals, 1945–1958)," http://history.machaon.ru/all/number_02analiti4/3.
11. See for instance, the very informative article of S. Pons, "Stalin, Togliatti and the Origins of the Cold War in Europe," *Journal of Cold War Studies* 3, no. 2 (Spring 2001), 3–27.
12. George Kennan, "The Long Telegram," February 22, 1946, www.ntanet.net/KENNAN.html.
13. "The Sources of Soviet Conduct," signed by Mr. X, www.historyguide.org/europe/kennan.html.
14. Kennan, "The Long Telegram."
15. President Harry S. Truman's Library (HSTL), Independence, MO, President Secretary's Files, Subject File: "Greece."
16. Records of the Department of State, 1940–1947, Records Group 59, Decimal Files. File No 847.00 (Internal Affairs of Bulgaria, 1945–1947).
17. Dr. Rafael Madoff, "Syria Sheltering War Criminals? Not the First Time," www.wymaninstitute.org/articles/2003–04-syria.php.

18.   Jeffrey Herf, "Hate Radio: Nazi Propaganda in the Arab World," *The Chronicle Review*, http://chronicle.com/article/Hate-Radio-Nazi-Propaganda-in/49199.
19.   Ibid.
20.   Mark Curtis, *Secret Affairs: Britain's Collusion with Radical Islam* (London: Serpent's Tail, 2010).
21.   Youssef Aboul-Enein, "The Egyptian-Yemeni War: Egyptian Perspective on Guerilla Warfare," *Infantry Magazine* (Jan–Feb 2004).
22.   Lorenzo Vidino, "The Muslim Brotherhood's Conquest of Europe," *The Middle East Quarterly* (Winter 2005), 25–34.
23.   Michael B. Oren, *Six Days of War—June 1967 and the Making of the Modern Middle East* (New York: Ballantine Books, 2002).
24.   Ibid., 335–336.
25.   "Muslim Brotherhood (Ikhwan) Infiltration and Influence in America," www.freepublic.com/focus/f-news/2584941/posts.
26.   Ibid.

3

On the Road to Al-Qaeda

Inevitably, the outcome of the Six Day War of June 1967 brought up a lot of bitterness and confusion throughout the Arab world. It also produced many burning questions involving the responsibility for the debacle. Finally, as far as the Arab countries were concerned, the defeat of 1967 yielded an intense search for new approaches and new politics that would not allow the repetition of the disaster. To make a complicated issue simple, while the others had questions, the radical Islamists were the only ones that had answers. Having emerged from the rubble of the secular legacy of Nasserism, radical Islam was able to influence the hearts and minds of many young Arabs.

During the 1960s and 1970s, the Muslim Brotherhood was the largest organization propagating the tenets of radical Islam, but it was not the only one. The year 1953 marked the creation of the Islamic Party of Liberation (Hizb-ut-Tahrir).[1] The founder of the organization was Taqiuddin an-Nabhani, a Palestinian Arab born in Haifa, who had been a judge during the times of the British Mandate. After the war of 1948, an-Nabhani immigrated to Lebanon. As far as the ideology of Hizb-ut-Tahrir (or HT, for convenience) was concerned, it was almost undistinguishable from the tenets of the Muslim Brotherhood. Similar to the Brotherhood, HT was founded upon the premise that ever since the formal dissolution of the last Islamic caliphate in 1924, the Muslim community had lost all sense of belonging and purpose. The abandonment of the rules and laws of Islam had determined all failures and humiliations the community was facing. The main goal of HT was the establishment of an Islamic state ruled according to the requirements of sharia law. The program of HT contained three stages:

> The First Stage: The stage of culturing to produce people who believe in the idea and the method of the Party, so that they form the Party group.
> The Second Stage: The stage of interaction with the global Muslim Community (the Ummah) to let the Ummah embrace and carry Islam,

so that the Ummah takes it up as its issue and thus works to establish it in the affairs of life.

The Third Stage: The stage of establishing government, implementing Islam generally and comprehensively, and carrying it as a message to the world.[2]

HT always has claimed that it is against the use of violence as an instrument for achieving its goals. At the same time, however, its leaders never denied that Hizb is against any form of political democracy, and for this reason, the Islamists from HT were boycotting all national and local elections. The reason for this opposition is twofold: On the one hand, the Western democracy is rejected by the Islamists because of its secular character. On the other hand, the political institution based on the expression of free will of the citizens is considered a non-Islamic phenomenon serving the interests of the Christian and Jewish enemies of Islam.

Once again, the leadership of HT was (and still is) insisting that their organization is nonviolent. To put it mildly, this claim is not accepted in Europe where Hizb-ut-Tahrir has been banned in several countries, including even the usually tolerant Germany. Going back into the turbulent Middle East of 1970s and 1980s, there cannot be any doubt that a growing number of individuals have rejected the secular approach to the political and social issues. They instead adopted a view of the world according to which only the creation of an Islamic state ruled by sharia law can solve the problems of the embittered and divided Muslims. Those were the individuals who were prepared to respond to al-Qaeda's appeal.

The Egyptian Connection

It seemed logical and understandable that the only politicians who had taken into account the appearance of the new trends in the Middle East were the Egyptian and Israeli statesmen. What is interesting, however, was that the leaders of the mutually hostile countries had committed the same mistake in their attempt not to confront but rather to use radical Islam as a barrier against forces they wrongly considered more dangerous.

In Egypt, this trend was connected with the intent of President Sadat to counter the internal threat that emerged as a counter measure to the pro-Soviet opposition to his pro-Western politics. This pressure prompted Sadat to use the power of Islam as an effective antidote against his enemies.[3] As a result, he released from jail a large number of Muslim Brotherhood detainees who had been imprisoned during the times of his predecessor. The numerous explanations of what happened next could be reduced to the following: instead of being grateful to Sadat for their release from the notorious jails of Egypt, the Islamists started conspiring against the new president.[4] Basically this version of the events is correct, but there are too many missing elements of a development that brought about the transformation of radical Islam into the main danger threatening the world today.

To start with, there were powerful social factors at work that contributed to the popularization of the cause of radical Islam in Egypt. The most important political conflict that shook the country throughout the 1950s ended with a seemingly permanent victory of the secular brand of Nasser's nationalism and socialism over the theocratic Muslim Brotherhood. Nasser was triumphant while the Islamists seemed to be on the losing side of the battle. Their leaders used to be executed, the organizational structure of the Brotherhood had been torn apart, and many Islamic activists who did not emigrate to Saudi Arabia or Qatar were subjected to the rough treatment of Nasser's jails and concentration camps.

Later, however, things started to change. The government regulation of economic activities and the clumsiness and corruption of the Nasser-era bureaucracy resulted in lower living standards. This process was powerfully reinforced by the uncontrollable growth of Cairo and the other large cities of Egypt. The impact of this dislocation had not only economic but also very important social consequences. The most important among them was the feeling of alienation and the loss of identity. The extremely powerful reaction of the majority of the Egyptians to the humiliating defeat of the country's armed forces during the Six Day War of June 1967 added a lot of frustration to those negative emotions.

The contradiction between the outright stupid official propaganda that included Nasser's firebrand speeches, the main content of which was the repetitive line "We shall throw the Jews into the sea," and the magnitude of the Arab defeat could not have been any bigger.[5] Neither a growing capitalism under the previous regime nor socialism under Nasser was working in their country. A growing number of Egyptians started asking themselves, isn't it time to start listening more carefully to the forbidden message of the Muslim Brotherhood?

The practical implementation of President Sadat's plan to attract the Islamists on his side involved the gradual development of Islamic societies as institutions designed to offer moral leadership and guid-ance. On a practical level, those societies acted as substitutes for the fail-ing government structures by providing health- and education-related services to the community. To accommodate the radical Islamists, President Sadat twice changed the constitution of the country. In the immediate aftermath of his predecessor's death and while the future jihadists were still in jails and concentration camps, Sadat proclaimed Islam the state religion.[6]

This act, to which very few people paid attention at the time, in real-ity played the role of a death sentence imposed on Egyptian secularism and socialism. President Sadat also introduced a second clause to the main legislative document of the country that stipulated that sharia law inspired Egyptian legislation. For the Islamists, however, such a formula was a highly unsatisfactory one, and in his attempt to accom-modate them, the president added a point containing the declaration that sharia law is not just one of the sources and inspirations for the entire process of serving justice, but the main one. What the president of Egypt did not realize was that instead of stabilizing the country by eliminating the bureaucratic inefficiency and showing the way for the establishment of a new kind of bond between the people of Egypt and its rulers, he had led the genie of radical Islam out of the bottle.

By the way, in the aftermath of the Six Day War, the Israeli military authorities in the West Bank faced the secular challenge of Fatah. Similar to the Egyptian authorities, the military administrators of the newly occupied territories wrongly considered the secular challenge as the most dangerous. In other words, the Israeli leaders decided to use the Islamists against their secular enemies.[7] Not only did the Israeli military administration release detained Islamists, but it provided financial support for the expansion of their activities with the absurd hope that the Islamic propaganda would detach the Palestinian youth from the influence of Yasser Arafat's Fatah. The results though were catastrophic for all proponents of this strategy. In Egypt, President Sadat got his bullet from the radical Islamists, and the Israelis later realized that the Islamist Hamas was (and still is) far more dangerous than the secular Fatah.

First of all, the new strategy of President Sadat opened the doors for large-scale financial assistance to funnel into the coffers of the Islamic societies from the ubiquitous Wahhabi foundations of Saudi Arabia. Second, this support made possible the significant growth of independent and private mosques that remained out of any form of government control. In the beginning, they served as a meeting ground for the newly activated radical Islamists, but a short time later, they became the ideal places for terrorist recruitment.

Another fatal misconception of President Sadat was his belief that he could make a deal with the Muslim Brotherhood. In his view, in exchange for the opportunity to propagate its belief system, the Brotherhood would accept the role of a peaceful participant in the political and social life of Egypt. In reality, nothing could have been further from the truth. While President Sadat and his associates were living in their dream world, with the help of the Wahhabi Saudi foundations, the Brotherhood expanded its activities abroad. No American security agency at the time suspected that the financial resources acquired by the Brotherhood would one day be used for the organization of terrorist acts against the United States.

The leaders of the Brotherhood established their own bank, Al Taqwa (Fear of God).[8] The new financial structure came into being in the border area between Switzerland and Italy. A bit later, important branches of the same bank were established in Liechtenstein and the Bahamas and used as offshore tax havens.

There was something else: a number of the Brotherhood financial experts had well-established Nazi ties.[9] The director of the bank, Ahmad Huber, was a Swiss convert to Islam who was previously known as Albert Huber. An open Nazi, with very dubious connections and functions during WWII, he found a new cause in radical Islam. A demonstration of the continuity of his loyalties could be found in the living room of his house, where every visitor faced the portraits of Adolph Hitler and Osama bin Laden. Huber's office offered an even more impressive panorama that included the portraits of Hitler and Himmler next to the portraits of the leading Islamic militants.[10]

A Brotherhood memorandum was obtained by the FBI and presented during a terrorism-financing trial in 2007. The document in question was titled "An Explanatory Memorandum on the General Strategic Goal for the Group in North America."[11] The author of the document was Mohammed Akram, one of the closest associates of Sheikh al-Qaradawi, who for decades was the main theoretician of the Muslim Brotherhood. The text of the document is self-explanatory to a degree that it does not need any comment: "The Ikhvan (the Arabic name of the Brotherhood), must understand that their work in America is a kind of grand Jihad in eliminating and destroying the Western civilization from within and sabotaging its miserable house by their hands and the hands of the believers so that it is eliminated and God's religion is made victorious over all other religions."[12]

What is very interesting in the document is the open proclamation of two main principles of radical Islam that, as a rule, are never discussed in open. The Islamic principle of Taqiyya expresses itself in "concealing or disguising one's beliefs, convictions, ideas, feelings, opinions, and/or strategies at a time of imminent danger, whether now or later in time, to save oneself from physical and/or mental injury."[13] This is the principle used as justification for the use of lies and deceit when they are applied for defense or for the expansion of Islam. In other words, the most basic moral rules and principles are applicable only in the dealings of the radical Islamists with the Muslim population.

Da'wa represents an act of invitation issued by Muslims to non-Muslims to accept their religion. The practical implementation of Da'wa involves a carefully designed effort by devoted Islamists to present their belief system in the best possible light to non-Muslim neighbors or audiences, thus motivating them to convert. The "Explanatory Memorandum" demonstrates in the most convincing way the unchangeable totalitarian nature of the Brotherhood. It also makes something else abundantly clear: given that "the Brothers" were planning to undermine the United States of America, one could only wonder about the degree of the naiveté of the Egyptian leaders of the 1970s who had hoped to lure the Brothers to be "good boys" within the borders of Egypt. The only consequence of the amnesty announced by President Sadat, besides the reanimation of the Brotherhood, was the appearance of two very dangerous radical Islamic groups.

Takfir wal-Hijra (Atonement and Emigration) was the name of one of the radical Islamist groups that came into being during the 1970s.[14] The term "emigration" represented a rather awkward attempt to translate "hidjra," the escape of Prophet Mohammed from Mecca to Medina that started the Muslim calendar. For the members of Takfir, "hidjra" was a symbol of a decisive move designed to leave a corrupted and nonspiritual surrounding for an Islamic world that will be an epitome of supreme justice and happiness. Such a fanatical organization is unthinkable without the presence of an even more fanatical and charismatic leader who is able to inspire and to evoke fear whenever necessary, even among his followers.

The leader of Takfir, Shukri Mustafa, was such a person.[15] Born and raised in Upper Egypt and an agricultural engineer by training, Mustafa joined the Muslim Brotherhood in the 1960s. He was arrested and detained during the brutal crackdown organized by Nasser's police on the Brotherhood. Instead of frightening him, however, his prison term transformed the young man into an extremely radical and outright fanatical Islamist. Influenced by the ideas of Sayyid Qutb, Shukri Mustafa reached the conclusion that the numerous negative dimensions of the Egyptian society were born out of the deviation of the majority of the population from the values and laws of early Islam. After reaching the conclusion that most of his compatriots do not have the right to call themselves Muslims, Mustafa created his organization as a tightly controlled and highly secretive unit. On a theoretical level, the purpose was to purify Islam and to expand it among the sinful population.

In the beginning, it seemed the purpose of the members of the organization had been to isolate them from the rest of the world. They cut all contacts with their families and established a commune in the caves of Upper Egypt. Considering the degree of conservatism in the rural areas of a Muslim country, it is not difficult to imagine the general feeling of shock when the rumor spread that Shukri Mustafa was accepting girls and women in the caves who were ready to join his organization. Firmly convinced that he was destined to be a supreme political and religious leader of the radical adherents of Islam, Shukri Mustafa declared his decision to proclaim null and void the existing marriages between Takfir members and their abusive partners and to encourage the establishment of new families within the ranks of the organization.[16]

The sharpening of the social climate in Egypt prompted the relocation of Takfir to Cairo. The reason for the rising tensions in the country manifested in the sad fact that if Gamal Abdel Nasser had convinced the people of Egypt that socialism did not work, his successor, Anwar Sadat, was successful in proving that capitalism did not work either. Under both opposing strategies and politics, the bureaucracy and corruption were powerful enough to destroy any attempt for positive change. It was within the frame of this tense situation that Takfir took an active part in the slowly brewing social upheaval. In January of 1977, "bread riots" broke out as a protest against President Sadat's administration strategy to reduce the direct government control over the economy in general and price control in particular.[17]

In Cairo alone, hundreds of buildings and 120 buses were set on fire. Takfir took an active role in the organization and execution of the orgy of pillaging and destruction. Far from incidental, the anger of the crowd, led by Takfir activists, was directed at the night clubs on the famous

Pyramids street regarded by the Islamists as an ultimate expression of Western decadence and the alienation of the Egyptian society from the rules and requirements of the Muslim religion.[18]

Takfir acquired national prominence by kidnapping Muhammad al-Dhahabi, a former minister and well-known and respected moderate cleric. The demands of the kidnappers were so outrageous that it was highly unlikely to find any government in the world to satisfy them. An incomplete list included 200,000 Egyptian pounds in cash, the immediate release of sixty members of the organization (most of them detained during and in the aftermath of the January riots), public apologies from the press, and the publication of the religious writings of Shukri Mustafa. The government did not react to those demands, and the kidnapped cleric was brutally murdered.[19]

This crime yielded an extremely hostile public reaction that prompted the authorities to act with utmost resolution and cruelty to wipe the Takfir terrorists off the face of earth. The sweeping police operation conducted simultaneously over the entire territory of the country resulted in 410 arrests. In other words, the majority of the Takfir membership found itself behind bars during the late fall of 1977. On March 19, 1978, Shukri Mustafa and four of his top associates were hanged. All together, the authorities executed twenty-three radical Islamists implicated in the kidnapping and murder of Muhammad al-Dhahabi.[20]

The second important Islamist splinter group from the large but disorganized body of the Muslim Brotherhood that made its appearance on the Egyptian political scene in 1979 was the Society of Struggle (Jamaat al-Jihad).[21] The society was created by an individual as fanatical and maniacal as Shukri Mustafa by the name of Muhammad Abd al-Salam Faraj.[22] Faraj was an engineer by training who had chosen to become a professional revolutionary instead of trying to follow any career fitting his excellent educational credentials.

The comparison between both radical Islamist groups would reveal many similarities stemming from the influence of Sayyid Qutb's ideas over both of them. The members of Takfir and Jihad were sharing the basic premise of Qutb's worldview involving the return to the legacy of early Islam by bringing down the secular and corrupt monarchies pretending to have a Muslim identity and replacing them by a theocratic totalitarian dictatorship. The final purpose of the radical Islamist movements, of course, is always the same: the creation of a global Muslim caliphate.

At the same time, there were some important differences between both branches of the Egyptian version of radical Islam. For instance, Takfir was propagating the idea of the retreat of the followers of the "only true Islam" from the rest of the population in Egypt while waiting for the right moment to strike against its numerous enemies. Taking a page straight from the book of Leninism, which required its followers to contribute to the defeat of their own country during WWI to unleash the fire of the global revolution, Takfir was instructing its adherents to fight in the ranks of the Egyptian Army under no circumstances. Meanwhile, the jihadists were categorically opposed to such a strategy, which for them was not only defeatist but also absolutely deprived of any chance of success.

Another major difference involved the structure of both organizations and the nature of their leadership. While Takfir was totally centralized and united around one single leader whose authority was large enough to transform him into the only decision maker, the Jihad used to have a collective leadership. The Jihad used to have a ten-member-strong consultation committee under the guidance of Sheikh Umar Abd al-Rahman. There were two branches of the organization, one based in Cairo and the other in Upper Egypt. Each of those branches was composed of semiautonomous cells headed by leaders (amirs) who met once a week to coordinate their actions in keeping with the general strategy of the organization.[23] In the area of recruiting, both organizations were concentrating their efforts on the new university students. Their intense propaganda efforts and contacts were able to create a larger organizational infrastructure that included teachers, students, low-ranking government officials, and military officers.

It was in November of 1977 when the firm decision to bring peace to his country prompted President Sadat to undertake his historic trip to Jerusalem. Upon his return, the president was greeted as a hero by a huge and enthusiastic crowd. As far as the radical Islamists were concerned, however, given that one of the main points on their agenda was the destruction of Israel, their reaction to Sadat's peace initiative was, predictably, very hostile. The Jihad took immediate steps to create a large-scale conspiracy that was successful in planning and executing the assassination of President Anwar Sadat in October of 1981.[24]

The murder of President Sadat, the participation of some young radical Islamists in the Afghan war, and the hate-filled sermons of the radical imams in Western Europe that influenced the minds of many young visitors to their mosques marked the Egyptian connection to the emergence of the Jihad. What was not so well-known at the time was the fact that the goal of the murderers was much more ambitious. According to their original design, the assassination of the president was supposed to create the necessary conditions for a coup d'état.

If we look more carefully into the structure of Jihad, it could be regarded as a prototype of present-day al-Qaeda. This opinion could be supported by a very strong argument: al-Qaeda's number two, Ayman al-Zawahiri was one of the codefendants during the trial of the assassins of President Sadat. Although considered the number two in the al-Qaeda hierarchy, al-Zawahiri is the main ideologue of the largest Islamic terrorist network today.[25]

Dr. Ayman al-Zawahiri was born in 1951 into a wealthy and privileged family. His paternal grandfather was an imam at Al-Azhar mosque, while his other grandfather was a literature professor who later became president of Cairo University. Later he became a diplomat who represented his country at an ambassadorial level in Pakistan, Saudi Arabia, and Yemen. His father, Dr. Mohammad Rabi' al-Zawahiri was one of the most famous Egyptian doctors, who at the same time was a professor at the medical school of Ain Shams University.[26]

In 1974, Ayman al-Zawahiri graduated as an honor student from the medical school of Cairo University. He had become active in politics during his student years when President Sadat's government lifted the ban on Islamist activities and the Egyptian universities became a hot bed for the circulation of Islamic ideas.

The young doctor quickly became popular with his concepts, which have been considered extremist, even within the context of radical Islam. According to al-Zawahiri,

> The rulers governing Islamic countries according to something other than what God has revealed in terms of situational laws, are unbelieving apostates who must be confronted, fought against, expelled from their positions, and Muslim rulers installed in their place; and that the democracy that was adopted by different countries as their policy system has an unbeliever democracy where their supporters and followers are illegal.[27]

The world saw al-Zawahiri for the first time shouting out the Islamic message of President Sadat's murderers from the cage where the defendants were locked.[28] Speaking of yelling, the young doctor undoubtedly demonstrated a lot of bravery because there was no guarantee that the court would not increase his prison term for such outrageous behavior. There was an additional problem with regard to this behavior. During the investigation, the young intellectual was brutally tortured, and under duress he talked to his torturers. Once released, Ayman al-Zawahiri left his native country of Egypt forever. The long journey he undertook ended in Afghanistan, where he met Osama bin Laden. In a relatively short time, given the personality of bin Laden, who was extremely mistrustful of everyone, Dr. al-Zawahiri nevertheless became the closest confidant and associate of the jihadist number one.

An important point that should not be forgotten or ignored is that al-Qaeda was born at the confluence of two streams of totalitarian Islamic fundamentalism—the Egyptian and the Saudi one. The Egyptian component of the contemporary jihad marked the beginning of a radical Islamist movement that finally merged into a large-scale international Islamic assault against Christianity, Jews, the state of Israel, and both dimensions of democracy—as a concept and as a political system. At the same time, it was the Saudi component of the Islamo-totalitarian assault on the world that provided the ideology of political Islam.[29]

The perfect harmony that existed for decades between the Saudi monarchy and the Wahhabi clergy started to breakdown when the unprecedented revenue generated by the oil sales flooded the Saudi coffers. The newly found wealth created a subculture of la dolce vita among the privileged elite of the Desert Kingdom. Once their private jets were leaving the airspace of Saudi Arabia, everything the princes had been taught by their Wahhabi instructors momentarily evaporated. Upon the landing of the jets at the European and American airports, the Saudi aristocrats were sinking into sinful indulgence financed by the deep pockets of their fathers. Their spending at the bars, casinos, hotels, and brothels and their purchases of luxurious real estate and outrageously expensive yachts and cars became legendary.

It was this lifestyle that marked the beginning of a potentially extremely dangerous, for the very existence of the Saudi monarchy, process of alienation between the rulers and those who were ruled by them. There is even more to it. If at this moment fair elections were called in Saudi Arabia, Osama bin Laden would end up as the winner. The sharp contrast between the 6,000-strong crowds of ignorant and wasteful princes and the austere image of a billionaire who, instead of enjoying his wealth in some luxurious and exotic location, had chosen to spend his life in the inhospitable Afghan and Pakistani mountains was a powerful factor working in his favor.

The first individual who made Osama bin Laden's name famous was his father.[30] Mohammed bin Laden was born in the most inhospitable mountainous area of Yemen called Hadramaut. The burning sun and the rocky ground forced the locals to look for a way to survive outside the scope of the traditional areas of agriculture and livestock. Similar to so many residents of the area, Mohammed bin Laden became a construction worker. Unlike the largest majority among them, however, he became rich and famous. His talent attracted the attention of King Saud, and the family fortune of the bin Laden clan skyrocketed. The ambition of the senior bin Laden to have more of everything life has to offer evidently dominated his personal life as well, considering that he married twenty-two women with whom he fathered fifty-four children.

The only child Mohammed bin Laden had with his fourth wife, who was fourteen when he married her at the age of forty-eight, was born in 1958 and was given the name Osama, which in Arabic means "lion." The father remained a distant and fear-inspiring figure who died in a car accident when the young boy was nine. The people around Osama observed some important changes in the psychological makeup of the boy when he turned fourteen.[31] Prior to that Osama was shy and aloof in his own way. He sported Western attire and loved to watch American cowboy movies. After the change, which according to some witnesses of his early adolescence took place under the influence of a Syrian gym teacher who was a member of the Muslim Brotherhood, religion became the most important topic in his life. According to the testimony of his mother, the boy became not only a deeply religious person who started praying five times a day, but he also developed strong interests in politics in general and toward the Israeli-Palestinian conflict in particular.

As a student at King Abdul Aziz University in Jeddah, although studying economics, Osama bin Laden formed a religious charity whose members discussed many issues, including jihad. At the same time, bin Laden was a regular visitor to the lectures of Mohammad Qutb, the brother of the jihadist martyr executed by Nasser.

Sheikh Abdullah Azzam was another individual who exercised an even stronger influence over bin Laden.[32] He prompted the young Islamic fanatic to join the Afghan resistance against the Soviet occupation of the country. After the Israeli occupation of the West Bank of the Jordan River, Abdullah Azzam fled to Jordan. Upon acquiring his doctorate in Islamic jurisprudence, he started teaching at the University of Jordan. In 1980, his teaching career was interrupted because of his involvement with the Palestinian movement. For about a year, Azzam found refuge in Saudi Arabia, where he offered to lead the prayers at the school mosque where bin Laden was conducting his studies. It was there where he delivered his fiery sermons in front of the enthusiastic student audiences. Sheikh Azzam's main message, which was repeated in front of the enthusiastic audiences, was taken straight from Sayyed Qutb's ideas: the duty of every Muslim is to fight for the global triumph of Islam.

A year later, Sheikh Azzam moved to Pakistan, and in the aftermath of the Soviet occupation of Afghanistan, he established himself in Peshawar, which had become the rallying point for the volunteers that started coming from all parts of the Muslim world. It was Azzam who brought Osama bin Laden to Peshawar. The arrival of bin Laden to this place marked the beginning of his long-term Afghan-related activities that brought him so much fame and so many followers.[33]

The birth of the bin Laden phenomenon was preceded by two decades of a spread of the radical Islamist network. The Saudi petrodollars were creating mosques and madrassas managed by fanatical Wahhabi missionaries (imams and teachers) throughout the world with a particular accent on the Islamization of the growing Muslim community of Western Europe. The majority of the Arab volunteers who took part in the Afghan war had left the country after the withdrawal of the Soviet troops from Afghanistan. Part of them went to Chechnya and another part to Bosnia, while the rest, having nothing good to expect from the police forces of the authoritarian regimes ruling their native countries, arrived in Europe as political refugees.[34] In other words, although not seen by the rest of the world at the time, during the 1970s and 1980s the seeds of the Islamo-totalitarian hatred and aggression were widely spread throughout the Muslim communities of the Middle East and Western Europe. In the next decade, the fire of this hatred and this aggression would touch the saturated soil of Chechnya and Bosnia. It was also the first decade of the murderous legacy of al-Qaeda.

On one hand, the creation of the al-Qaeda network was made possible and powerfully reinforced by the dynamics of the Egyptian-born jihadism, the Saudi financing of the jihadist network, and the transformation of Iran into a totalitarian theocratic state. On the other hand, there was the blindness, the lack of understanding, and the passivity of the West toward the newly emerged deadly danger symbolized by the totalitarian brand of Islam that had also made their important contribution to the creation of the global terrorist network.

The emergence of Osama bin Laden as a leader of the Sunni branch of the Islamist jihad could be viewed as one of those historical events when the development of some important phenomenon has reached a level making possible the match between the situation and the personality who was able to make the best possible use of it. There are some important questions that involve bin Laden's leadership. The eyewitness testimonies are unanimous with regard to the dramatic difference between bin Laden's behavior before and after his participation in the anti-Soviet resistance in Afghanistan. During his adolescence and early youth, Osama bin Laden was quite a likable individual whose deep religiosity shined through his modesty, shyness, and a certain level of aloofness. At the same time, even during this period, the young Osama was impressing people with his extreme stubbornness and certain attraction to risk taking to the point of jeopardizing his life and the lives of others while riding or driving. Completely indifferent toward the temptations of a glamorous lifestyle his share of Mohammed bin Laden's fabulous wealth would have been able to offer him, the pious and very emotional youngster was deeply influenced by his Wahhabi teachers and the radical Saudi preachers. Having embraced the cause of radical Islam, Osama bin Laden was ready to invest his last penny for the needs of the cause in which he believed.

If we accept the premise that before his involvement with the Afghan mujahideen bin Laden had a complex personality that offered a rare mix of character features that as a rule we are accustomed to finding in different individuals, the Afghan period of his life transformed him completely. The evolution of his character was clearly visible along several different lines. To start, the pious young man had become a religious fanatic. Even more, bin Laden belonged to the worst possible brand of fanatics, who see themselves not as rank-and-file believers but rather like supreme leaders who are teaching the average folks what is right and wrong with their lives and belief systems.

But there was more to it: the once modest young man had returned from Afghanistan as an arrogant, egotistical maniac who sincerely believed in his right to conduct his own foreign policy! Case in point, upon his return bin Laden decided to unsettle the military government of southern Yemen, which was the only pro-communist regime in the Arab world. He funneled money to Yemeni jihadists, and after arriving in the country, he started preaching in the Wahhabi mosques against the country's rulers.

The decade preceding 9/11 was a period of additional strengthening of the grip of radical Islam over the Muslim communities of Europe.[35] In the beginning of the 1990s, bin Laden established himself in Sudan, where he enjoyed the hospitality of the newly established Islamist regime of the country. It was from the Sudanese capital that bin Laden financed the operation planned by the blind Sheikh Abdul Rahman that became the first attack against the Twin Towers. After the consolidation of Taliban control over Afghanistan, bin Laden relocated himself and his closest associates once again. During the 1990s, the al-Qaeda leader organized the mass murder that took place in the bombings of the US embassies in Kenya and Tanzania and the attack against the USS *Cole* and expanded his terrorist network.

There were, however, many American mistakes that paved the way to 9/11. President Clinton's administration missed several good opportunities to rid the world of bin Laden. Later, it was the lack of the ability of the intelligence and security agencies in the beginning of President George W. Bush's mandate to combine their resources and activities that had made possible the arrival and the training of the suicidal murderers on the American soil.[36]

The overexposure of the al-Qaeda and bin Laden phenomena had created some important misunderstandings of the nature and the magnitude of the Islamo-totalitarian danger. The complexity of those phenomena stems from the different dimensions of the nature of the terrorist network. Starting with its ideology, there are many people (not necessarily Muslims) who in their heart of hearts believe that Osama bin Laden and al-Qaeda were trying to transplant the tenets of medieval Islam into the twenty-first century. While it is absolutely true that the Islamo-totalitarians are trying to bring a lot of barbarity from the past into the future, it is highly debatable that their belief system is in keeping with all rules and requirements of the religion created by Prophet Mohammed.

Two examples are enough to say it all. It is a well-known fact that bin Laden liked to brag about his achievements in the art of murdering human beings. The world has heard many times the jihadist harangues about the attack on the USS *Cole*, the bombings in Spain, and, of course, about 9/11. What is interesting, however, is the complete silence with which jihadist number one and his huge propaganda apparatus reacted to the bombings of the American embassies in Kenya and Tanzania. The problem with those bombings was that among all casualties, hundreds of them were Muslims.

Even a fanatic and maniac of the magnitude of bin Laden was not able to deny the fact that, from the point of view of early Islam, the mass murder of Muslims, who on top of that were completely innocent, constitutes nothing less than an unbelievable crime of huge proportions. During Prophet Mohammed's times, the mass murder of Muslims would have been punished with the entire severity of sharia law. That is why the main criminal preferred to remain silent about the crime committed on the distant shores of Africa. Later, the Iraq War brought about thousands of Muslim casualties who became victims of the Wahhabi fanaticism for which every Muslim who does not belong to the most extreme branch of Islam deserves to die for the same reason the Jews and Christians deserve death.

Bin Laden preferred as well to forget another basic tenet of early Islam: its categorical ban on suicide that was considered by the Prophet of the new religion as one of the deadliest sins. Consequently, the use of suicidal murderers in to kill completely innocent people undoubtedly also represents a dramatic violation of the rules and laws of the religion al-Qaeda is trying to impose on the world. In reality, what al-Qaeda and the numerous imitations or direct franchises of the terrorist organization are trying to impose on the world is an outright totalitarian tyranny that is theocratic only in the sense that it is based on the most extreme branch of Islam.

Notes

1. www.hizb-ut-tahrir.org/english/english.html.
2. "The Method of Hizb-ut-Tahrir," www.hizb-ut-tahrir.org/english/english.html.
3. Kirk J. Beattie, *Egypt during the Sadat Years* (New York: St. Martin's Press, 2000).
4. One of the best books on the subject is Julles Kepel, *Muslim Extremism in Egypt: The Prophet and the Pharaoh* (London: Al Sagi Books, 1985).
5. David Zeidan, "Radical Islam in Egypt: A Comparison of Two Groups," *Middle Eastern Review of International Affairs* 3, no. 3 (September 1999); Kepel, *Muslim Extremism in Egypt: The Prophet and the Pharaoh*.
6. David Hirst and Irene Beeson, *Sadat* (London: Faber and Faber, 1981
7. Brendan O'Neil, "How Israel Helped to Create Hamas," www.amconmag.com/print.html?Id=I amConservative-2007Feb12–00017.
8. Interview with a relative of a former member of Takfir.
9. "The Nazi-Muslim Terrorist Connection: Francois Genoud and Al Takwa Bank," www.antifascistencyclopedia.com/allposts/the-nazi-muslim-terrorist-connection-fr.
10. Ibid.
11. Patric Pool, "The Muslim Brotherhood Project," www.frontpagemag.com/Articles.

12. Ibid.
13. Ibid.
14. Zeidan, "Radical Islam in Egypt: A Comparison of Two Groups."
15. Interview with a relative of a member of Takfir.
16. Ibid.
17. Kirk J. Beattie, *Egypt during the Sadat Years* (New York: St. Martin's Press, 2000).
18. Ibid.
19. Ibid.
20. Interview with a relative of a Takfir member; see as well "Perspectives on World History and Current Events," *Middle East Project: Mujammad abd al-Salaam Faraj and al-Jihad*, www.pwhce.org/faraj.html.
21. Kepel, *Muslim Extremism in Egypt: The Prophet and the Pharaoh.*
22. "Perspectives on World History and Current Events."
23. An interview with a family member of Takfir.
24. Zvi Mazel, "How Egypt Molded Modern Radical Islam," *Jerusalem Center for Public Affairs*, Issue Brief 4, no. 18 (February 16, 2005).
25. "Combating Terrorism Center at West Point: Translation from Original Text," Dr. Ayman al-Zawahiri, www.ctc.ucma.edu/harmony/harmony.usp.
26. Ibid.
27. Ibid.
28. Ibid.
29. See the interesting and thought-provoking article of Uriya Shavit, "Al-Qaeda Saudi Origins," *Middle East Quarterly* (Fall 2006), 3–13.
30. About the biography of Osama bin Laden, see Carmen bin Ladin, *Inside the Kingdom: My Life in Saudi Arabia* (New York: Warner Books, 2004; Peter L. Bergen, *The Osama bin Laden I Know: An Oral History of Al-Qaeda Leader* (New York: Free Press, 2006).
31. John L. Esposito, *Unholy War: Terror in the Name of Islam* (New York: Oxford University Press, 2002), 92–93.
32. "Middle East Project: Abdullah Azzam, the Godfather of Jihad (Biography/ Profile)," www.pwhce.org/azzam.html.
33. Ibid.
34. Mark Sageman, *Understanding Terror Networks* (Philadelphia: University of Pennsylvania Press, 2004).
35. Ibid.
36. John Miller and Michael Stone, with Chris Mitchell, *The Cell: Inside the 9/11 Plot, and Why the FBI and CIA Failed to Stop It* (New York: Hyperion, 2002).

4

The Beginning of the Islamization of Europe

During a mild, gloomy October afternoon in 2009, although jet-lagged after a long transatlantic flight, I took a stroll through the streets of the British city of Luton. Although the city is located only about twenty-five miles north of London, a large part of it could hardly be called British. In front of my tired, unbelieving eyes, as if in slow motion, paraded a kaleidoscope of faces and scenes that I could not connect with my image of Britain. The overcrowded streets were full of men (very few women) who looked as part of the street panorama of any city in the Middle East. The traditional Muslim attire completely dominated the scene. The heads and faces of the few women (with the exception of a teen-aged Pakistani girl) were covered, and most of the street names were not English. Within a thirty-minute walking range, there were three mosques. There was a church in sight as well, but it was empty, locked, overgrown, and its entrance was blocked with heavy iron chains. No, not by the Muslims but, most probably, by the owners of the property who had no candidates to buy it.

It was Friday and time for Friday prayer, called Namaz. The mosques were overcrowded. When the religious service was over, the streets suddenly became too narrow for the hordes of people. The men leaving the mosques wore beards and baggy pants and looked inspired. Some of them strolled in a somewhat pensive mood; others formed large groups while engaged in intense discussions. Having lost my way, I approached one of those groups and asked for directions. In a most polite manner, the young people addressed my issue, and I left the premises with more questions than answers.

Maybe the problem was the complexity of the phenomenon I was observing. Let's start with the expressions on the faces of the people I saw. Those people were so cordial to each other! I saw so many smiles, embraces, and many men talking with visible pleasure to each other.

When, however, the eyes of those sociable gentlemen were locked for a short instant with mine, there was no more cordiality. No, I am not saying that the friendliness was replaced by hatred, or any kind of hostility, but my impression was that those positive emotions were for local consumption only.

The most interesting aspect of this almost surreal journey into the future was that at the moment when under the influence of some particularly impressive street scene unfolding in front of your eyes you managed to reach some conclusion about the surrounding reality, the next one seems to have been intentionally designed to destroy your conclusion. Case in point, I had already been firmly convinced that traditional Muslim female attire was absolutely mandatory for every woman in Luton when a few hundred yards away from one of the mosques, and next to a food store, I saw a young girl walking toward me. Her face was uncovered, and she was wearing an outfit that would have suited any teenaged British girl. I dared to stop her to initiate a short conversation. A group of teenaged Muslim boys passed us by without paying any attention to us. The girl did not look disturbed a bit while she was talking to me. By the way, she said that she would like to visit the United States, which was for her "a very interesting country."

Encouraged by this conversation and ready to change my stereotype about Luton, I decided to enter the food store. For some unknown reason, the place was overcrowded. For a few minutes I remained frozen next to the entrance, struck by the unusual scene. The visitors, most of them Muslims but a lot of non-Muslims as well, were completely ignoring each other while selecting the items they wanted to buy and while waiting in line to pay for them. There were no more smiles, no more animated conversations. The place was as quiet as a church. But it was only a food store. The impressive scene was leading to the only possible conclusion: what I had been looking at was nothing but a fragment of the parallel existence on British soil of two completely different societies that have nothing in common. This conclusion presented a torturous question: if British society is not able to integrate the Muslim residents, what is in store for Great Britain's future? Or maybe because I am not Muslim I am biased? Or maybe Luton is an exception?

What follows is from an article that contains the impressions of a female Turkish journalist from a community situated within the boundaries of the British capital. The name of the journalist is Ekif Safak, and the name of London's neighborhood is Harringay. Safak wrote, "I walk around in Harringay. You know, that part of London where all green grocers are Turkish, where the white cheese is all imported from Turkey, and where the donner kebap sellers are more than you can count. Barbers, restaurants, 'kahve houses' . . . newspaper sellers, corner stores—they are all run by Turks speaking Turkish in Harringay."[1]

The article ends up with an amazing story that provides a lot of food for thought, not just about the realities in Harringay but, in a larger context, about the future of England. The story starts when a group of British ladies ask the owner of the Turkish restaurant about the varieties of soup the place has to offer. The owner, who does not speak a word of English, asks his thirteen-year-old daughter to translate the words of the "tourists." Safak's comment on this situation deserves to be quoted verbatim: "And so, the Turkish merchant who calls Brits 'tourists' in their own land lives comfortably on, without even having to leave Harringay."[2]

Going back to my Luton-based impressions, on my way back to the parking lot I had another conversation, this time with a British man who was obviously very well educated and in an extremely bad mood that he was not trying to hide. He did not wait for my questions. Instead, he shot back his opinion right away: "They will take out the country! The people here are afraid even to talk about that!" What he did not realize was that he had lowered his voice while saying those words. As someone who was born and raised in a communist country, I know perfectly well that people tend to lower their voices when they are expressing an opinion that could be dangerous.

Professionally speaking, my visit to Luton had been too short, but it nevertheless allowed me to grasp at least some dimensions of the Islamization of Europe in general and of Great Britain in particular. It became abundantly clear to me that, unlike the United States, Great Britain was not a melting pot. If some long-term solution capable of integrating both communities in the British political and social system is not be found, these societies are heading toward a major conflict. They are like two geological plates pressing on each other; the different cultures and attitudes are threatening the very foundations of British Society and statehood. The clash could end up with the Islamization of Great Britain or with a civil war that will break out to prevent it.

My thoughts went back to the short conversation I'd had with the young Pakistani girl back in Luton. Did her uncovered beautiful, radiant face and her warm and friendly smile offer some hope that the deadly collision can be prevented? Or maybe in her own eyes she was just a British girl with a Pakistani background. What about the future role of the millions of Muslims who do not have anything to do with the jihadist assault on Western civilization, culture, and political system? Are we right in our hope that when the hour of confrontation comes they will not follow the jihadist lead? If that is the case, then why are there not large-scale Muslim protests against the crimes of the jihadists?

More than two millenniums ago, the fathers of history from ancient Greece left timeless advice to the next generations, the essence of which is that our past is the area that holds the key to our future. Very often throughout history, the initial stage of some groundbreaking historical event makes its appearance on the world scene while the attention of the contemporaries are distracted by less important developments that impair their ability to see the most meaningful outlines of the future. One of the most important components of the future of Europe that the Europeans have so far ignored is the impact of postwar immigration over the ethnic, cultural, religious, and political makeup of the continent.

The Demographics and Economics of the Islamization of Europe

Beyond any doubt, the primary reason for the emergence of the Islamization of Europe is a demographic one. The demographers have reached a consensus that the world population is set to grow by 17 percent from the beginning of the century to 2020. The numerical expression of this growth has the following dynamics: from 5 billion in 2005, it will reach 6.5 billion by 2025.[3] The long-established trend demonstrates that we should expect a sharp increase of the population in the least-developed countries, and the stagnation, aging, and reduction of the number of residents in the most-advanced regions will continue. As far as the age of the population is concerned, the percentage of the youngest group (0–16) will continue to grow in the developing countries. At the same time, the numbers of the representatives in that group who live in the so-called first world will continue to shrink. The projection of the size of the population of the different continents speaks for itself: While Europe had 728.3 million inhabitants in 2005, in 2020 it will have about 714 million. And while Africa had a population of 906 million in 2005, by 2020 it will have 1.228 million inhabitants.[4]

An inevitable consequence of this situation is the steady increase of the migration of huge numbers of people from the countries where there are too many children and not enough resources to countries having trouble supporting their growing number of retirees. Let's look at the numbers again. While in 1960 there were 75 million migrant workers who moved from the least-developed countries into the most-developed, today the number of those workers is about 191 million. Between 2007 and 2020, the migratory process will add at least 100 million more immigrants to the already radically changed demographic scene of the developed part of the world.[5]

This unprecedented movement of huge human masses makes the famous "great resettlement of the people" look like an innocent collective walk. The most important dimension of the migratory process with regard to the subject area of this book is its Muslim component because it is the Muslim community that represents the fastest-growing part of the world's population. Some examples are very impressive indeed.

To make some important points abundantly clear, it is useful to examine some data from the research of the Greek demographer Ioannis Micheletos. The changing dynamics of the European demographic map could be demonstrated by the increased gap between the sizes of the population of two neighboring countries—one of them Christian and the other Muslim. During the 1950s the population of Greece was 7 million, while the Turkish population was 21 million, a ratio of three to one in favor of Turkey. Today Greece has slightly more than 11 million inhabitants, while Turkey is the home to more than 70 million people. In other words, today the proportion is already seven to one in favor of Turkey.[6]

If we look at the picture in a larger context, in the early 1970s, the population of the Muslim countries of northern Africa, Algeria, Tunisia, Libya, Morocco, and Egypt, was 70 million. At the same time, the combined populations of France, Italy, Spain, Portugal, and Greece—in other words, the European countries bordering the Mediterranean Sea—numbered 160 million. Today the numbers are 180 million for southern Europe and 150 million for northern Africa.[7] According to the calculations of the demographers, Afghanistan, which had slightly more than 25 million in 2005, will be home to 79.4 million people in 2050. The numbers for Pakistan are respectively 158 and 292 million inhabitants. And for Iran, which in 2005 was populated by 69.4 million people, it will have 100.2 million residents in 2050.[8]

Theoretically speaking, the dramatic increase of the Muslim component of the gigantic migration process represents only one of the aspects of the phenomenon that is occurring and expanding in the ethnic and religious makeup of the world's population. It is a situation, however, that in the long run will bring about a complete change of the social, cultural, and political structures of whole continents. Inevitably, this process will have a deep impact on the entire fabric of international relations as well.

According to some official European assessments, there are currently between 15 million and 20 million Muslims living on the Old Continent.[9] Some American assessments place the number of the representatives of the Muslim minority on European soil at more than 23 million.[10] The main ingredient of the powerful current of Muslim settlers flowing into Europe comes from the Middle East and North Africa, and it consists almost entirely of Muslims. While in 1973, for instance, there were 600,000 Muslims living in Germany, in 2005 their numbers had reached 2.4 million and now exceeds 3 million.[11] According to a survey prepared for the *London Times*, during a relatively short period of time, the Muslim population of Great Britain swelled to more than 1.5 million.[12]

Particularly intense were the dynamics of the increase of the Muslim population in Holland and France. In 1974, there were only 48,000 Muslim residents living in Holland. By 2005, there were already 585,000, and in 2010, this number was in the neighborhood of 1 million. In 1975, there were 1.1 million primarily North African Muslims living in France. By 2002, this number had tripled to 3 million, and today it exceeds 5 million.[13]

Given that the birthrate of the new Muslim residents of Europe remains higher than the birthrate of the Europeans, the ratio between the traditional population and the newcomers quickly changes in favor of the latter category. What is critically important is the Muslim superiority among the members of the most crucial age group, 0–16, that will determine the future demographic structure of the continent. Even today, for instance, one quarter of the population of Brussels under sixteen is Muslim, and the most popular boy's name is Mohammed.

The accuracy of the demographic data concerning the population of Europe is seriously impaired by the fact that, in many countries, no questions are asked concerning the ethnic and religious identity of the residents. Nevertheless, the official statistics do not leave any doubt about the changing panorama of the continent. In France, for instance, the percentage of the Muslim population is somewhere around 10 percent.[14] The situation involving the nature and the dynamics of the Muslim immigration to Europe leaves enough room for the validation of the numerous predictions and warnings that somewhere in the not too distant future the Old Continent will be thoroughly Islamized. Bernard Lewis, who arguably is the best expert on Islam in the world, is a little bit more generous in predicting that this transformation will take place only at the very end of the century.[15]

There are several factors contributing to the Islamization of Europe. The most important among them, undoubtedly, involves the requirements of the shrinking labor market. It could be argued that the oil embargo imposed by OPEC against the Western world in the aftermath of the Yom Kippur/Ramadan War of 1973 not only initiated the process but also determined its dynamics.

The fateful decision of OPEC was made during their conference in Kuwait on October 16 and 17 in 1973. The purpose of the high-level gathering was "to punish" the countries that, according to the participants, helped Israel during the war. The importers of the precious commodity who before the war were paying $2.46 per barrel had to pay $10.46 for the same barrel of oil after the OPEC's Kuwaiti meeting. OPEC also declared an oil embargo against the United States, Denmark, and Holland, who were obviously perceived by the Arab world as the staunchest supporters of Israel.[16] The European statesmen panicked, and led by German Chancellor Brandt and the president of France, George Pompidou, they were in a hurry to declare that Western Europe was ready to cooperate with the League of Arab States to establish a mutually beneficial relationship with the Arab world.

At the initial meeting in Damascus, Arab delegates presented their political preconditions that were supposed to be met before the members of the Arab League would contemplate the signing of any kind of economic or cultural agreement with Western Europe. The list of those preconditions ran as follows:

1. Unconditional Israeli withdrawal to the 1949 armistice lines
2. Arab sovereignty over the Old City of Jerusalem
3. Participation of the Palestinian Organization (PLO) in any negotiations
4. European Community pressure on the United States to detach it from Israel and to bring its policies closer to those of the Arab states[17]

With the uninterrupted flow of oil into the thirsty European markets in mind, the statesmen of the Old Continent were in a hurry to meet all the demands of their future Arab partners. Similar, however, to the classic relationship between every blackmailer and his victim, the satisfaction of the first set of Arab requirements was immediately followed by a second set of demands. Two of the new requirements were designed to play a crucial role in the later stages of the Islamization of Europe.

The first requirement (let's call it a cultural one) sounded like: "If they want to cooperate with the Arab world, the European governments and political leaders have an obligation to protest against the denigration of Arabs in their media. They must reaffirm their confidence in the Euro-Arab friendship and their respect for the millennial contribution of the Arabs to world civilization."[18]

It can be assumed with reasonable certainty that the politicians who had initiated the European-Arab "dialogue" believed they had been doing something beneficial for both parties. The first result from the Arab blackmail of frightened Europe was the unsuspected dynamics of the numerical growth of the Muslim community on the Old Continent.

Why Was Europe So Well-prepared for Islamization?

One of the least-understood aspects of the developments that had made the Islamization of Europe not only possible but in the long-term inevitable, if some dramatic change does not occur, is the fact that the postwar years have brought about the full realization of almost all the dreams of the residents of Western Europe. An important part of the long-forgotten truth was the role the unparalleled generosity of the Marshall Plan played for the economic recovery of Western Europe. Besides, the decades-long American military protection rendered to the Old Continent had allowed the free part of Europe to reinvest its financial gains into its prosperous economy and into the growing welfare sector. In addition to their booming economies, the Western Europeans created the largest and the most-sophisticated system of social services that the world has ever seen. At the same time, the most tragic component of the present-day intense Islamization of the continent reflects the fact that the realization of the huge amount of materialistic desires failed to bring Europe into the perpetuity of a free, affluent, and secure world dreamed about by its residents. Instead, the realization of those dreams became the main reason for the gradual extinction of the European culture, civilization, and political system.

What the happy, until recently, residents of Western Europe had failed to understand (and many of them do not grasp it even today) was the correlation between the accumulation of material wealth and social benefits on the one hand and the gradual disappearance of the traditional moral values on the other. There were many wrongs and failures that are part of European history, but at least for centuries there was also a common belief system and the feeling of belonging to the land of their fathers and grandfathers. Those were powerful emotions that on numerous occasions provided the defenders of the faith and the land with strength, bravery, and a readiness to sacrifice. Speaking of faith, the crisis of European Christianity contributed in a very substantial way to the development of the present-day situation when Western Europe is displaying an amazing lack of ability to defend its traditions, culture, and political and social systems.

Again a voice from the recent past expressed in an incredibly powerful way the problems of contemporary Western civilization, but there were very few European listeners able to benefit from its prophetic power. The voice belonged to the exiled Russian writer Alexander Solzhenitsyn, who back in the already distant 1978 had addressed the students and faculty of Harvard University. Solzhenitsyn made abundantly clear one of his main points:

> A decline in courage may be the most striking feature which an outside observer notices in the West in our days. The Western world has lost its civil courage, both as a whole and separately, in each country, each government each political party and, of course, in the United Nations. Such a decline in courage is particularly noticeable among the ruling groups and the intellectual elite, causing an impression of loss of courage by the entire society. Of course, there are many courageous individuals, but they have no determining influence on public life.[19]

Coming from a completely different belief system, Yusuf al-Qaradawi, who is a highly respected Muslim cleric in the European Muslim community and one of the most influential Sunni theologians, also reached the conclusion that the Western world had lost its spirituality and moral strength: "We condemn the excessive materialism of the West. We deplore the loss of solidarity and brotherliness, the decay of morals and the daily violations of human dignity. God has disappeared—almost nobody in the West talks about Him anymore."[20]

Inevitably, the moral crisis of Western Europe was connected with the crisis in the quality and the very nature of the European leaders. The institutions and the leaders that in the past had forged a sense of unity across the different social groups during the challenging or demanding times do not play the same role anymore. The institutions of Christianity are so weakened that no spiritual leader is able to raise his voice to offer some guidance that leads to a solution of the problems the region is facing. As a matter of fact, the majority of the political and the spiritual leaders of Western Europe have turned a blind eye to the aggressive advancement of radical Islam. In this respect, particularly shocking is the attitude of Prince Charles of the British royal family who has chosen a very strange strategy to not confront but rather to appease the Muslim conquerors of his native country.

Some of the opinions of His Royal Highness are so shocking that one can hardly see any difference between his worldview and the concepts expressed by some Islamic clerics. What should be, for instance, the correct assessment of the following excerpt from one of his statements?

> Islamic culture in its traditional form has striven to preserve this integrated, spiritual view of the world in a way we have not seen fit to do in recent generations in the West. There is much we can learn from that Islamic world view in this respect.
>
> There are many ways in which mutual understanding and appreciation can be built. Perhaps, for instance, we could begin by having more Muslim teachers in British schools, or by encouraging exchanges of teachers. Everywhere in the world people want to learn English. But in the West, in turn, we need to be taught by Islamic teachers how to learn with our hearts, as well with our heads.[21]

Where Did the European Treatment of Muslim Immigrants Go Wrong?

The short answer to where Europe went wrong is very simple: *everything went wrong from the very beginning.* To start, no Western European agency or organization investigated the impact of the conflict between the cultures and the social conditions in the large Western European cities and the substance living in the distant mountainous or desert villages of Morocco, Algeria, and eastern Turkey during the earliest stages of the Muslim immigration.

Maybe many tragedies could have been avoided had someone provided some basic information to the new residents of Europe regarding the political systems and the social conditions existing in their countries of choice. Someone should have explained to the newcomers that the current European societies had been established on the basis of freedom of choice and on a strict division between religion and the state. In other words, no one made any effort to explain to the new Europeans that no religious belief system claiming monopoly over the truth should be imposed upon the rest of the society. Denmark has recently introduced a new set of rules stipulating that everyone who claims Danish citizenship must learn Danish and must pass a basic exam on the nature and the function of the county's political system.

Unfortunately, those requirements should have been reinforced *before* the mass Muslim immigration to Europe, not *after* it.

According to the politically correct interpretations such an approach would have represented a discriminatory act against the Muslims. The politically correct individuals are wrong: the above-mentioned body of information would have been the only way to set up a correct future relationship between the newcomers and their adopted countries. The only possible correct message to them would have been a clear-cut statement made by the authorized agencies dealing with immigration issues to the effect that the gates of Europe are wide open to everyone who accepts the existing rules and closely shut in front of any individual who for whatever reasons does not like them.

On the other hand, no effort has been made by the government institutions or by private agencies to integrate the young Muslims into society by organizing effective programs designed to encourage the process of their integration. Special efforts are urgently needed to prevent the formation of gangs in the Muslim-populated areas by offering language classes and knowledge about the nature and function of the Western world. The material and intellectual potential of the highly developed European states are perfectly capable of providing these kinds of integration-related programs. What has prevented their planning and implementation is not the lack of human or financial resources.

It is political correctness and multicultural dogmas that have established the completely wrong outlook among the government bureaucracy according to which the Muslims should be considered a separate group left alone to develop its own lifestyle within Western European societies. Because of the pathology of the multicultural approach, even if some residents of a Muslim country had expressed interest toward the culture and the social and political system of the country that had accepted them, the reaction of the hosts had been very far from encouraging.

A story that took place in Norway is quite revealing in this respect. At the expense of the taxpayers, the government bureaucracy created the so-called International Cultural Center where the Muslims were supposed to enjoy the opportunity to inform the rest of the visitors about their culture. An Iraqi writer by the name of Walid al-Kubaisi gave the director of the center a hard time by asking him a very logical question: "But isn't it more important for the immigrants to learn about the Norwegian culture and values?"[22] The answer of the cultural bureaucrat from Norway was quite revealing: "It isn't our job to teach them (the Muslim immigrants) the Norwegian culture. They can decide about that for themselves if they wish. . . . You have your culture and we have ours."[23]

Al-Kubaisi, however, asked an even more disturbing question about whether the Muslims should have the right to criticize their own religion. Again, the director's answer deserves to be quoted verbatim: "You are a Muslim, Walid, and you must not to lose your identity. . . . We want to create a multicultural society, and we don't want to dissolve these foreign cultures. Your attitude alters all our plans. It creates conflicts between the immigrants."[24] The adoption of those politically correct concepts and approaches did not bring about the Europeanization of the new residents of the Old Continent, but rather had made possible the Islamization of Europe.

The second huge mistake of the Western Europeans with regard to their new neighbors was the automatic, unconditional, and limitless inclusion of a huge number of Muslim immigrants into the very sophisticated and all-inclusive welfare system of the region. This approach had (and continues to have) disastrous consequences because of the incredibly large, according to developing world standards, perks and benefits indiscriminately given to the immigrants. Understandably and inevitably, it continues to bring new cohorts of candidates for a better life who are coming not to work in Europe but just to live there at the expense of the European taxpayers.

Before addressing the details of a relationship that went very wrong, some important facts should be taken into account. It would be impossible to imagine the German economic miracle without the contribution of the Turkish guest workers. During my early teaching years, while working in a small but heavily industrialized city in my native country of Bulgaria, I observed on a daily basis the early morning arrival to the railway station of large groups of ethnic Turks. They were coming from the nearby villages to work at the industrial facilities where they earned the reputation of being the hardest and most-dependable workers.

The majority of the new wave of Muslim immigration to Europe, however, had a completely different mentality and behavior. Those immigrants were driven to the shores of the Old Continent by the opportunity to live there without working. The dynamics of the process involving the replacement of the hard-working Muslims by a welfare-paychecks-receiving crowd is quite complicated, and its details differ from country to country.

In general, some important changes took place at the European labor market before the appearance of the new Muslim immigrants. In France, for instance, the decreasing need for unskilled labor and the protection offered by the trade unions to their members sharply increased the unemployment rate among the unqualified labor force. This fact stirred the discontent among the young Muslims, who became much more alienated from the French society and much more receptive to the jihadist message of the radical imams. Meanwhile, many Muslim families started receiving unemployment benefits that were gradually replaced by welfare payments.

At the same time, in Holland, the Dutch government no longer needed the contributions of a large number of Moroccan construction workers who had been brought to the country during the years of steady growth. A careful check of the labor-related legislation found that because those workers had arrived in Holland on long-term visas, they were entitled to unemployment and welfare payments. The law was meticulously followed, but its strict application brought about an unexpected and very unpleasant consequence.

What the Dutch social services did not take into account was that unlike the female component of the Dutch labor force, the Muslim women were primarily stay-at-home moms, and given the much larger number of children in their families, the welfare payments, courtesy of the Dutch taxpayers, skyrocketed. Meanwhile, the stream of Muslim immigrants flowed uninterrupted through the largely opened gates of the wealthy Scandinavian countries without having anything to do with the requirements of the labor market.

The multiculturalism that was so wholeheartedly accepted by the bureaucracies and the majority of the European academics created a culture of capitulation that made a jihadist takeover of Europe a real probability. That included a concept according to which the new Muslim immigrants should not only be entitled to welfare payments, but they also should be treated with extreme caution because of their perception that all Muslims are permanent victims of prejudice and discrimination.

The inevitable and easily predictable result of those approaches was the gradual appearance of two parallel societies in each country of Western Europe possessing a higher percentage of Muslim residents. In the beginning of this uneasy cohabitation, each of the countries saw the growth of a brand-new group of citizens whose only connection with their European hosts was the monthly visits to the social security offices to receive their paychecks. This practice led to the emergence of a brand-new social category of nonintegrated individuals united by completely different values and customs in comparison with the European population. Because of its higher birthrate, this category is raising unexpectedly fast. Its representatives populate the Muslim ghettoes surrounding cities such as Marseille, France; Malmo, Sweden; and Rotterdam, Holland, just to name a few.

Most of the Muslim recipients of the financial support do not speak the language of the host country, do not study, and do not work. In Holland, I interviewed a social worker who temporarily worked as a translator for one single immigrant of Azerbaijan. It turned, though, that the future citizen of Holland did not have even the slightest incentive to learn Dutch, preferring instead to spend his days at some café chatting with fellow welfare recipients.

A Moroccan girl working as a waitress to support her studies at a university located in Southern California once asked me with real amazement what kind of country Sweden is, where her sister had immigrated with her family. It was extremely difficult for me to explain the reason why both the sister and her husband were receiving paychecks every month without being required to study or to work.

It would be well worth it to try to establish the general pattern of the problems facing all countries that have accepted the growing streams of the welfare-driven Muslim immigrants. Given that many of the immigrants came from the most backward rural areas of the Middle East and North Africa, their mentality immediately clashed with the tradition and attitudes of the modern Western European societies. The fact that many of the new immigrants never received a modern and systemic education in their countries in addition to their complete lack of familiarity with the Western European society, traditions, and culture created a wall between the immigrants and their new surroundings.

The Europeans evidently thought that they had established the right kind of relationship with their new Muslim countrymen, who would live quietly in their ghettoes while spending their generous welfare payments. The Europeans were wrong on this issue. The parallel coexistence of two completely different societies within the boundaries of the same country did not take too long before producing a lot of problems. The first one involved the emergence of many street gangs consisting of the children of the welfare-receiving residents of the overcrowded communal projects. This problem led to another one: the growth of the crime rate in the Muslim neighborhoods. Some of the most heinous crimes have been committed by the youngsters who have never been made familiar with the culture of the country they live in and who have never learned the lesson that the crime does not pay.

Let's take, for example, such an important issue as the attitude with regard to women. The most negative dimensions of the tradition born many centuries ago in the deserts of North Africa and the Middle East involving the social status of women have determined the social behavior of many young uneducated and nonworking residents of the Muslim ghettoes of Europe. This situation has produced several consequences. There are several important women-related negative developments that emerged as a result of the indiscriminate acceptance of everyone who wanted to live at the expense of the European taxpayers. They could be summarized as the transfer of the tradition of arranged marriages to European soil, the so-called honor killings, female genital mutilation, and the specifics of the rape wave that swept the European metropolises after the emergence of the gangs composed of Muslim youngsters. One of the first visible consequences of the acceptance of so many individuals who did not fit the lifestyle of a contemporary Western society was the dramatic increase of the cases of brutal rape of primarily teenaged and minor girls.

For a boy that grew up in a North African or Middle Eastern village where the only women he had seen were covered from head to toe, the sight of a Western European or Scandinavian girl wearing shorts and a T-shirt was a sight bordering on the rim of his wildest teenage fantasies. On one hand, what turns those youngsters into rapists is the upbringing that had taught them that women are not equal to men. On the other hand, the future rapists had been taught that a woman who does not hide herself behind the traditional outfit is a kind of prostitute who was challenging the males to have sex with her. This is the main explanation for the rape wave that seized Western Europe from Norway all the way to Gibraltar.[25]

There were Scandinavian countries that indeed turned out to be particularly attractive magnets for Muslim newcomers who wanted to have an easy life benefiting from the extremely generous welfare payments—courtesy of the prosperous and generous northerners. The difference between the earlier generations of hard-working Muslims who had arrived in Germany or France after the war and the receivers of social services paychecks of today has already been mentioned. There is another difference, however, that should not be ignored. The generous contributors to the well-being of the new Muslim residents of the Scandinavian countries were directed by very noble purposes, the very premise of which, however, turned out to be very wrong.

The Swedish case turned out to be particularly dramatic to a degree deserving more detailed analysis. Besides, the Swedish situation is worth exploring because of the almost total capitulation of the country in front of the Islamic assault. Unlike the case with the rest of Western Europe, Swedish acceptance of a very large quota of Muslim immigrants has not been dictated entirely, or even primarily, by oil-related considerations. Having been ruled by the Social-Democratic Party ever since 1934, and having been successful in avoiding the calamity of WWII, Sweden had created the most comprehensive welfare system not only in Europe but also in the world. One of the dimensions of the national pride of Sweden often expressed by the Swedish politicians circa the 1970s and 1980s has been the alleged status of the country as a small country but a moral superpower, offering its hospitality to all people who suffered the persecution of different dictatorships.

This opinion could be accepted only if we add some important clarification. During the Cold War, for instance, the neutral Sweden ideologically had tilted to the left. The Swedish policymakers were extremely critical of the United States, having even accepted some American deserters from the Vietnam War. Sweden had also become a home to many immigrants from Latin America who had left Chile and Argentina, which were ruled by dictatorial regimes at the time.

At the same time, however, the Swedish government was extremely docile with regard to Soviet totalitarianism. It did not dare to press Moscow hard enough for the criminal kidnapping in Budapest of the remarkable Swedish diplomat Raul Wallenberg, who had saved many Jewish lives. When the greatest Russian writer of the twentieth century received the Nobel Prize, they did not dare to satisfy the requirement of Alexander Solzhenitsyn to be given the opportunity to accept his award at the Swedish embassy in Moscow. Given that the Soviet regime would not have allowed Solzhenitsyn to come back to his country after the acceptance of the prestigious award, the satisfaction of the completely legitimate request of the writer would have been an act fitting the definition of Sweden as a moral superpower.

As far as Muslim immigration is concerned, the government of the country not only repeated *all* mistakes committed by the rest of Western Europe, but it surpassed by far their magnitude. To start, Sweden continued to accept new Muslim immigrants, which brought about new heights in crimes and the emergence of areas over which the Swedish state de facto had lost its sovereignty. The most shocking example of that is the situation that developed in the third-largest city of Sweden, Malmo, where the police and the fire teams are afraid to respond to the calls coming from the predominantly Muslim-populated neighborhoods. Robberies and rape are on a constant rise, including the shocking increase of cases involving the rape of children under the age of fifteen.

The Muslim quarters of the Swedish cities, together with the Muslim quarters of the Dutch, Belgian, French, and German cities, have been transformed into growing islands of a completely different lifestyle and culture that is deeply hostile to the countries that have been generous enough to accept the "islanders" without caring to present them with a very simple and obvious truth.

Everyone, or almost everyone, I believe, would accept the logic of the premise that if you do not like the rules of a beautiful home you would like to share with its residents, you should not be accepted into it. Such an approach is very reasonable, honest, and necessary. Had its requirements been applied at the earliest stages of the mass Muslim immigration to Europe, there would not have been any problems. Unfortunately, however, the gates of the Old Continent have been left wide open to everyone, including to those who have not arrived with work or studies in mind. Far worse, those gates largely remained open even to individuals whose purpose had been (and still is) to bury the European freedom under the thick ice cap of theocratic and totalitarian dictatorship. In keeping with their dreams, the new Islamic order should outlast even the thousand-year Reich of Adolph Hitler.

Notes

1. *Turkish Daily News*, London, May 21, 2006.
2. Ibid.
3. Ernst Hillebrand, "Too Many or Too Few?: Demographic Growth and International Migration," *Compass 2020* (Berlin: Friedrich Ebert Stiftung, 2007), 2.
4. www.meforum,org/2107/europe-shifting-immigration-dynamic.
5. Ibid.
6. www.serbianna.com/columns/michaletos/003.shtml.
7. "Critical Demographics of the Greater Middle East: A New Lens for Understanding Regional Issues," March 13, 2009, Stanford Center of Longevity, Global Aging Program, http://longevity.stanford.edu/myworld.
8. http://islamicweb.com/begin/population.htm.
9. Ibid.
10. US Department of State, *Annual Report on International Religious Freedom*, 2003.

11. http://euro-islam.info/pages/about.html.
12. http://islamicweb.com/begin/population.htm.
13. www.meforum,org/2107/europe-shifting-immigration-dynamic.
14. http://euro-islam.info/pages/about.html.
15. "Die Welt," Hamburg, 07.28.200411.
16. For the full details about the birth of the so-called Eurabia and for its cultural aspects, see the Egyptian-born Jewish-British author Ba'or *Eurabia—The Euro-Arab Axis* (Farleigh Dickinson University Press/Associate University Press, 2005).
17. "Middle East History: It Happened in November," www.washington-report. org/backissues/1099/9910081.html.
18. The Hamburg Symposium, 1983, Section "Prospect for Cultural Exchange," http://74.6.146.127/search/cache?ei=UTF-8&p=Euro-Arab+Dialogue&icp=1&w=euro; Andrew G. Bostom, "Eurabia—Conspiracy or Policy," *American Thinker*, June 13, 2007.
19. www.americanrhetoric.com/speeches/alexandersolzhenitsynharvard.htm.
20. Michael Radu, *Europe's Ghost: Tolerance, Jihadism, and the Crisis in the West* (New York: Encounter Books, 2009), 88.
21. "Prince Charles Praises Islam," www.sunnah.org/nl/v0104/prince.htm.
22. Quoted from Bruce Bower, *While Europe Slept—How Radical Islam Is Destroying the West from Within* (New York: Broadway Books, 2006), 66.
23. Ibid.
24. Ibid.
25. See for details a site very rich in factual information about the crime wave that had seized the Muslim-populated quarters of cities in Sweden and Norway, but the crime wave follows the same pattern if not the same magnitude throughout Western Europe: http://fjordman.blogspot.com/2005/02/muslim-rape-epidemic-in-sweden-and.html.

5

The Jihadist Assault
on Europe

The remarkable and absolutely correct observation of the famous British historian and philosopher of history Arnold Toynbee, that civilizations do not die of murder but, rather, of suicide, came forcefully to my mind while I was looking at the unexpectedly heavy early morning traffic of Prishtina, Kosovo. The place looked to me as a mother utterly devastated by the impact of the long conflict between her constantly fighting children.

The first murder was seen by the entire world when the Albanian residents of the city were ethnically cleansed by the Serbians during the dictatorial regime of Slobodan Milosevic. The second one was invisible to an indifferent world and took place when the Serbian residents of the city became victims of a no less merciless Albanian ethnic cleansing. Looking at the intense traffic, I was receiving indifferent and occasionally hostile glances from the Albanian drivers because of the Serbian license plates on the van in which I was traveling. It was a battered vehicle that transported doctors, nurses, and teachers who worked at the hospital and at the school of a small Serbian enclave located in the outskirts of Prishtina.

All of the passengers of the battered van were former residents of the city who are currently refugees living in southern Serbia and forced to cross the border each day that separated them from the city where they were born. Then a terrifying thought crossed my mind: what if the fate of the refugees was destined to be the fate of millions of Europeans who could easily be ethnically cleansed in the case of a jihadist triumph over Western civilization. It was the moment when the wise but not consoling thought of Arnold Toynbee came to my mind.

An hour later, I was facing the fragile frame but powerful spirit of Bishop Artemije, the spiritual leader of the remnants of the Serbian community of Kosovo. I asked him point blank what he thought of the sad message of Toynbee. The bishop, however, did not even think for a second before he came up with his powerful answer: "Don't you think that regardless of the magnitude of all calamities it had to endure, the Faith managed to survive among the ruins of all fallen civilizations? By the way, I agree with Toynbee, that they have committed suicide before their enemies managed to kill them."

Faith turned out to be an unexplored angle missing from the illustrious Englishman's definition. At the same time, the statement of Bishop Artemije raised a question that was both important and painful: wasn't it the decrease of moral values and the belief system that had unified Europeans in the past that was the main factor that enabled the jihadist onslaught on the Western civilization?

What Is the Name of the Enemy?

Many people are convinced that Western civilization in general and the United States in particular are threatened by the cancerous growth of a conflict that is becoming sharper and more ominous on a daily basis. There is a paradox involved with this issue though that stems from the fact that there is no clear-cut answer to a seemingly very simple question: *who* is our enemy?

Let's start with the semantics of the problem. What is the real context of the commonly used term "War on Terror"? This definition is outright absurd because terror is only the *method* used by the terrorists. If we agree on that, then the next question could only be this: *who* are the users of this method? This question has a much clearer answer than the first one: the users are the members of the worldwide network of terrorists inspired by the ideology of radical Islam. There is a lot of confusion around this ideology as well.

The numerous attempts designed to determine the nature of radical Islam did not produce a unanimously accepted definition. For many enemies of the jihadists, their ideology represents a kind of "religious Fascism." It could be successfully argued though that the most popular terms designed to describe the essence of the ideology of radical Islam are "Islamic Fundamentalism" and "Islamic Fascism." Many scholars have expressed their reservations with regard to the term "Islamic Fundamentalism" because of its indiscriminate application to completely different phenomena. The definition of radical Islam as "Islamo-Fascism" was introduced as early as 1990 by the Scottish writer Malise Ruthven, but it has been made popular in the United States by the author Christopher Hitchens. According to Hitchens, the similarity between Fascism and radical Islam had been determined by the fact that both movements are extremely violent, anti-intellectual, antidemocratic, and anti-Semitic.[1]

All those analogies are correct, but there is a serious problem with the seemingly unbeatable definition as well. From the point of view of historical and terminological precision, it would be more correct to define the ideology of radical Islam as "Islamo-Nazism" and its adherents as "Islamo-Nazis." Let's not forget that Fascism was an Italian invention that was substantially milder than German Nazism, which with its fierce antidemocratism and pathological anti-Semitism bears a much closer similarity to the ideology of the Islamic jihadists. At the same time, it is beyond any doubt that radical Islam has a lot in common with the left-wing totalitarianism as well. It would be enough to mention the mandatory ideology, the large apparatus of repression, the anti-Americanism, the anti-Semitism (masked as anti-Israelism), and, above all, the endless expansion determined by an aggressive worldview.

Perhaps the best definition of the ideology of radical Islam would be Islamo-totalitarianism. The advantage of this formulation is obvious; it reflects the link between radical Islam on one hand and *both* varieties of totalitarianism on the other. The deficiency of it is also obvious; the term is too intellectual and too heavy duty for everyday use.

Given all those inconveniencies, the best option would be to call things by their real names. The fact that the goal of radical Islam is to impose a global totalitarian dictatorship that combines the worst features of the "classical" branches of Nazism and Stalinism makes its out-and-out totalitarian ideology repellant enough to be called "Islamo-totalitarianism."

The Islamization of the Muslims

Every attempt to analyze the mechanism of the most profound change the European continent has been subjected to inevitably brings about more questions than answers. Or to be more precise, every answer provides ground for a new question. Case in point, it is obvious that the jihadist cells that performed the terrorist acts in Madrid and London are the smallest but deadliest components of the gigantic apparatus of the Islamization rolling across the continent. A very logical question would be the following: who is creating those cells? Is it the individuals who share the basics of the jihadist belief system, or someone who is occupying a higher position within the Islamic terrorist hierarchy?

As a matter of fact, some of the sleeping and active Islamic terrorist cells have been created from below, so to speak, while the others have been organized by emissaries sent from the top leadership of al-Qaeda. What is more important, however, is the realization that the Islamic terrorist cells are the *final product* of the ongoing and intense process of the Islamization of Europe. In other words, the creation of the deadly cells became possible because of the existence of much larger Islamic structures. The largest of them all is Tablighi Jamaat. This organization is as big as it is secretive.[2]

Established in 1926, in the territory of British Colonial India, the purpose of Tablighi Jamaat had been to preach a return to the real (or pure) Islamic values. The preferred way the organization conducts its activities is through missionaries who visit mosques and community and cultural centers throughout the world to propagate those values. The fact that Tablighi is considered controversial by some Islamic circles and outright heretical by others did not affect its popularity at all. Back in 1988, for instance, its annual conference that took place in Raiwind near Lahor, Pakistan, was attended by one million followers. This remarkable achievement transformed Tablighi into the only organization able to put together the second-largest Muslim gathering, surpassed only by the pilgrimage to Mecca, which is mandatory for every Muslim.

Is there any reason to consider Tablighi Jamaat a terrorist organization? The question does not have an easy or simple answer. On one hand, its leaders claim that the only purpose of Tablighi is to propagate the tenets of the Islamic religion the way they were presented by its founder. There is no proof of any coordination between the activities of al-Qaeda and Tablighi Jamaat.

The growth of the European Muslim community and the advancement of the ideology of radical Islam brought about the radicalization of Tablighi Jamaat. It also brought substantial Saudi financial support because of the deeply conservative variety of Islam propagated by the organization. Tablighi became particularly active in Central Asia, where its propaganda activities prepared the ground for the triumph of radical Islam in the area that could emerge as the only option in the case of a Vietnam-style termination of the American military effort in Afghanistan.

The Turkish American author Zeyno Baran provides the following description of the activities performed by the members of Tablighi

Jamaat and of their impact on the Muslim communities exposed to those activities:

> Members are also required to conduct "Tablighi," that is, to try and convert others to Islam, on a regular basis. . . . Members can spend this time camping in small groups in order to preach "the Prophet's way" in the mosques. In Central Asia, they also preach in bazaars. . . . In recent years, like many other Islamic movements, TJ has also become radicalized. Consequently, those who learn about Islam via the TJ are today at risk of supporting or joining terrorist groups. . . . TJ came to the attention of US terrorism experts after it became known that American Muslim terrorist John Walker Lindh was inspired to go to Afghanistan after first traveling to Pakistan with Tablighi.[3]

Particularly active and dangerous are the members of Hizb ut-Tahrir, who left Egypt in the aftermath of the government reprisals that followed the assassination of President Sadat. They formed the hard core of the Egyptian terrorist underground in Western Europe. An interview conducted by the journalist Shiv Malik for *New Statesman* with a disappointed former recruiter for Hizb reveals some interesting details.[4] Well educated, like many other recruits, "Walid" (not his real name) worked across the north of England for five years as a recruiter for the organization. He ran workshops and distributed leaflets, even on the premises of the Leeds Grand Mosque.

Walid made a very interesting difference between Hizb's words and actions. For instance, he pointed out that if you approach the organization to share your desire to become a suicide bomber, "they will try to dissuade you." At the same time, however, there is a large number of Islamic preachers in Great Britain "who offer a violent vision" to their audiences. He reminded the journalist as well that the twenty-seven-year-old British would-be bomber Omar Sharif, who in 2003 tried to blow up a pub in Tel-Aviv, was a regular reader of Hizb's propaganda material. As far as numbers are concerned, Walid stated that in only the United Kingdom Hizb ut-Tahrir has between two and three thousand members.[5]

Particularly important is the role of the Egyptian jihadists in the underworld of radical Islamic terror. The French expert on terrorism Roland Jacquard was absolutely convinced that Mohammed Atta, the leader of the suicidal hijackers who carried out the 9/11 calamity, was strongly influenced by the ideology of Egyptian jihadist organizations.[6] Jacquard was also convinced that "The members of the radical Islamist organization called 'Takfir' are the hard core of the hard core: they are the ones who will be called upon to organize and execute the really big attacks."[7] Another French official voiced the opinion that "The goal of Takfir is to blend into corrupt societies in order to plot attacks against them better. Members will live together, will drink alcohol, eat during Ramadan, become smart dressers and ladies men to show just how integrated they are."[8]

If we accept the premise that the radical Islamist formations that preceded al-Qaeda supplied bin Laden's jihadists with experienced fighters, there were radical imams who played the most important role in influencing the minds of many representatives of the young generation of Muslims living in Europe to the point of pushing them straight into the hands of the jihadists. Not many people realize, however, that it has been the weakness of Europe that created the strength, magnitude, and intensity of radical Islam's assault on the world. What even fewer numbers of Europeans realized was that their ability to resist the impending attack was held in such low esteem by the jihadist planners that the Middle East, North Africa, and South Asia were not selected as an operational base during the first phase of their global quest for power. Wisely, the jihadists chose Europe instead.

The situation that greatly enhanced the process of the Islamization of the continent was born out of the simultaneous emergence of two equally important contributing factors. To present a complicated situation in the simplest possible way, it could be said that when the Muslim immigration wave hit European shores, most of the future organizers of the Islamic jihad and the recruiters of the future jihadists were already there! Its center became the capital of the United Kingdom, not incidentally called by many authors and experts "Londonistan." Because the rise of the immigration tide was getting out of control, which was noticed as early as 1968 by Sir Enoch Powell, many radical Islamists arrived in Great Britain under the guise of political refugees.

Let me make this point clear because it will play a very important role in the development and direction of the jihadist assault. The authorities of the autocratic regimes of Saudi Arabia, Egypt, Syria, Algeria, Morocco, and Jordan were quite rough on the radical Islamists for whom the governments of those countries were too secular and too pro-American. The role of Saudi Arabia with regard to the Islamists was a complicated one: On one hand, the desert kingdom was funneling money into the coffers of the mushrooming "foundations" and "charities" that created the numerous madrassas suddenly appearing all over the world with their only purpose to spread the most radical version of the Islamic religion. On the other hand, however, to put it mildly, the Saudi regime did not act in keeping with the requirements of the human rights organizations while dealing with the Islamists who were trying to organize antigovernment activities inside the country.

At first the arrival of too many sinister characters to the friendly shores of the United Kingdom did not provide reason for any worries. The radical newcomers just immersed themselves in the uncontrolled and gradually getting more uncontrollable waters of the immigrant tide that flooded the United Kingdom. They established contacts between themselves, and gradually London became the place where the most radical publications in the Arabic language started their circulation.

The hospitable Brits were not worried at all. Obviously, they were assuming that if the political immigrants do not have the right to express what they had not been allowed to publish in their countries of origins, what would they be doing in the country that had accepted them? Besides, wasn't it Great Britain that gave birth to the very idea of freedom of speech? The situation, however, started changing during the 1980s with the arrival of some of the war-hardened jihadists from the battlefields of Afghanistan and the unconditional acceptance of a score of fanatical and aggressive imams who quickly became spokesmen for the communities exposed to their vitriolic and hate-filled sermons.

At London's Heathrow Airport I had an interesting conversation with a well-spoken and well-educated Bangladeshi man, who, having arrived as a penniless young immigrant to the country, had worked his way up to a prestigious position as a highly qualified expert in the field of modern technology. I asked why people like him, who were respecting and enjoying everything the British society was able to offer, did not assume a leading position within the Muslim communities instead of the radical imams. The man smiled (it was a sad smile though) and said, "I didn't have time for the mosques and their ignorant imams, sir. At a certain point I had to work two jobs in addition to my attendance of high school in the beginning and the university later."

The Imams

Let's take the case of the most notorious imam among them. Mustafa Kamel Mustafa, who later will became famous under the name Abu Hamza, was born in 1958 in Alexandria, Egypt.[9] His father was a naval officer, and his mother was the headmistress of a primary school. In 1979, the young man arrived in London to continue his education in civil engineering at Brighton Polytechnic College. Most probably under the influence of the process of the radicalization of the young generation of the European Muslim community, in the aftermath of the Iranian Revolution, Abu Hamza adopted the ideology of radical Islam. During the mandatory pilgrimage to Mecca, Hamza met the founder of the Afghan Islamic resistance against the Soviet occupation, Sheikh Abdullah Azzam. Possibly as a result of this meeting, Abu Hamza went to Afghanistan, and if we use the evidence from his trial, "he went there intending never to return."[10]

However, Hamza did return to Great Britain. The comeback was neither a voluntary nor a happy one. While working on a mine-diffusing project in the area of Jalalabad, an explosion took place, and Hamza lost both of his hands and an eye. After his hospitalization and getting accustomed to the use of his right-hand prosthesis, Hamza was again en route in the 1990s. This time the destination was Bosnia, which was embroiled in a civil war between the Muslims, Croats, and Serbs.

Upon his return to Great Britain, in his own words, the radical Islamist was invited to the Finsbury Park Mosque to help normalize the tense relationship between the Pakistani and Bangladeshi attendants of the mosque and those who had come from Morocco, Algeria, Syria, and Egypt.[11] Hamza, who had become a radical cleric by then, acquired national prominence in 1999 when he attracted the attention of Scotland Yard in connection with a conspiracy involving the organization of bomb plots in Yemen. At the time when Abu Hamza was leaving his interrogators as a free man because of the lack of evidence against him, one of his sons was arrested in Yemen, where he later received a jail sentence for his role in the conspiracy.

A moment came when the American authorities also became interested in Hamza's Yemeni connections in the aftermath of the terrorist attack on the USS *Cole* at the Port of Aden. In the end, even the British authorities had enough of Hamza, and he was arrested and finally convicted. After an endless going back and forth, the leading jihadist was sentenced to seven years in jail after which he should be extradited to the United States to be prosecuted for his involvement in the planning of many terrorist acts. There was a report that Abu Hamza continued his jihadist sermons by using the water pipes in his cell. Or, if we use the words of the journalist from the *Daily Mail*, "He is able to give his lectures through the plumbing that connects to neighboring cells in Belmarsh prison."[12]

The most shocking page of the undeservedly long saga of Abu Hamza would be the story of how the British bureaucracy continued to support the criminal's expensive lifestyle by providing welfare to him, his wife, and the eight children he had managed to bring into the world while enjoying substantial financial support courtesy of the British taxpayers. Some numbers may help to grasp the magnitude of the undeserved generosity: According to the estimates of the British Taxpayers' Alliance, the continuous support to a criminal who had devoted his life to recruiting murderous associates and his large parasitic family cost Great Britain £2,750,000, or around $5 million, in welfare payments, council housing, prison bills, trials, and legal appeals. Hamza's legal fight against his impending deportation to the United States would add another £250,000 to this already exorbitant amount.[13]

Another prominent Islamo-Nazi was an individual by the name of Omar Bakri Muhammad. If we use the popular idiomatic expression, the future jihadist was born with a silver spoon in his mouth to a rich family in the ancient Syrian city of Aleppo. His childhood took place among chauffeurs and servants who offered their services to the privileged masters at the luxurious homes and villas spread across three countries: Syria, Turkey, and Lebanon.[14] Unlike Abu Hamza, Omar Bakri Muhammad received a systemic religious education that started at an Islamic boarding school when he was only five years old. The continuation of his studies led him through Islamic universities in Syria, Lebanon, Egypt, and Saudi Arabia, although he never graduated from any of them.

Since his late teens, Bakri Muhammad was an active member of different Islamist organizations. The most important connection in this respect was his association with Hizb-ut-Tahrir. As far as the organizational activities of Bakri Muhammad are concerned, his record got somewhat murky during the 1980s. To start with, it was in Lebanon where Muhammad joined Hizb-ut-Tahrir. After his move to Cairo, he established contacts with the Egyptian branch of the organization. A bit later, however, the future jihadist became disappointed with his political partners.

Most probably well financed by the cautious Saudis, who were (and still are) always ready to bribe their way out of trouble by financing every terrorist group, provided that it conducts its activities anywhere but on Saudi soil, the leadership of Hizb-ut-Tahrir forbade its members to operate within the borders of the desert kingdom.

Following two brief detentions by the Saudi authorities, in 1986, Bakri decided to move to Great Britain, where he tried to establish a computer company but failed. Having brought seven children into the world, the Syria-born jihadist decided to put his family at the mercy of the generous British taxpayers from whom he managed to milk £300,000 in social security payments and, in addition to that, was given a car worth £31,000![15]

What makes this situation even more puzzling is that, for all those twenty years he resided in the United Kingdom, Omar Bakri retained his dual Lebanese and Syrian citizenship but never cared to acquire a British citizenship. In all fairness, Sheikh Bakri never hid the fact that he was on welfare. In an interview, the cleric admitted that he was getting almost £300 per week for himself and his growing family. His comment on this fact deserves to be quoted: "Islam allows me to take the benefit the system offers. I am fully eligible. It is very difficult for me to get a job. Anyway, *most of the leadership of the Islamic movement are on state benefits*" (italics mine).[16]

The virulent but totally parasitic jihadist cleric paid back the generous Brits by preaching vitriolic hatred toward their people, their country, and their political system—an activity that earned him the nickname "Tottenham Ayatollah." In an interview with a London-based Arab newspaper that took place in 1998, Omar Bakri provided an explanation of the Islamic generosity toward the United Kingdom: "I work here in accordance with the covenant of peace which I made with the British Government when I got political asylum. . . . We respect the terms of the bond as Allah orders us to do."[17]

In the process of declaring his peaceful nature, Omar Bakri had forgotten his first conversation with some representatives of the British agency MI5 that took place seven years before the interview with the Arabic newspaper. The British investigators had a serious reason to break the privacy of the welfare receiver and peaceful observer of the covenant with the government of the United Kingdom. As it turned out, at the outbreak of the Gulf War, Sheikh Bakri called for the assassination of the then British Prime Minister John Major. According to one of London's newspapers, Bakri said, "Major is a legitimate target. If anyone gets the opportunity to assassinate him, I don't think they should save it. It is our Islamic duty and we will celebrate his death."[18]

In Bakri's eyes, the participation of Great Britain in a conflict designed to restore the sovereignty of an independent Arab country occupied by Saddam's regime was a crime punishable by the death of the prime minister of the country. Neither he nor any other radical imam, for that matter, had raised his voice against the murderous dictator that had caused suffering and death to millions of Muslims.

It was a regime that had occupied and incorporated the territory of the sovereign Muslim nation of Kuwait and invaded Iran. It was the same regime that had used the deadliest weapons of mass destruction against its own citizens of Kurdish descent.

This situation left Bakri completely indifferent. Instead, on several occasions, the sheikh was a spokesman for the political wing of the so-called International Front for Jihad against Jews and Crusaders, established in 1996 by Osama bin Laden. While denying any direct organizational links with al-Qaeda, Bakri had made abundantly clear his respect and admiration for the founder of al-Qaeda: "We may agree with him in something and disagree with him in something. At the end of the day, *there is no proof yet that he is involved in any terrorist activity*" (italics mine).[19]

Another prominent radical imam is Mullah Krakar, and by no accident, he was also a welfare beneficiary (this time at the courtesy of the Norwegian taxpayers). Mullah Krakar, whose real name is Nahm al-Din-Faraj Ahmad, came to Norway as a "political refugee," got his welfare payments for himself and his expanding family, and started actively propagating jihadist and radical Islamic ideology among the growing Muslim population of Norway. As always in the case of radical imams, there are some unclear moments involving the biography and political career of Mullah Kreker. For instance, there are many experts and scholars who consider him the founder of the radical Islamist organization Ansar-al-Islam (Partisans of Islam), which is an extremely cruel and violent brand of jihadist guerillas operating in the Kurdish-populated areas of northern Iraq along the Iran-Iraq border.[20] The organization acquired a lot of notoriety after the establishment of a Taliban-like regime in the villages it controls in the areas of its operations.

At the same time, however, there is a consensus that Ansar had been created in the mid-1990s at the earliest. If this statement is true, then given the fact that Kreker arrived to Norway in 1991, he could not have been the founder of the organization. Consequently, there are two options to remove the aforementioned contradiction. First, perhaps Kreker was the leading figure among the future members of Ansar, and when followed by Saddam's police, he had to leave the country. Second, Kreker may have formally inaugurated Ansar-al-Islam during some of his trips outside Norway. What is beyond any doubt is that his name is the only well-known one that came from the ranks of the secretive and fanatical group.

Kreker managed to make his name popular in Norway as well by earning the reputation of the most vitriolic and outright jihadist imam residing in, until recently, the very pleasant and extremely quaint capital city of Oslo. Evidently the legal status of the jihadists in Norway is more protected and privileged than in Great Britain, judging by the interview given by Kreker to a Norwegian newspaper. In answer to the question of the interviewing journalist about whether the purpose of the Islamists could be defined as the reestablishment of the rule that had been promulgated by the Prophet, Kreker immediately shot back, "Yes. Our Caliph is dead and we are orphans. Therefore we are fighting, like the Jews fought under David Ben Gurion, for our own state, a state ruled by a true Islamic ruler."[21]

In the next part of the interview, the receiver of the generous Norwegian-style benefits calmly explained to the stunned journalist that "Muslims in the West and Norway don't want to understand that this is not their country. The Muslim state will be their home, *no matter where it is located* (italics mine). . . . Our position is to maintain our numerical strength. . . . It is you and the West who should be telling us what the West can do for us. The West should protect Islam, and not the other way around."[22]

There is an Islamic cleric who is far more important than the receiver of welfare payments from the undeservedly generous social services of Norway. Yusuf al-Qaradawi is an Egyptian-born, extremely respected, and influential Muslim scholar and Islamic preacher. Qaradawi is the head of a religious institute in Qatar, where has lived since the mid-1960s. He is a trustee of the Oxford University Center for Islamic Studies. Because of his program titled "ash-Shariah wal Hayat" (Shariah and Life), which is beamed to the 40 million–strong audience of Al Jazeera—the most popular TV station throughout the Arab world—Sheikh Qaradawi has the largest audience a Muslim cleric has ever had. A 2008 *Foreign Policy* poll put him at number three on the list of the top twenty public intellectuals worldwide.[23]

Yusuf Qaradawi was born in a small Egyptian village in 1926. His father died when he was only two years old. Having the good luck to have loving and nurturing relatives who took excellent care of him, the pious and sensitive boy started his religious education even before his enrollment in a secular school.[24] Upon receiving modest financial support for his excellent record as a high school student, Qaradawi started his studies at Fuad I University (later called Cairo University).[25]

During his student years, Qaradawi joined the Muslim Brotherhood—
an act that earned him several months of imprisonment under Nasser
but at the same time elevated him to a new level of popularity. This
growing amount of prestige enabled the leadership of the Muslim
Brotherhood to offer Qaradawi the position of a supreme leader, not
once but twice, in 1975 and 2004.[26]

Qaradawi's intellectual response to the secular challenges of
Nasser's presidency was the publication of the first of his four books,
published under the title *The Inevitability of the Islamist Solution.*[27]
The very title of the book makes its author one of the predecessors
of the powerful outbreak of radical Islamist and jihadist ideology a
couple of decades later.

Qaradawi's worldview represents a subject area that involves a lot
of controversy and a lot of diametrically opposed interpretations. For
instance, for some people, the sheikh is a living symbol of the cause of
radical Islam because of his firm belief that sooner or later Islam will
triumph over the world. In one of his fatwas, Qaradawi is very specific
on this issue:

> The Prophet Mohammed was asked: "What city will be conquered
> first, Constantinople or Romiyya?" He answered: "The city of Hirqil
> (the Byzantine emperor Heraclius) will be conquered first"—that is,
> Constantinople.
>
> Romiyya is the city called today Rome. Constantinople was con-
> quered by the young 23 year old Ottoman Muhammad bin Morad,
> known in history as Muhammad the Conqueror, in 1453. The other
> city, Romiyya, remains, and we hope and believe (that it too will be
> conquered).This means that Islam will return to Europe as a con-
> queror and victor, after being expelled from it twice—once from
> the South, from Andalusia (Spain) and a second time from the East
> when it knocked several times on the door of Athens. . . . I maintain
> that the conquest this time will not be by sword but by preaching
> and ideology. . . . We want an army of preachers and teachers who
> will present Islam in all languages and in all dialects.[28]

However, on the other hand, the sheikh has been accused of being
a heretic by some radical Islamists. One of their publications was very
explicit about that:

> Yusuf Qaradawi is now trying his best to become the worldwide leader
> of the Wahhabi cult. He controls the Ministry of Religious Affairs of
> Qatar, and has unlimited funds coming from Arab Emirates, from

Kuwait and from Saudiyyah. This is the reason why his campaign of heresy is so massive, and why he and his followers can spend billions of dollars every year to publish his books, to broadcast his videos, to publish everything he writes on the Internet, etc.[29]

What is the truth about Yusuf Qaradawi's moderation? The individuals who are supporting this definition of the Sheikh's ideology are quoting the fatwa issued in the immediate aftermath of 9/11 that was cosigned by Qaradawi and contains a statement that is in a clear-cut contradiction with the basic tenets of radical Islam: "According to the Islamic law the terrorist acts constitute the crime of hirabah, (waging war against the society)."[30]

The key question, however, was how *explicit* was Qaradawi's condemnation of the crime committed on 9/11? Let's turn again to his statements—this time our attention will be focused on one involving the connection between Osama bin Laden and al-Qaeda and their crime:

> We condemn their acts, but I am categorically opposed to the idea of expulsion from the ranks of Muslims. That would be committing the same sort of sin as these people themselves commit: They want to make us and their other critics out to be heretics. . . . The day will come when they will stand in front of the Kadi (Islamic Judge), but at this point, we are not so far along. First we have to decide who should be their judges.[31]

Unlike his condemnation of the crime committed on 9/11, the attitude of Sheikh Qaradawi with regard to the actions of the suicidal murderers on Israeli soil is completely different:

> I was the first who condemned the crimes of 9/11—even before it was clear to many that al-Qaeda was behind the attacks. There is certainly a difference if violence is used in a blind terrorist act if it is. The Israelis might have nuclear bombs but we have the children bomb and there are human bombs that must continue until liberation. . . . We cannot describe the society as civilian. . . . They are not civilian or innocent.[32]

What is particularly disturbing is that one of the precious few Muslim voices that could have exposed the jihadist strategy and jihadist global ambitions and would have contributed to the isolation of the Islamo-totalitarian forces from the rest of the Muslim community had, in a way, supported the jihadist agenda. The following statement by Qaradawi excludes any other interpretation: "Islam is a single nation, there is only one Islamic law and we all pray to the single God. Eventually such a nation will also become a political reality. . . . Obviously, since the Caliphate is the ultimate goal, Muslims, if not the entire world, belong to their own nation—*not to the nations they live in*" (italics mine).[33]

Another Islamic cleric who had the same reputation as the "moderate" thinker and spiritual leader is the Turkish imam by the name of Fethullah Gulen. The only way to address the legacy of the controversial leader would be to investigate his ideas and activities in the light of the process of the Islamization of Turkey that marks the most recent history of the country. There is some arguably boring but absolutely necessary statistical data:

> Today, Turkey has over 85,000 active mosques, one for every 350 citizens—compared to one hospital for every 60,000 citizens—the highest number per capita in the world and, with 90,000 imams, more imams than doctors or teachers. It has thousands of madrassas—like Imam-hatip schools and about four thousand more official Quran schools which may expand the total number tenfold. Spending by the governmental Directorate of Religious Affairs has grown five-fold, from 533 trillion Turkish lira (approximately $325 million) to 2.7 quadrillion lira during the first four and a half years of the AKP government (the current government of Turkey); it has a larger budget than eight other ministries combined.[34]

The Islamization of Turkey is performed at two levels. The first dimension of this process that takes place on Turkish soil is executed by the ruling Islamist Justice and Development Party (AKP by its Turkish acronym). However, the transformation of Turkish society and its politics is advanced with a lot of caution and subtlety. It is this government that is following a strategy of gradual alienation from its long-term allies, such as the United States and Israel. Instead, the Turkish government is executing a gradual rapprochement with Russia, Iran, and Syria. Internally, the AKP government led by Prime Minister Erdogan "has changed textbooks, emphasized religious courses and transferred thousands of certified imams from their positions in the Directorate of Religious Affairs to positions as teachers and administrators in Turkey's public schools."[35]

This is the visible part of the ongoing Islamization of Turkey. As with the icebergs, far more important is the invisible one, symbolized by the personality and activity of the aforementioned "hocaefendi" (Master Lord), Fethullah Gulen. In many ways, this is a mysterious individual who is extremely private and who exercises his enormous influence behind the scenes. The tools of his influence are his numerous followers from the ranks of the AKP—the party that rules Turkey today—his huge media empire, banks, and, above all, his schools, which one day could equal the number of the jihadist madrassas. So, we have every reason to ask some questions about this enigmatic religious, spiritual, and, as a matter of fact, political leader as well.

Fethullah Gulen was born in 1941 (but according to other sources in 1942), in a small village in the vicinity of Erzerum (eastern Turkey). Although he had completed only five classes of school, he is treated not only by his followers but by the condescending academia and by sycophantic journalists as a first-rate intellectual and thinker. At the same time, there can be no doubt that the lack of formal education has to a large degree been compensated for by a high level of natural intelligence and the ability to impress and convince people.[36] Upon obtaining his imam's certificate, Gulen started preaching at different mosques. His sermons were deeply influenced by the views of a famous Turkish cleric and religious thinker of Kurdish nationality by the name of Sheikh Said—i Kurdi, also known as Said i Nursi, who was the founder of the Islamist movement called Nur (Light).[37]

Being too Islamic for the tough secular legislation of Turkey, Gulen's first brush with the law occurred as early as 1971, when he was arrested for violating the strict laws regulating the relationship between the state and the religion. Much later, Gulen avoided an arrest for a much more serious violation of the Turkish law when he was accused of promoting the idea of an armed insurrection. The dynamic cleric avoided the problem by leaving Turkey for the United States. The reason for his desire to visit the United States as presented to the American authorities was health related: Gulen was hoping to find a better treatment for his diabetes. Obviously his health required an extended stay on American soil because Gulen has lived on American soil since 1998.

One of the many mysteries surrounding his personality and to a certain degree his ideology is his incredible wealth. The formerly modest cleric currently enjoys the opulence of a large estate in eastern Pennsylvania, where he lives with about a hundred of his followers, who protect him and cater to his every need. What is the source of the money paying for the upkeep of this kind of lifestyle in addition to the means necessary to maintain the function of hundreds of high schools and dozens of the universities in 110 countries around the world? This is an excellent question, but there is no answer to it.

Formally, Fethullah Gulen does not have anything to do with radical Islam. Just the opposite, he maintains contact with Christian and

Jewish organizations and institutions and is an active proponent for an interreligious dialogue. Is this dimension of Gulen's ideology and activities the main one and the only one?

Bayram Balchi is a French scholar with a Turkish ethnic background who has spent three years in Central Asia investigating the large network of Gulen's schools for his doctoral thesis. Balci has offered a completely different interpretation of Fethullah Gulen's ideology and goals: "Fethullah's aim is the Islamization of Turkish nationality and the Turkification of Islam in the foreign countries. Dozens of Fethullah's Turkish schools abroad—most of which are for the boys—are used to covertly 'convert,' not so much 'in school,' but through direct proselytism 'outside school.'"[38]

By no means is this opinion an isolated one. In 2008, Holland cut several million Euros in government funding for any organizations affiliated with "the Turkish Imam Fethullah Gulen" based on the testimonies of former followers of Gulen who had warned the Dutch authorities that the purpose of the Gulen followers is to bring down the secular order and to replace it with an Islamic one. A nonrelated statement of another disappointed disciple of Gulen pointed out that the followers of the Imam Gulen were referring to Dutch people as "filthy and blasphemous infidels" who "must be made Muslims."[39]

Obviously, the actions of Fethullah Gulen and his followers are in keeping with the Islamic principle of Taqiyya that allows the use of every lie that could be beneficial to the cause of the Islamists. What is most important is that the activities of Fethullah Gulen and his numerous followers and supporters are designed to restore the Islamic caliphate from the times of the Ottoman Empire and to spread the Turkish version of radical Islam throughout the Central Asian, Balkan, and European domains of the new version of the old empire.

The Foot Soldiers of Radical Islam

The first (out of so many!) mysteries involving the jihadist assault on the rest of the world would be the answer to the question of why a French-born person whose father was from Benin and mother from Paris would die in the Chechen War or why a British-born Pakistani man would blow himself up in an Israeli café? Here is the answer: those anomalies have been made possible by the jihadist imams who were able to convince many Muslim residents of Europe that there is no higher calling in life than the blind following of the instructions of the jihadists. This answer, however, immediately creates a follow-up question: why is the propaganda of the imams, who except for Sheikh Qaradawi could hardly be qualified as intellectuals, so successful?

In the pursuit of the answer to this question, careful research will confront the observer with an unexpected discovery; at least part of the success of the jihadist propaganda is because it operates within the *only* link that provides the connection between the majority of the Muslim population and the radical Islamists. This connection has been established and is maintained by the feeling of belonging to a community that is discriminated against by the Europeans but which at the same time is vastly morally superior to the capitalistic West.

Speaking of the minority, actively engaged in the Islamization of Europe, it consists of several distinctive categories of jihadists. The first of them is composed of individuals who have accepted the message of the radical imams and perceive themselves as warriors in the fight against the infidels. This group offers the biggest possible diversity because even a superficial review of the jihadist ranks would reveal the presence of noneducated and socially nonintegrated youngsters from the Muslim ghettoes of the large European metropolises and well-educated individuals who have every chance to succeed in all levels of the modern Western society.

What is the common denominator between the German-educated 9/11 hijacker Mohammed Atta from a well-to-do Egyptian family and the illiterate and slightly deranged Palestinian teenaged suicidal murderer who took the necessary measures to protect his private parts before the fatal blast that tore the upper part of his body apart?[40] The only possible explanation for this absurd act could have been the anticipation of the sexual pleasure promised to him by the unscrupulous recruiters. The difference between both individuals is the most convincing proof for the effectiveness of the jihadist propaganda based upon the premise that the invisible but powerful bond of the Muslim religion connects Muslims from all over the world. The second message that got a positive response was that with the readiness to sacrifice their own lives, the jihadists are not only securing their place in the eternal life after death, but they are also contributing to the global victory of Islam.

Another category of jihadists, not as numerous as the first one but much more monolithic, consists of individuals who have been involved in conflicts with the governments of their countries long before the Soviet occupation of Afghanistan. The generous American financial and material support designed for the needs of the anti-Soviet resistance was masterfully manipulated by the Pakistani intermediaries who made sure that it primarily went to the theocratic wing of the Afghan resistance. Many of the Arab enemies of the dictatorial and pro-American regimes ruling their countries who volunteered to take part in the growing guerilla movement in Afghanistan found them involved in the merciless fight that erupted amid the majestic mountains. The end of the Soviet occupation of Afghanistan did not interrupt the flow of jihadists but rather inaugurated a new phase in the conflict that ended with the establishment of Taliban control over the country. It was this stage that forged the connection between al-Qaeda and the volunteers who had come from all corners of the Muslim world and whose numbers, according to numerous assessments, ranged from 12,000 to 70,000.[41]

The bulk of the recruits had received their basic training in the camps established on Afghan soil by Osama bin Laden's organization. In most of the cases, the European volunteers used to be assigned to a training facility located in Khalden. The best "graduates" from this training received invitations to attend an advanced six-week course that included bomb manufacturing at the Darunta camp. Osama bin Laden received a wonderful opportunity to expand his activities on a global scale, and he used it in the most effective way. It was this situation that enabled al-Qaeda to spread its tentacles into Western Europe, North Africa, the western part of the Balkans, northern Caucasus, and Central Asia and to create the necessary preconditions for further expansion.

Bosnia was the first area of the European continent where about 3,000, according to most of the assessments, foreign mujahideen veterans from the Afghan War made their appearance.[42] Having established themselves in the beautiful old city of Travnik, the jihadists not only committed many acts of bestial cruelty but also became famous for documenting them. They tried really hard to organize their local infrastructure by recruiting a large number of local Muslims. Those efforts failed because the Muslims they were dealing with had been living for centuries in Europe, and while the jihadists were looking at the Balkan conflict as a religious one, for the locals it was a clash between different nations.[43]

The result of those developments would be realized much later, but the very end of the twentieth century was the period of the consolidation and expansion of Islamo-totalitarianism. Given that only the calamity of 9/11 played the role of an eye-opener for the Western world for the danger of Islamic terrorism and, also, given the numerous specifics of that danger, there are many dimensions of the jihadist assault that had received different explanations throughout the years. Some of those issues remain debatable even today. The example of the Hamburg-based radical Islamist cell, historically the most important so far because its creation and evolution brought about the carnage of 9/11, is quite interesting. If we use the terminology of the report prepared for the Danish Ministry of Justice, it states: "The Hamburg cell emerged from a convergence of nine people in an upper-middle-class expatriate student community."[44]

Everything started with the visits of two students with Middle Eastern backgrounds, Mohammed Atta and Ziad Jarrah, to the services at the radical Hamburg mosque, Al Quds. The preachers at the mosque were propagating the same ideas that had created the connection between Atta and Jarrah—virulent anti-Semitism and anti-Americanism. Gradually the group of Middle Eastern radicals studying in Hamburg grew to nine people who started meeting on a regular basis three or four times a week. By the fall of 1999, four of the members of this group decided to join the ranks of the Islamists fighting in Chechnya. An accidental meeting in a train, however, changed everything for them. Directed by the fellow radical Islamist, the members of the Hamburg cell went to Duisburg, where they met an al-Qaeda recruiter who enabled them to reach Afghanistan, where they met Osama bin Laden, who had been looking for candidates for suicide missions.[45]

The continuation of the story is tragically well-known, so I will not repeat it here. What is interesting is that the Hamburg cell came into being independently from the activities of al-Qaeda, and there were organizers of the cell who found their way to the leader of the global jihad to offer him their services. Consequently, there were numerous groups of enthusiastic Islamists ready to kill and to get killed in the process who were looking for al-Qaeda guidance, training, and instructions.

It would be interesting to explore those developments through the eyes of an Algerian Islamist who some years ago was living illegally in Great Britain after serving a jail term in his native Algeria. First of all, let's hear what he had to say about bin Laden, because this is the image shared by a frighteningly large number of people: "For sure, Algerians admire Osama for shaking the notion that the superpowers are invincible. His beauty and poetry recall the noble Islamic warriors of the medieval age, and in our time, the brave mujahedeen who stood up to the tanks of the Soviet atheists invading Afghanistan."[46]

It is also worthwhile to hear "Rashid's" opinion about the impact of the Afghan campaign over the minds of the North African fundamentalists:

> We all felt excited by the victory against the Soviets in Afghanistan. Suddenly our people were not just bare-footed beggars but the conquerors of a superpower. Many rushed to join the fundamentalist movement as an alternative to our corrupt government. . . . The explosive malcontent becomes a tightly controlled member of al-Qaeda. Before an action, the recruit prays until he is in trance-like state. The psychological, spiritual and emotional support given to the brothers fills their hearts to overflowing. The fear of arrest is transcended. The terrorist senses only the pleas of his brothers, a deep anger and a limitless passion for God, for whom he could even, like Abraham, kill his own son.[47]

There is another excerpt from the same author that makes a comment absolutely necessary: "The terrorists fear God alone, and believe Him to be on their side. The Algerian who stabbed a British policeman in Manchester earlier this year, *did so not out of hatred but out of habit* (italics mine), coming from a country where the government's use of torture and the death penalty has made capture fatal. The innocent British policeman was the scapegoat for evils engendered thousands of miles from his home."[48] Obviously the only way for the British authorities not to expose innocent British lives to the knife or to the bullet of individuals who simply are killing "out of habit" would be to not allow their appearance on British soil. Another necessary step would be to deport them immediately upon establishing their whereabouts in the United Kingdom.

Unfortunately for Europe, those measures have not been taken. Many people are living under the illusion that the Islamo-totalitarian assault on the democratic West exists only in the imagination of right-wingers and Islamophobes. There is another category of Europeans who realize the danger but who are assuming that the Americans, who are not welcome during times of peace but who are so badly needed during the times of war, will save the day once again. Unfortunately, there is only a tiny minority of Europeans capable of realizing the huge difference between the battle when you are facing invaders who are trying to enter your country and a conflict when the enemy is already within your country.

Notes

1. Christopher Hitchens, "Defending Islamo-Fascism—It's a Valid Term—Here Is Why," *Slate*, October 22, 2007, www.slate.com/id/2176389.
2. Alex Alexiev, "Tablighi Jamaat: Jihad's Stealthy Legions," *Middle East Quarterly* (January 2005). See also www.meforum/org/article/686.
3. Michael Radu, Op Cit, 203–204.
4. Michael Elliott, "Hate Club," *Time*, November 4, 2001.
5. Ibid.
6. Ibid
7. Ibid.
8. Ibid.
9. "Profile: Aby Hamza," http://news.bbc.co.uk/2/hi/uk_news/4644960.stm.
10. Ibid.
11. www.dailymail.co.uk/news/article-1228195/Hate-preacher-Abu-Hamza-gets-n.
12. Ibid.
13. Jon Ronson, *Them: Adventures with Extremists* (New York: Simon and Schuster), 20.
14. Michael Radu Op. Cit., 228.
15. *The Daily Mirror*, September 7, 1996, http://msanews.mynet.net/MSANE WS/199610/19961911.1.html.
16. www.militantislammonitor.org/article/id/2659.
17. Ibid. Mail on Sunday, November 12, 1995.
18. Ibid.
19. Ibid.
20. Jonathan Schanzer, "Ansar-al-Islam—Back in Iraq," *Middle East Quarterly* (Winter 2004), 41–50.
21. Dagbladet (Norway), March 13, 2006, www.memri.org/report/en/0/0/0/0//0/0/1656.htm.
22. Ibid.
23. http://en.wikipedia.org/wiki/yusuf_al-Qaradawi.
24. "Global Politician—Sheikh Yusuf al-Qaradawi: Portrait of a Leading Islamic Cleric," www.globalpolitician.com/24328-islam.
25. Ibid.
26 "Al-Qaradawi Turns Down Offer to Assume Leadership of the Muslim Brotherhood," Center for Studies on New Religions, *al Jazeera*, January 12, 2004, www.cesnur.org/2004/garadawi.htm.
27. "Global Politician—Sheikh Yusuf al-Qaradawi: Portrait of a Leading Islamic Cleric."
28. Brigitte Gabriel, *They Must Be Stopped—Why We Must Defeat Radical Islam and How We Can Do It* (New York: St. Martin's Griffin, 2008), 147.
29. "Against the Heretic Yusuf al-Qaradawi," www.amislam.com/garadawi.htm.
30. Michael Radu, Op. Cit., 240.
31. Ibid., 241–242.
32. Ibid.
33. Ibid., 243.
34. Rachel Sharon-Krespin, "Fethullah Gulen's Grand Ambition: Turkey's Islamic Danger," *Middle East Quarterly* (Winter 2009), 55–66, www.meforum.org/2045/fethullah-gulens-grand-ambition.

35. Ibid.
36. J. J. Rogers, "Giants of Light: Fethullah Gulen and Meister Echart in Dialogue," The University of Texas, San Antonio, Texas, November 3, 2007.
37. See more about Nursi in Camila Nereid T., *In the Light of Said Nursi: Turkish Nationalism and the Religious Alternative* (London: C. Hurst Publishers, 1998).
38. Sharon-Krespin, "Fethullah Gulen's Grand Ambition: Turkey's Islamic Danger."
39. Ibid.
40. This information was provided by a former Israeli policewoman.
41. Michael Taarnby, "Recruitment of Islamic Terrorists in Europe: Trends and Perspectives," a Research Report for the Danish Ministry of Justice, submitted January 14, 2005, www.jm.dk/image.asp?page=images&objno=71157.
42. Ibid.
43. "Bin Laden's Balkan Connections," http://balkaninfo.wordpress.com/2010/01/12/bin-Laden%E2%80%99s-balkan-connections.
44. "National Commission on Terrorist Attacks upon the United States," www.9–11commission.gov/report/911Report_Ch5.htm.
45. Ibid.
46. "Inside the Mind of a Terrorist," *The Observer*, March 9, 2003.
47. Ibid.
48. Ibid.

6

The Islamo-Totalitarian Challenge to Russia

First among the numerous problems every researcher of the Islam-related issues of Russia encounter involves the number of the country's Muslim residents. The radical Islamists claim that there are 25 million Muslims living in Russia, while according to the scholars, this number fluctuates anywhere from 5 million all the way up to 20 million.[1]

A closer look at the problem reveals a complicated picture. It was back in 2001 when the scholars of the Russian Academy of Civil Service asserted that the number of Russian Muslims did not exceed 15 million.[2] However, given the higher birthrate of the Muslim community and, also, the extremely important fact that Russian women married to Muslims are converting to their husbands' faith, the total number of Muslims should be at least 20 million. According to Ravil Gaynutdin, who is the leader of the Council of Muftis in Russia, the number of Muslim residents of the country is no less than 23 million.[3]

In addition, the demographic calamity plaguing the Slavic and Christian populations contributes to the increase of the percentage of the Muslim component. Alexei Malashenko, who is one of the leading experts on the problems of Russian Islam, pointed out the danger of confusing the issue instead of clarifying it. According to him, the strict following of the polling rules without realizing the numerous specifics marking the mentality of the Muslim population of Russia is leading to erroneous conclusions.[4] The pollsters, for instance, are asking the Muslims how many times a day they pray and how familiar are they with the basic tenets of Islam. Theoretically, this approach is spotless, but in practice it brings a lot of confusion.

A resident of a Tatar village lost somewhere in the endless spread of Russia would say that he does not pray on a daily basis and that he has not read the Koran. In most of the cases, the pollster would also learn that the villager visits a mosque only once in a blue moon. Having heard all that, the pollster would qualify the Tatar farmer as a non-Muslim, and he would be dead wrong because the farmer was been raised in a family whose predecessors have been Muslims for many generations. Even more, such a farmer would not only consider himself a Muslim, but possibly, under certain conditions, he could join the ranks of the Islamo-totalitarians. To avoid this kind of confusion, Malashenko recommends the acceptance of the decisive role of the ethnicity of the Russian Muslims as a criterion for their identity rather than the observance of the rules and rites of the religion itself.

The role of Islam has shaped the personality and identity of the Russian and particularly of the Central Asian Muslims regardless of its severe suppression during the long decades of communist rule. The religious feelings of the representatives of the Muslim communities of Russia have been a very important factor for the preservation of their national and cultural identity. As a matter of fact, historically speaking, Islam appeared in some of the present-day Russian regions before Christianity. It was the Russians who in sixteenth century conquered the lands of the Tartars and the Bashkirs, which have ever since been a part of Russian society.

The second large component of the Russian Muslim community consists of the residents of the regions of Central Asia and the Caucasus that had been conquered by czarist Russia after a long and bloody conflict that took place during the nineteenth century. Traditionally, the majority of the Muslim population of Russia has been concentrated in two major areas: the Volga-Urals region that includes Tatarstan, Bashkortostan (or Bashkiria), Udmurtia, Chuvashia, and Mari-El and pockets in the Ulyanovsk, Samara, Astrakhan, Perm, Nizhniy Novgorod, Yekaterinburg oblasts (districts).[5]

Another large area of the Muslim component of the Russian population is the northern Caucasus, which is home to about four and a half million Muslims. They are divided into a number of ethnic groups: Chechens, Ingushes, Avars, Dargins, Kumyks (or Kalmiks), Lezgins, Chircassian, Karachai, and Balkar. The Muslim residents of the Volga-Ural area and North Caucasus are very different in every possible respect, including their religious identity. The majority of the Russian Muslims are Sunnis, while the Azeris and some small ethnic groups in Dagestan are Shias.

The current demographic trends have transformed the largest city agglomerations of Russia—Moscow, Saint Petersburg, and their surroundings—into the fourth-largest Muslim-populated area of the country. A demographer who is trying to calculate the number of Muslims residing in the capital city of Russia and in the second-largest metropolis of the country would be facing precisely the same problem an American colleague would in an attempt to come up with the number of illegal aliens living in New York City or Los Angeles.

The problem is that because of the economic magnetism of the fast-growing and expanding capital of Russia for the impoverished multitudes of the Caucasian and Central Asian Muslims, huge numbers of them flocked into Moscow and its outskirts. Consequently, there is not a consensus about the number of economic migrants from the new Muslim states of Central Asia; the estimates vary all the way between one and a half to over two million.

Unlike the situation existing today in Western Europe, where newly arrived large groups of Muslims have created a society of their own parallel to the traditional society of the country that accepted them, the Russian Muslims have been a part of the Russian society for centuries. Imperial Russia did not interfere in their religious affairs, and the tiny educated stratum of the Muslim community in particular had all the opportunities existing under the czars and was suffering from all of the deficiencies of the "ancient regime."

After the establishment of communist rule, the status of the Muslim community in Russia changed completely. One of the most essential features of the left-wing totalitarianism was the consistent antireligious policy of the regime toward all forms of religious faith and practice. There was no discrimination in this respect, and the KGB treated with the same level of harshness the active practitioners of religious faith regardless of whether they were Christians, Jews, or Muslims. The famous Russian dissident and gifted poetess Natalia Gorbanevskaia created a remarkable definition of the religious freedom the citizens of the Soviet Union were enjoying: she wrote that they have the full right to pray to God, but on the condition that only God was supposed to hear their prayers.

Joking aside, in the immediate aftermath of the collapse of communism in 1991, there were only three hundred mosques remaining in the country's territory. Entire generations have been raised without the opportunity to practice the religion of their forefathers. At the same time, however, the universal and mandatory education that the czarist regime was never able to develop became a reality during the Soviet period. This situation produced a large group of educated Muslims who were considered and who felt equal to all other residents of the Soviet

111

Union. And they were treated like all other Soviet citizens, receiving free education and health care, but were constantly monitored by the all-powerful and ubiquitous secret police.

The assumption has been that the Soviet regime was successful in eliminating the influence of the Muslim religion over the hearts and minds of the new Soviet-era generations. The reality, however, was more complicated than the assumptions and generalizations. The religious feelings of the representatives of the Muslim communities of Russia have been a very important factor for the preservation of their national and cultural identity.

I clearly recall the impression that an incidental meeting with a young Tadjik poet left on me that took place in Moscow during the early 1970s. We are talking about an individual who, having being raised in a hard-core Communist family of Party apparatchiks, had never read the Koran and had never set his foot inside a mosque. Nevertheless, he expressed the thought that without his vague but emotional and very real attachment to Islam, he would have been a completely different person. And, according to him, he would not have been able to create one single piece of poetry.

Maybe this episode would explain the impressive rebirth of Islam in Russia that occurred in the immediate aftermath of the breakup of the Soviet Union. What should be considered in the process of any attempt to analyze the status of the Muslim community of Russia is the realization that after the end of the Soviet Union there was an important difference with regard to the status of the main components of the Muslim community. On one hand, there are those who have lived for centuries in Russian territory (the Tartars and the Bashkirs, for instance) and who remained there after the demise of the Soviet Union while the residents of Central Asia ended up creating their own states.

The most important development prompted by the end of the Soviet empire within the Muslim communities of Russia and Central Asia was the powerful comeback of the Muslim religion in the areas where it had seemed to have been chased out of forever during the communist regime. The Russian expert Alexei Malashenko mentions the following main features of the "Islamic Renaissance" that took place on Russian soil: "Increased religious awareness and appreciation of being Tatars, Bashkirs, Avars, Chechen, etc.—not just an ethnic group but a part of a giant civilization."[6]

The material expression of the renaissance became the growth of the Islamic religious and educational facilities. In 2000, there were already

4,568 mosques and over 100 Muslim establishments of secondary and higher education.[7] Today, with its more than 8,000 mosques, Russia is in possession of more Muslim prayer institutions than Egypt!

Another very important factor for the growing role of Islam in the world outlook of the Russian Muslims was the elimination of the Iron Curtain—a development that enabled the isolated Muslim community of Russia to establish contacts with the rest of the Muslim world. The same situation of course enabled the inevitable and ubiquitous Saudi foundations to make their way into Russia and Central Asia.

The early 1990s of the last century were the period of the appearance on the political scene of the country of parties the ideology of which had been based on the principles and the teachings of Islam. Actually, the first Islamist party on Russian soil, the Islamic Rebirth Party, was created in 1990, during the last year of the Soviet Union's existence. The legacy of this organization offers too many complexities, and its membership never exceeded 5,000 individuals. Besides, primarily because of personal rivalries, the party terminated its existence only four years later.

Nevertheless, regardless of its short existence, the Islamic Rebirth Party played an important role in the involvement of Russian Muslims in the political process. The fact that the Russian authorities had allowed the registration of a political party whose ideology was based on the principles of Islam had established an extremely important precedent. Even more, after the breakup of the Soviet Union and the transformation of the Muslim republics into independent Muslim states, the Tadjik Party members detached from the party and established their own under the name National Islamic Rebirth Party of Tajikistan (IRP). The short history of IRP was followed by the formation of a score of Muslim political organizations in the territory of Tatarstan, such as Ittifak, the Muslims of Tatarstan, the Young Center of Islamic Culture, and Iman. Another Muslim party was registered in Dagestan under the name of the Dagestan's Islamic Democratic Party, later renamed the Islamic Party of Dagestan.

A typical phenomenon preceding the 1996 presidential elections was the ambition of the Muslim parties to achieve national prominence by associating themselves with the campaigns conducted by the Russian political parties. Given that the parliamentary elections did not bring any of their candidates into the Duma (the Russian Parliament), the role of the Muslim political parties started to fade in the aftermath of the electoral victory of Boris Yeltsin. The fact that even very large Muslim

113

communities such as the one in Tatarstan felt ignored by the rest of the participants in the Russian political process marked the beginning of potentially dangerous development. In Tatarstan, for instance, under the guidance of the gifted poetess Fauziya Bairamova, the Muslim political party Ittifak adopted a document titled "The Constitution of the Tatar People," which underlined the religious (Islamic) component of the Tatar national identity. At the same time, however, having decided to operate within the frame of the law, Ittifak did not call for the secession of Tatarstan from Russia or for the establishment of an Islamic state.

What should not be forgotten, however, is that any search for national identity and the future of any given nationality conducted through the ideology of radical Islam continues to be a potential delayed-action time bomb. In a conversation with the author, a Tatar emigrant to the United States—very anti-Soviet minded and a resolute enemy of radical Islam as well—offered a sincere opinion about the future of Tatarstan. According to him, the Muslims of Tatarstan are much smarter than the residents of Chechnya and Ingushetia because, instead of unleashing a bloody conflict, they will simply wait until the changing demography of the area prompted by the meltdown of the Slavic population will transform the Muslims into a dominating group.

Another attempt aimed at the consolidation of the Muslim political forces of Russia was made in 2001 with the formation of the Islamic Party of Russia by the Dagestani banker Magomet Radzhabov.[8] Regardless of the ambitious banker's claims that his party had a 3.5 million–strong membership, as a matter of fact it did not attract a substantial following. After a ban was imposed on the existence of all political organizations formed on the basis of some religion, the IRP was replaced by two other organizations, True Patriots of Russia and Justice and Development of Russia. They made a coalition that during the parliamentary elections of 2003 managed to gain about 0.25 percent of the vote. After their disappearance from the Russian political scene, the Muslim presence was symbolized by the activities of the following five centers, each of them pretending to be the most genuine representative of the Muslim community in Russia:

1. The Central Spiritual Board of the Muslims of Russia and the European States of CIS, headed by the Mufti Talgat Tadzhuddin
2. The Council of Muftis, headed by the Mufti Ravil Gaynutdin
3. The Supreme Coordinating Center of the Muslims of Russia, the chairman of which calls himself supreme mufti of Russia, Abdul Wahed Nyazov

4. The Islamic Cultural Center in Moscow, also organized by Nyazov
5. The Union of the Moslems of Russia, initially led by Nadirishah Khachilaev

There is also the Coordinating Center of the Moslems of the Northern Caucasus, headed by the Mufti Ismail Berdiev.[9]

The contradiction between the numerical rise of the Muslim community of Russia and its failure to produce a political party able to attract the support of the majority of the Muslims brought about an increase of the authority and prestige of the religious leaders of this community. What is very important to know is that the religious leaders of the Muslim community did not take advantage of the disintegration of the Soviet Union to appeal for the establishment of Muslim states in the territory of the Russian Federation. Even the potentially dangerous and somewhat problematic Tatarstan did not pose any problems in this respect. At the same time, the Muslim clergymen, possibly encouraged by the changing demography of the country, raised some demands that could constitute a future danger for the unity of the country.

In September 2005, Ravil Gaynutdin, the leader of the Council of the Russian Muftis, for instance, publicly addressed the possibility that "at some point in the future" Russia could consider introducing the position of a vice presidency to be occupied by a Muslim.[10] A couple of months later, Nafigul Ashirov, who was a chairman of the Spiritual Administration of Moslems of the Asian Part of Russia, called for the removal of Christian symbols from the Russian Federation's coat of arms.[11] Two years after that, a group of Muslim clergymen initiated a discussion about the possibility for the creation of Muslim detachments in the Russian Army.[12]

Isn't this trend of thought strongly reminiscent of the earliest phase of the Islamic demands raised by the Western European radical imams? There is more to it: are we right to reach the conclusion that the continuing change of the demographic panorama of Russia will bring the further escalation of radical Islamist demands? Or, to put an immensely complicated question in the simplest possible terms, given the deafening beat of the drums of Islamic propaganda, how long will the Russian Muslim community continue to regard itself as a part of Russia?

The Ordeal of Chechnya

The situation in the area of North Caucasus took a completely different turn. The most important difference between that area and the rest of the Muslim-populated areas of Russia has been determined by the different historical traditions and social conditions. Geographically, the area is located between the Black and the Caspian Seas. Besides the ethnically Russian sections of Krasnodar, and Stavropol, moving from west to east, we will find territories possessing the status of autonomous republics: Adygeia, Karachai-Cherkessia, Kabardino-Balkaria, North Osetia-Alania, Ingushetia, Chechnya, and Dagestan.

A short review of the history and traditions of the Muslim population of Chechnya, Ingushetia, and Dagestan could provide some insights about the nature and dynamics of the conflict ravaging the area for years. The Chechens are one of the most ancient population groups living in the present-day territory of Russia, and some scholars have expressed the opinion that they were among the residents of one of the earliest state formations in human history, called Urartu. The isolation provided by the mostly inaccessible mountainous setting forged a kind of society typical of many isolated mountainous parts of the world and some islands.

By tradition, the Chechen society consisted of 9 taips (tribes) and 150 separate clans. The taips never had individual leaders, while the clans have been ruled by the councils of the elders whose power was undisputed and respected to the point of transforming every village into an autonomous unit. Temporary alliances emerged only in case of some dangerous common threat. The mentality of the residents of those clannish societies, shaped by a tradition that goes as far back as history acquired its voice, includes the rejection of any outside form of power.

The best way to judge the character of not just of the individuals but of the nations as well is to analyze their behavior under extraordinary circumstances. The Muslim resistance against the Russian conquest of North Caucasus was so stubborn and so fanatical that it took decades for the Imperial Army to impose Russian rule.[13] The inclusion of Chechnya and Ingushetia into the frame of the Russian Empire did not affect the traditional way of living in the hardly accessible mountainous villages much, where the day-to-day living continued to be regulated by the traditional clannish structure and functions. Similar to the pattern of strategy applied in Tatarstan and Bashkiria, the Russians did not try to intervene in the religious universe of the Muslim population, so it is small wonder that the traditional society established long ago in the Caucasian mountains managed to survive the Russian monarchy that crumbled in 1917.

Unlike the defunct czarist regime, the Soviet totalitarianism had a much larger impact on the traditional society that had continued its existence in the depth of the Caucasian mountains. The region as a whole, and the Chechens in particular, resisted the brutal campaign of forcible collectivization of the land and the intense antireligious (in the Chechen- and Ingush-related case, anti-Islamic) campaign. It is no wonder then that during the summer of 1942 the population of North Caucasus granted a warm welcome to the advancing German troops.[14]

After the end of the short German military presence in the Caucasus area and the restoration of the Soviet control over it, Joseph Stalin decided that the payback time had arrived. In keeping with the genocidal impulses hidden in the very essence of every variety of totalitarianism, the dictator ordered the exile of the entire Chechen nation in some of the most inhospitable areas of the Soviet Union. The roundup of the Chechen villagers in the depth of winter was accompanied by a lot of cruelties and bestialities performed by Stalin's henchmen, such as the murders of people who were not able to walk, the burning of many villages, and the destruction of every trace of the centuries-old Chechen presence by the destruction of mosques and graveyards. Almost half of the internees died in the icy-cold railway cars en route to the place selected by Joseph Stalin to be their grave.

A well-educated Chechen man who was born in exile related to me the terrifying ordeal of his family. His parents, a young couple at the time, had lost both of their very young daughters during the journey that lasted up to several weeks to the distant steppes of northern Kazakhstan. Given that food and water had been distributed only once in several days, the parents had to keep the tiny bodies locked in their hopeless embrace while waiting for a longer stop, which was the time when all dead bodies had to be buried by the internees. The winter ground was very firm, so the graves were really shallow. The Chechen man who carried the terrible legacy of his family story ended his tale with the revelation that upon the return of his family to Caucasus, neither he nor his parents have *ever* boarded a train again.[15]

Speaking of the Chechen national character, quite revealing examples could be found in the unwritten pages of the history of the collective punishment imposed on the Chechens by Joseph Stalin. The first amazing feature displayed by the exiled Caucasians was the almost complete absence of cooperation between them and their tormentors. According to an astute observation of Alexander Solzhenitsyn in his monumental history of gulags, the exiles from Chechnya and Ingushetia turned out to be the only groups among the endless victims of the Stalinist repression who remained free of traitors. The fate of the real or even the potential informers was decided by the elders, and the condemned person disappeared, together with his family.

Khrushchev's amnesty of 1957 and the comeback of the exiled nations did not heal the old wounds. In a way, it was only the educated strata of the young intelligentsia that was able to move with an amazing dexterity within the frame of two completely different words. They felt equally at ease within the realm of their universities, institutes, and working places and the unchanged and in many ways unchangeable world of their parents and grandparents when they were visiting their home areas.

The sudden and unexpected downfall of Soviet totalitarianism and the breakup of the Soviet Union had a different impact in Chechnya and Ingushetia than in any other Muslim-populated area of the country. Unlike the situation in Tatarstan, where a renaissance of the long-suppressed Muslim religion took place, Chechnya was burning not in religious but in nationalist fever. It was in November 1990 when Dzokhar Dudayev was elected as a leader of the so-called All-National Congress of the Chechen People.[16] Let's not forget that to start with nothing of the biography of Dudayev provides any reason for the conclusion that he had anything to do with Islam in general or with its radical version in particular.

Born in exile, Dudayev was thirteen years old when he saw the mountains of Chechnya for the first time. He had a distinguished military career, which was a real rarity for a Chechen because they were considered unreliable, regardless of Khrushchev's amnesty. Dudayev upgraded his sophistication as a fighter pilot at the prestigious Soviet Air Force Academy named after Yuri Gagarin. Besides meeting the extremely high criteria, the ambitious Chechen managed to enroll in Yuri Gagarin Academy by hiding his Chechen background and presenting himself as an Osetin.

Dzokhar Dudayev became the first Chechen to achieve the rank of general. In addition to the fact that the successful military leader was not at all interested in Islam, he became a member of the Communist Party of the Soviet Union, which had been one of the reasons for his career advancement that during the last years of the Soviet Union had brought him the command of the 23rd Strategic Bomber Division.

A defining moment in Dudayev's life was his assignment to Tartu (Estonia), where he became involved in the whirlwind of the Estonian push for independence. The riotous Chechen in Dudayev overcame his status of Soviet general, and he refused to follow an order for his division to put down the fire of Estonian nationalism. Instead, the former Soviet general went back to Chechnya, where he started his political activity. The grateful Estonians, however, remembered his behavior in their country and named a street in Tartu after Dudayev.

The other interesting dimension of the first act of the Chechen drama was the indisputable fact that the goal of the committee that had selected Dudayev as its leader was to achieve sovereignty *within* the borders of the Soviet Union. The referendum that took place in October of 1991, in other words, *after* the breakup of the Soviet Union, did not authorize the complete independence of the tiny republic either.

Dudayev, however, in his capacity as the president of the Republic of Ichkeria, as Chechnya had been quickly renamed, unilaterally proclaimed the independence of the country and its secession from the Soviet Union and Russia. My attempts to establish what the reaction of the Chechens to this act by Dudayev did not produce a convincing result because of the radically different reactions to it on the part of the interviewees. For instance, a man who had left the area in 1994 told me that the decision by Dudayev had been extremely popular with Chechnya's population.[17]

A second emigrant, however, expressed a very different opinion, and he claimed that his attitude is shared by the majority of his copatriots. The essence of the explanation offered by him was that the population of Chechnya was enjoying the fullest possible degree of autonomy *within* the borders of the Russian Federation.[18] According to the second witness of the events, Dudayev was a popular and respected leader and probably could have led Chechnya to democracy and prosperity by accepting the symbolic connection with Moscow.

Given the importance of such factors as age and education, the first interviewee was sixteen years old in 1991, had completed his education in the West, and was employed as an independent contractor. The second one was thirty-nine years old in 1991, and he had obtained his education in the former Soviet Union, outside of Chechnya.

There is enough evidence supporting the thesis that the period between the proclamation of the Chechen independence and the first Chechen War (1991–1994) was not a happy time for the newly "independent" Chechnya. There is no contradiction between the opinions of the people holding different political views that it was a time of corruption, lawlessness, and an exodus from the territory by the minorities, primarily the Slavic residents.

The initial Russian reaction to Chechen independence was determined by the consideration to find some alternative to a military option. Guided by this choice, President Yeltsin's administration offered substate (in other words, the fullest possible) autonomy along the lines of the one enjoyed by Tatarstan. In all fairness, this Russian offer would have been the best and mutually beneficial solution to the problem because it would have offered a preservation of the territorial integrity of Russia and the de facto self-rule for the people of Chechnya.

At the same time, however, there are strong reasons to believe that the Russian offer was not a sincere one. President Yeltsin's government, for instance, provided substantial financial and military support to a pro-Russian organization, Congress of the Peoples of Chechnya, created by Umar Avturkhanov in June of 1994, with the purpose of confronting Dudayev's government. Taking advantage of this support, Avturkhanov, acting upon instructions from Moscow, invaded the capital city of Grozny in October of 1994. His military force consisted of Chechens only. Against his expectations, the pro-Russian leader did not meet serious resistance from the almost anarchistic and disorganized army of Dudayev.[19]

If the Russians have been expecting smooth sailing in Grozny, they should have been bitterly disappointed. The lack of law and order in the Chechen capital evidently was contagious because the money given to Avturkhanov's warriors quickly disappeared and the military equipment was sold to anonymous buyers.

Convinced that Chechnya would not be taken back with the help of the locals, President Yeltsin authorized the taking of the Chechen capital by the Russian Army. This attack, which turned out to be unsuccessful, prompted the start of the First Chechen War that lasted through the summer of 1996.[20] The war was both shameful and unsuccessful for the former totalitarian superpower. The Russian troops turned out to be undersupplied, undertrained, and, above all, undermotivated.

Distracted by the day-to-day activities on the newly established front line, the world missed the development of a very important phenomenon that could be described as the emergence of radical Islam as an extremely important factor that gradually transformed into one of the major components of the conflict.

In April of 1995, the Russian Special Forces managed to kill the president of Chechnya, Dzokhar Dudayev. The event proved to be extremely important because the murdered leader had been an anti-Russian politician in the sense that he had been a strong supporter of the Chechen independence, but at the same time, he had undoubtedly been a secular leader. His death inaugurated the era of the radical Islamists who became instrumental in enlarging and maintaining the fire of the Russian-Chechen conflict.

This moment is very important and deserves closer scrutiny. To start with, radical Islam did not play any role during the earliest phase of the process that led to the proclamation of Chechnya's independence. The first president of independent Chechnya, Dzokhar Dudayev, was a former general-lieutenant from the Soviet Air Force and a former member of the Communist Party of the Soviet Union. It is true that, during the ceremony of his inauguration, Dudayev was sworn in holding a copy of the Koran. He promised as well that, in his capacity as president of the republic, he would protect the Islamic faith. At the same time, though, Dudayev assured his audience that his purpose was to create "a secular, constitutional state with equal rights, obligations and opportunities for all citizens."[21]

A closer look into the background of the rest of the leaders of the Chechen nationalists would reveal the same pattern typical of Dudayev. During the Soviet times, for instance, the second (temporary) president of the Chechen republic, Zelimkhan Yandarbiyev, was a nationalist poet and author of children's book. Aslan Maskhadov, who became the third president of the little country in the aftermath of amazingly fair elections observed by the representatives of twenty countries, was a professional military man who graduated from the military school in Tbilisi and later continued his education at the Artillery Academy of Leningrad. His successful military career afterward only confirms the guess that the man had anything to do with radical Islam.

The appearance of the Islamic and jihadist components in the ideology and practice of Chechen nationalism was determined by two equally important factors.[22] The first is the fact that, with the exception of Georgia, no one else recognized the independence of Chechnya. In this respect, the Chechens have shared the tragic fate of the Kurds, who remained stateless because the creation of an independent Kurdish state would have affected too many interests and too many powerful international players. Second, the Chechen conflict offered a tremendous opportunity to al-Qaeda to establish its military presence in a very strategically located area. The Chechen lands are close to the Caspian oil, Central Asia, and Turkey, and, in addition, the bloody conflict offered the radical Islamists the opportunity to pour some oil on the fire of a conflict that undermined the stability and territorial integrity of Russia.

Not incidentally, the number two in the al-Qaeda hierarchy, Dr. Ayman al-Zawahiri, tried to reach the Islamist stronghold in Chechnya. The looting of his computer some time later and its resale to a reporter with *Wall Street Journal* revealed the amazing saga of the jihadist on Russian soil. On December 1, 1996, during his attempt to cross the Chechen border, al-Zawahiri was detained with a false passport, advanced communication equipment, and a large sum of money in different denominations. Unfortunately, the Russian security police did not show any interest in the content of the Arabic text, and for this reason, the trial that took place in April of 1997 ended up with the dismissal of the case.[23]

Meanwhile, a stream of Muslim volunteers made their way into the distant and isolated mountains of Chechnya. The Islamic financial network of international terrorism, supported primarily by American oil dollars, had been put at disposal of the fast-growing number of Islamic enemies of Russia. There were two waves of Muslim volunteers that are often confused by the authors trying to make sense and to describe the jihadist aspect of the conflict ravaging the Caucasian area. The important point is that the first outsiders who made their appearance on the battlefield were Chechen nationals who came from the Chechen expatriate communities of Turkey and in lesser numbers from Jordan.[24] Regardless of the fact that undoubtedly there were some Islamists among them, the majority of the volunteers were motivated by nationalist rather than religious considerations.

The non-Chechen jihadist participants in the Chechen Wars primarily came from the Arab countries. There were many representatives of other nations: Pakistanis, Kosovo Albanians, Tadjiks, Uzbeks, Turkmens, and also jihadists from some Muslim-populated countries of tropical Africa. It was not the nationality-related issues that had prompted their decisions to risk their lives in the distant Caucasian mountains, about the existence of which most of them had little knowledge. What mattered was their devotion to the Wahhabi branch of Islam promoted by the al-Qaeda terrorists and some dubious Saudi "foundations." It was very clear who was calling the shots as far as the Islamist component of the conflict was concerned.

Some of the jihadists were veterans from the battlefields of the anti-Soviet war they had waged in Afghanistan. Some of them (about 2,000 individuals) had received their training in seven training facilities located in mostly inaccessible areas of Chechnya and Dagestan. Their presence became particularly visible during the Second Chechen War.[25]

The jihadists unleashed an intense recruitment campaign designed to attract young Chechens into their ranks. Strangely, at first glance, they had not counted on the attractiveness of the paradise waiting for the Muslim warriors after their death on the battlefields. Instead, the recruiters offered $1,000 to every potential volunteer. Any new recruit who would be able to bring five more warriors received $5,000.[26]

The transformation of the Chechen elite from nationalists to Islamic fundamentalists was a very logical process because the jihadists turned out to be the only foreign supporters of the Chechen independence. One of the many developments neglected by the main-line media was the growing contradictions between the secular Chechen nationalists and their recent partners. The conflict reached the very top of the social Chechen pyramid when President Aslan Makhsadov accused his temporary predecessor, Zemilkhan Yanderliev, of establishing a too close relationship with the jihadists and of involving himself in shady financial deals with them.

The main content of the fast Islamization of the Chechen conflict, however, was not connected with the murky deals of Yanderliev, but rather with the personality and activities of Shamil Bassaev.[27] Unlike the representatives of the older generation of Chechen nationalists, Baseyev was born after the return of the Chechen nation from the Stalinist exile. He was born into a family that possessed a long-standing tradition of anti-Russian and anti-Soviet resistance. His grandfather happened to be one of the leaders of a Muslim insurrection, the purpose of which had been the establishment of a North Caucasian emirate. Unlike the case with the nationalistic Chechen leaders, the Soviet period of Baseyev's life had been a complete failure. The future leader of the Chechen Islamists was unable to obtain either higher education or qualifications to open the door to some better job.

Evidently not fitted for studies, ever since his earlier years, Shamil Baseyev was an adventurer who possessed enormous bravery and the uncanny ability to take risks. His name hit media releases for the first time in 1991. It was the time when, together with two associates, Baseyev had organized the kidnapping of a Russian passenger plane to Ankara, Turkey. The demands of the kidnappers purposefully attracted the world's attention to the situation in Chechnya, the independence of which had been threatened by the possibility of all-out Russian assault. The Turks returned the passengers and the plane, but they allowed the kidnappers a free return to Chechnya, where the nationwide prominence greatly facilitated the political career of Basayev.

During the early 1990s, Basayev made his appearance in the Georgian area of Abkhazia where the tension brewing between the 250,000-strong Georgian majority and about 90,000-strong Abkhasian Muslim minority took a turn toward open conflict. It turned out as well that the minority was much better armed and prepared for that, and, as a result, the Georgian majority was ethnically cleansed and forced to leave Abkhazia. By the way, almost no one living outside of the area paid any attention to those dramatic events whatsoever.

The next destination of the indefatigable warrior turned out to be Nagorno Karabah, an Armenian enclave located in Azerbaijani territory that during the bitter post-Soviet feuds had been transformed into a battlefield. Basayev's participation in the military campaign in the territory confirmed his image as a resolute and smart military leader. One of the high-level Azeri officers left the following description of Baseyev's participation in the war between the Armenians and the Azeris: "The Chechen volunteers led by Shamil Basayev and Salmon Rachiev have rendered us an invaluable help in the battles."

Basayev also took a very active part in the First Chechen War, where he masterfully commanded the unit that had distinguished itself during the intense street fights for the capital city of Grozny. His popularity in Chechnya had increased even more as a result of the partisan raid conducted in summer of 1995 of the Russian city of Budyonnovsk, organized and personally led by Baseyev.[28]

Although the original target of the attack had been a Russian military base located in the city, on their way back, the participants in the attack fortified themselves in the city hospital and took a large number of hostages. Baseyev's daring raid at Budyonnovsk ended up a complete success as it forced the Russian government to accept the main condition of the attackers who wanted a public declaration from Moscow about the Russian readiness to start negotiations. Using the living shield of some of their kidnapped victims, the participants in the raid managed to reach a safe refuge in the mountains of Chechnya. They did not care that their operation left 129 dead bodies behind.

After the end of the First Chechen War in 1996 and in the aftermath of the assassination of President Dudayev, Shamil Basayev raised his candidacy for president, but he was defeated by his rival, Aslan Maskhadov. During the following years, Basayev became the leader of the Islamist trend that was getting more and more pronounced on the Chechen side of the conflict. This trend to a certain degree became inevitable in light of the bitter feeling of being abandoned by the rest of the world that started to prevail among the Chechens. The bitterness was so strong that it had filled to the rim the heart of an eight-year-old Chechen boy who wrote in his notebook: "Why Putin doesn't understand that we are people too?"

Shamil Basayev decided to use this powerful emotion to establish his leadership over the Chechens by following the pattern of the Budyonnovsk raid and transferring the hostile actions to the enemy's territory. There was an important additional consideration to the effect that any assault on Russian soil would have larger propaganda-related impact over the world with regard to the Chechen plight and cause. There were some Chechens who tended to believe that this strategy was a right one. Their expectation, however, did not materialize simply because no one can correct one wrong action by committing an even more wrong action in return.

What Baseyev organized and did on Russian soil represented a series of the most appalling and heinous crimes committed by a terrorist network against an innocent civilian population. He planned and executed the apartment explosions in Moscow and in several other Russian cities and the nightmarish hostage crises in one of the leading theaters of Moscow and the school in Beslan, that brought about hundreds of casualties. Basayev managed as well to expand the jihadist war into neighboring Dagestan.

Regardless of the official statements periodically issued by Moscow to the effect that the Chechen conflict was over, the situation in the area was far from being calm and clear. In short, the combined actions of the Russian armed forces and intelligence agencies managed to eliminate almost completely both the nationalist and Islamic wings of Chechen nationalism. Dudayev, Maskhadov, and Basayev were all dead, and Yanderbiyev had been murdered on the distant shores of Qatar.

For their part, the jihadists were successful in killing the pro-Russian president of the Chechen autonomous republic, Kadyrov, whose son is the current president and with the fullest possible Russian support rules his small country with an iron fist. That he is a wholehearted supporter of the Islamic political and judicial system does not disturb Moscow.

All in all, the number of active jihadists hidden in their mountainous hideaways and led by Doku Umarov, who is as fanatical and possessing of the same amount of suicidal bravery as Basayev, could hardly be more than 1,000 individuals. How large is the Islamic underground leading a "legal" way of living while waiting for the moment to reappear on the surface is an open question. For the time being, Chechnya looks calm. No one knows though for how long.

The Russian Strategy with Regard to the Muslims

There are couple of very important considerations guiding the Russian strategy with regard to the Muslim community of Russia developed during Mr. Putin's presidency that have remained unchanged. Starting with Tatarstan, containing the highest compact Muslim population within the federation, Russia has guaranteed the largest possible autonomy to that republic.

In Tatarstan, President Putin got personally involved in an effort designed to produce and reinforce a diametrically opposed image of Russia compared to the one existing among the population of North Caucasus. On August 29, 2005, the president made his personal appearance at the opening session of the World Congress of the Tatars in the capital city of Kazan.[29] The event had attracted representatives of sixty-one regions of Russia and guests from twenty-six primarily Muslim foreign countries, including the general secretary of the Conference of the Islamic States, General Ekmeleddin Ihsanoglu. One can only imagine the impact of the decision by President Putin to deliver his speech in the Tatar language.

The result of this well-planned and well-executed strategy was the peaceful and remarkably stable functioning of the government of Tatarstan. The first change at the highest level of power took place only in March 2010, when President Mintimer Shaimiyev, who had been in power since 1991, was replaced by his prime minister, Rustam Minnikhanov.[30]

The Islamic religion is protected by the local government up to the point of acceptance of what is officially called "the non-traditional Islamic groups," which is a cover name for the jihadists who are involved in propaganda activities and during the Chechen wars with the recruitment of volunteers. The government has reached the correct decision that given the insignificant level of the popularity of those groups, it does not make any sense to provide them with the opportunity to present themselves as martyrs. As a result, the impact of radical Islam in Tatarstan is much weaker than in Chechnya.

It is undeniable fact that many accusations against the ruling elite of Tatarstan, of corruption and nepotism in particular, are well founded. Evidently, however, the assumption has been that if this is the price that must be paid for good relations between Kazan and Moscow, then it is well worth it to pay it. The same rule applies to the differences between the attitudes of both governments with regard to some international developments. The best example in this respect has been the attitude of the government of Tatarstan with regard to the ethnic conflict that had the former Yugoslavia torn apart. President Putin's policy was the one in support of the Serbs, while Tatarstan expressed its support for the Muslim communities of Bosnia and Kosovo. This difference did not produce any rift between Moscow and Kazan, and its existence has proven once more the wisdom of moderation.

At the same time, there can be little doubt that the Tatar population and its intelligentsia in particular are dreaming of expanding the independent status of their republic. The ethnic consideration is the most important component of this urge: there is a largely supported view that the Tatar language must be recognized as an official language of the republic together with Russian. Another source of the above-mentioned urge is connected with the economy: there is a consensus in Tatarstan that the republic must diversify its economic connections with the European Union along both lines of investments and trade. As far as the political dimension of the problem is concerned, the prevailing attitude among the Tatar population of Tatarstan with regard to the relationship with Moscow could be described as a partnership between equals.

The politics of President Putin toward the Republic of Tatarstan could be regarded as a part of his strategy designed to convince the Muslim world that for centuries Russia has been a home to Christians and Muslims and that the post-communist Russia is offering to the Muslims everything they have been deprived of under communism. To maintain its dialogue with the Muslim world, Russia applied and was granted the status of an observer within the frame of the Conference of the Islamic States—the most representative organization that includes all Muslim countries in the world.

As far as the Chechen conflict is concerned, it is just a nationalistic revolt Russia has to fight, as any country would, to save the integrity of its territory. Looked at through the lens of the government's rhetoric, the Chechen enemies of Russia are not Islamic terrorists inspired by the ideology of Wahhabism. Oh, no! They are just "extremists." One can only wonder about the degree of similarity between the American and Russian definitions of the most dangerous enemies of both countries. The big question remains: how big is the chance that this kind of terminology and the considerations behind it take both countries on the road to defeat?

The future conflict (for the time being almost invisible) is simultaneously brewing inside the country and also next to its borders. Some important symptoms marking the deepening of the rift between the religious leaders of the Muslim community of Russia, on one hand, and the Russian church and the government institutions, on the other, have made their appearance in 2010. The imam of Moscow's largest mosque, for instance, required the construction of one hundred new mosques in response to the appeal of the Christian organizations of Russia for the construction of two hundred churches.[31]

Even stranger was the letter that Fatih Garifullin, the Mufti of the Siberian region of Tumen, sent to the patriarch of Russia. It was a document containing the unprecedented requirement for a patriarch's approval of the use of the Russian churches by the Muslims from the areas of Russia where there are not enough mosques.[32] According to Garifullin, all the Russian church authorities would have to do would be to cover all crosses and icons before the start of the Muslim religious service. One is tempted to ask Mr. Garifullin what the reaction of the Muslims would be if someone offered the use of the mosques to Christian parishioners who would temporarily cover the walls of the mosques with crosses and icons for the duration of their service.

The growth and the magnitude of the Islamist threat hanging over the Russian borders is about to be determined by the outcome of the conflict in Afghanistan. The theoretical possibility for a Vietnam War–style American withdrawal would represent a real calamity for Russia. The establishment of a radical Islamist entity next to the borders of the former Muslim Soviet republics would enable the powerful Taliban to penetrate Central Asia, primarily Tajikistan and Kyrgyzstan. This development would transform the Taliban into a direct Russian neighbor with all the consequences.

One of the most dramatic consequences would be the skyrocketing of the already existing heroin addiction in Russia. There is a fact that should not be ignored: 21 percent of the Afghan heroin is consumed in Russia, where the victims of the addiction are about 1.5 million people. Somewhere between 30,000 and 40,000 of them die every year.[33] The profitability of the narcotrade is impressive indeed: a pound of heroin costs $750 in Afghanistan, $6,000 at the Kazakhs border (where it arrives via Tajikistan and Kyrgyzstan), and $50,000 in Moscow.[34]

One does not need to be a trained mathematician to evaluate the consequence of a potential unrestricted Taliban domination over Afghanistan, given that currently 90 percent of the world production of heroine is provided by the activities of only 12.9 percent of the population of Afghanistan who are involved in the growing of the poppy crop. What will happen if this number reaches, say, 60 percent?

Maybe the best explanation that involves the very essence of the radicalization of the Muslims from Russia and the former Muslim republics of the Soviet Union has been offered by Ilshat Alsayef, a former military officer and veteran of the Soviet-Afghan war, who retired as lieutenant colonel after the First Chechen War, and a founding member of Muslims against Sharia. There were two waves of radicalization of the ex-Soviet Muslims. The first wave started after the breakup of the Soviet Union in the early 1990s. After the fall of communism, former Soviet Asian republics, now independent countries (Kazakhstan, Kyrgyzstan, Tajikistan, Turkmenistan, and Uzbekistan), as well as the autonomous regions of Russia (Chechnya, Dagestan, and Ingushetia), experienced a resurgence of religious freedom.

The second wave of radicalization of parts of the Muslim population of Russia started at the turn of the century. Some people claim that it was a result of the American conflict with radical Islam, which many Muslims interpret as the American war on Islam, but in reality the real reason is the skyrocketing oil revenues by the Saudi monarchy at the disposal of the Wahhabi foundations. Centuries-old local mosques in the Russian cities are being replaced by modern, Wahhabi-built structures. Old imams who survived communism are being replaced by Wahhabi clerics. This is not only true for predominantly Muslim countries such as Tajikistan, but also for the autonomous regions inside of Russia such as Bashkortostan and Tatarstan, where most people consider themselves more Russians than Muslim. One can see similar developments in former Yugoslavia, where moderate imams with little financial backing are being replaced by radicals with virtually unlimited financing.

If current demographic trends hold, Muslims in Russia may become a majority by the midcentury. And if current radicalization trends hold, Russia may become a war theater comparable to Chechnya or Lebanon, but on a much larger scale.

Notes

1. See the numbers quoted by Dmitry Gorenberg, the Associate Director of the American Association for the Advancement of Slavic Studies in Current History, vol. 105, no. 693, October 2006.
2. Alexei Malashenko, "Islam and Politics in Present-day Russia," www.princeton.edu/~lisd/publications/wprussiaservices_malashenko.pdf.

3. Dr. Mark A. Smith, "Islam in the Russian Federation," *Conflict Studies Research Centre*, November 2006, 3.
4. Malashenko, "Islam and Politics in Present-day Russia."
5. Ibid.
6. Ibid.
7. "Islam in Russia and Central Asia," www.Witnesspioneer.org/vie/Books/SH_CA/Islam_in_RussiaandCentral_Asia.
8. Smith, "Islam in the Russian Federation."
9. Ibid.
10. Ibid.
11. "Nezavisimaia Gazeta," December 7, 2005.
12. Smith, "Islam in the Russian Federation."
13. One of the most informative works in English about the Russian conquest of North Caucasus is Moshe Gammer, *Muslim Resistance to the Tsar: Shamil and the Conquest of Chechnya and Dagestan* (London: Frank Cass, 2001).
14. Alexander Dallin, "Chapter 12," in *German Rule in Russia, 1941–1945* (London: MacMillan and Company, 1957).
15. Interview in Moscow, 1976.
16. Artem Kroupenev, "Radical Islam in Chechnya," http://us.mg201.mail.yahoo.com.
17. Interview, 2001.
18. Interview, 2006.
19. S. E. Cornell, "Chechnya, Russia and the Islamic Factor: A Source of Instability in the Northern Caucasus," www.ca-c.org/journaleng-04–2000/25.comshtml.
20. Ibid.
21. Ibid.
22. Kroupenev, "Radical Islam in Chechnya."
23. Nimrof Raphael, "Ayman Muhmamad Rabi' Al Zawahiri: The Making of an Arch-Terrorist," in *Terrorism and Political Violence* 14, no. 4 (Winter 2002), 13.
24. V. Akaev, "Religious-Political Conflict in the Chechen Republic of Ichkeria," www.c-c.org/dataeng/05akaev.shtml.
25. Ibid.
26. Kroupenev, "Radical Islam in Chechnya."
27. Akaev, "Religious-Political Conflict in the Chechen Republic of Ichkeria."
28. Kroupenev, "Radical Islam in Chechnya."
29. Radio Free Europe and Radio Liberty, "World Congress of Tatars Convenes in Kazan," www.rferl.org/content/article/1060999.html.
30. Radio Free Europe and Radio Liberty, "Tatarstan's New President Is Sworn In," http://ww.rferl.org/content/Tatarstan_New_President_Sworn_In.1993656.html.
31. "A Conflict Is Brewing between Christians and Muslims," www.inosmi.ru.social/20101019/163700260-print.html25.112010.
32. Ibid.
33. "Russia Is Sinking in Afghan Heroin," www.inosmi.ru/social/20101019/163700260-print.html.
34. Jamie Glazov and Ilshat Alsayef, "Russia: A Future Radical Muslim Superpower?," http://islam-watch.org/ExMuslims/Russia-Future-Radical-Muslim-Superpower.htm.

7

Iran: The Emergence of the Shia Branch of Theocratic Totalitarianism

It would be reasonable to expect questions along the following lines: Why do the events of already distant 1953 still deserve our attention as far as Iran is concerned? What do they have to do with the world we are living in? Even authors and scholars well familiar with Iranian history and politics continue to look at the dramatic events that unfolded during the last half of the twentieth century through the dense fog of their ideological agenda. Case in point is the following analysis of the most important events of the above period of Iranian history made by Dr. Samir Rihani:

> The CIA set operation Ajax in motion in 1953 and it took only two months and $200,000 to topple Mosaddegh and to restore the Shah to power. Mosaddegh on the other hand was sentenced to three years of solitary confinement. He ended his days under house arrest. The oil dispute was settled and the Shah resumed his headlong rush into total tyranny, enforced by the CIA trained officers of SAVAK. As conditions worsened in 1975, the Shah did what the local agents of foreign powers do under those circumstances: He annulled the multiparty system and created his own party. The opposition could only seek an outlet through religion. By the end of 1978 the writing was on the wall and it was only a matter of time before the Shah was toppled. The "experts" promptly swung into classic damage limitation. It was futile but they were doing something! The CIA sought a dialogue with opposition groups behind the Shah's back. Finally and inevitably, the Shah fled from Iran in January 1979 and Khomeini and his supporters assumed power.[1]

The very first phrase of this long quotation reveals an interesting paradox so typical for the politically correct outlook of the events in question. There is an inconvenient point, however: Dr. Rihani's description of the 1953 coup in Tehran leads the reader to the amazing conclusion that the government of Prime Minister Mossadegh was so unpopular at the time of the coup that "it took only two months and $200,000 to topple Mossadegh and to restore the Shah to power."

It would be worthwhile to make an attempt to look at the long-gone era of Prime Minister Mohammed Mossadegh without any bias. The man assumed the position of prime minister in 1951. The main item on his agenda was the nationalization of the most precious asset of Iran: its oil industry that was completely dominated at the time by the British-Iranian Company directly controlled by the government of the United Kingdom. The blood of every Iranian was boiling given that the company was paying only 16 percent from its profits to Iran. All attempts to convince the Brits to follow the American pattern in Saudi Arabia where the Saudis were getting half of the profit were unsuccessful.

Unlike so many politicians, Mosaddegh kept his promise and nationalized the assets of the British-Iranian Company. Most of the interpretations of this act continue to repeat completely wrong Cold War–era statements. In reality, Mosaddegh was neither a communist nor a socialist. Born into the family of one of the largest Iranian land-owners, he obtained his education at a prestigious European university. Later he became one of the leading experts of his country in the area of constitutional law. Politically, he was an ardent nationalist and firm believer in the principles of constitutional monarchy—a fact that created tension in his relationship with the young shah.

An important additional detail is that the Iranian prime minister was an unabashed admirer of American democracy. At the peak of the conflict with Great Britain, Mosaddegh made a long tour of the United States, and in his negotiations in Washington, he desperately tried to obtain American support. President Truman, however, refused to get involved in the Iranian-British conflict, and the only result of the visit was *Time*'s selection of Prime Minister Mosaddegh as the 1951 Man of the Year. This decision was justified by the following argument: "This strange old man represented one of the most profound problems of this time. Around this dizzy old wizard swirled a crisis of human destiny."[2]

Meanwhile, the Iranian economy took a dangerous plunge downward as a result of an effective boycott organized by the government of Great Britain. In order to not be blamed for the actions of the others, Mosaddegh's government broke diplomatic relations with Great Britain.[3] This act prompted the initiative of the new conservative government led by the indefatigable Winston Churchill to address the traditional American ally with its desperate plea for help.

There was a new administration in Washington as well. Only nine years earlier Churchill and Eisenhower were busy with the liberation of Western Europe initiated by the largest landing operation in the history of the world. It was not difficult for Prime Minister Churchill to convince the new president of the danger to the free world if they lost Iran to their Cold War Soviet rival. President Eisenhower satisfied the British demand by ordering the CIA to work together with the British agencies to prepare the removal of Prime Minister Mosaddegh's government.

The question to what extent the sovereignty of Iran had been threatened by the Soviet Union is a complicated one, and its correct answer does not coincide with either of the explanations generated by the conflicting ideologies. As already pointed out, Prime Minister Mosaddegh was neither a communist nor a Soviet stooge.

At the same time, however, the Iranian Communist Party (Tudeh) played a prominent role in the loose coalition of political organizations supporting the politics of Mosaddegh.[4] Given the rising tide of the social tension brought by the deterioration of the quality of life as a result of the effectiveness of the British boycott, there was indeed a real danger of disintegration of the political structure and the social fabric of Iranian society. Past experience had shown that such a situation could have provoked some form of indirect or direct Soviet involvement in the Iranian crisis.

The British and American intelligence services assigned to organize the coup coordinated their efforts in the course of two meetings that took place in June of 1953 in Nicosia, Cyprus, and Beirut, Lebanon.[5] The essence of the coordinated British-American plan for government change in Iran was not complicated at all. The CIA was supposed to stir some public disorder in Tehran and then the shah had to step into the game by dismissing Mohammad Mosaddegh from his position and to replace him with General Zahedi—a pro-Western military leader who was also an ardent monarchist.[6]

Back in 1953, Shah Mohammad Reza Pahlavi was a young, shy, and highly uncertain man. It was in 1941 when he inherited the throne at the age of twenty-two, after the British had interned his father in South Africa for his pro-German leanings. In 1953, against British and American expectations, Mohammad Reza Pahlavi was extremely reluctant to get involved in a risky adventure that could have placed at stake not only his throne but his life as well. The growing public discontent with the increasingly dictatorial and confusing politics of Mosaddegh finally terminated the hesitations of the monarch, and on August 13, 1953, he signed the document for the replacement of Mosaddegh with General Zahedi.[7] This act exhausted the bravery of the shah, and he decided to wait for the outcome of a very volatile situation first in Baghdad and then some days later in Rome. Following this brief emigration, the monarch returned to Tehran and was warmly welcomed by large crowds. The dramatic events changed the demeanor of the young man; upon his return, he decided that the only way to survive the unexpected twists and turns of Iranian political life is for the Iranian monarch to be the ultimate decision maker. The once shy young man became such a decision maker, and his unlimited power lasted for a quarter of a century.

Iran under the Shah's Rule (1953–1978)

At the end of those twenty-five years of the shah's absolute power over Iran, another whirlwind of unexpected events engulfed the country. Dr. Rihani caught their essence with a short and precise phrase: "Finally and inevitably, the Shah fled from Iran in January of 1979."[8] What is true in this statement, of course, is that the shah "finally fled from Iran in January of 1979." The statement to the effect that the departure of the Iranian monarch had been "inevitable," however, deserves closer scrutiny. To analyze it, let's try to take an objective look at the legacy of Shah Mohammad Reza Pahlavi and the Ayatollah Ruhollah Khomeini, whose actions played a decisive role in Iranian history over the last sixty years.

Starting with the monarch, upon his return from the short exile to Italy, the shah gradually established his complete control over the country. The realities of his authoritarian dictatorship have been described in full detail by many authors, and it will not be necessary to mention them in this review. Another aspect of the long reign of the shah, however, has been completely ignored by one-sided interpretations offered to the students of American and Western European universities. The primary goal of Mohammad Reza Pahlavi throughout his reign was the transformation of a poor, rural Iran into a modern, powerful state.[9]

To achieve this goal, the shah initiated his "White Revolution," which was an ambitious plan to transplant the backward and rural Iran into a modern state via effective agrarian reform, large-scale educational projects, and by providing full civil rights to the Iranian women.[10] In addition to the planned radical transformation of Iranian society, the shah initiated an oversized program, the purpose of which was to make Iran the strongest state in the strategically crucial area containing most of the world's oil deposits. Similar to the case with Saudi Arabia, Iran under the shah had spent billions of dollars on weaponry and equipment for which the armed forces of the country needed time to master the necessary technology.

Much more important, though, was the fact that the shah's strategy did not address the issues involving the Iranian political system. Mohammad Reza Pahlavi was assuming (wrongly!) that the coveted status of the main and only transformer of Iranian society requires the fullest possible concentration of political power in his own hands as a guaranty for the stability of his system and the success of his reforms.

It could be argued that it was this concept that pushed the shah to the point of no return, and that became the starting point of his tortuous exile that accelerated his death. The situation would have been completely different had the monarch decided to create a consensus among all components of the secular spectrum of Iranian society (except for the extreme left) by initiating a public discussion about the future of Iran and by allowing the creation of political parties whose programs supported the modernization of the country and opposed the Islamist danger.

He could have easily obtained the support of Mosaddegh by releasing the former prime minister from house arrest and encouraging him to enlist the support of the former participants in his broad coalition that had brought him to power a decade earlier. The argument of the shah could have been that, given that the country was finally independent and in full control of its precious natural resources, all individuals who were interested in developing a fully democratic political system in Iran must unite their efforts while facing the Islamist threat. Dr. Mosaddegh could have been most useful in that respect.

The shah, however, was not interested in such efforts. Contrary to the clichés of the Islamic and the leftist propaganda that presented him as a cruel despot, the Iranian monarch remained to a certain degree a shy and aloof man. In the eyes of his people, he was a distant figure living in sumptuous palaces and was changing his wives in search of one who would be able to provide him with a son. The monarch nailed a really big nail in his political coffin when back in 1971 he wasted $200 million for a lavish celebration of the 2,500th anniversary of the establishment of the first Persian kingdom.[11]

What the shah was not able to see was the growing alienation of all major social groups of the Iranian society in his regime. Considering this situation and adding its impact to the influence of the feudal and conservative Islamist clergy dominating the minds of the people from the countryside, the social base of the shah's regime started shrinking until, according to the politically correct analyses, it reached the point of no return during the late fall of 1978. Or did it? What is very often eliminated from the investigation of events that led to the ascension of Khomeini to power is the foreign factor contributing to the downfall of the shah.

Throughout the long years of his reign, Mohammad Reza Pahlavi must have well remembered how reluctantly the Soviet troops left the occupied areas of northern Iran. He knew as well that this withdrawal became possible only because of the firmness demonstrated by President Truman's administration. It is possible that only the American monopoly over the atomic bomb prompted Joseph Stalin to act against his instincts and desires. Let's not forget that the Soviet dictator felt so "comfortable" on Iranian territory that in 1945 he ordered the start of the geological survey designed to find oil deposits. Politically, Joseph Stalin created two small republics on Iranian territory—one designed to provide "statehood" to the Azeris, while the other one catered to the national aspirations of the Kurds.[12]

Strangely at first sight, while persecuting the Iranian communists who he had every reason to consider foreign agents, the shah maintained perfectly normal diplomatic and economic relations with the Soviet Union and the rest of the communist world, as a necessary antidote to a potentially dangerous confrontation. In the eyes of the Iranian monarch, the only guaranty that his country would not be invaded by its powerful communist neighbor would be the development of a strong alliance with the United States. That is why, since 1953, it was America that became the main ally and protector of Iran and its ruler. For a quarter of a century, the American-Iranian relationship worked in an almost perfect and mutually beneficial way. From the American point of view, the shah's Iran was a reliable ally providing protection and security in a very sensitive and volatile area, while at the same time satisfying the thirsty Western world with its most precious commodity.

The powerful bond between the shah's Iran and the United States was established during the first term of President Eisenhower. With its unconditional economic, military, and political support, the Eisenhower administration sent a message to the shah that an informal but very real alliance between both countries could be extremely beneficial to both sides.

The American-Iranian relations, however, became more complicated during the presidency of John F. Kennedy. Privately, the new president had been influenced by the negative image of the shah already existing in the Western media. During the mandate of President Lyndon Johnson because of the heavy involvement of the United States in the conflict burning in Southeast Asia on one hand and the growing economic and military potential of Iran on the other hand, Tehran started playing an even more important role in the American strategy to protect the Persian Gulf area.

President Johnson encouraged the fast economic and military development of Iran because, in his view, the more powerful Iran was the better the country would be able to protect the long-term American interests in the region. There was, however, more to it: Johnson was an ardent sympathizer of the reforms leading to the progress of poor countries. From his point of view, the president was looking at the shah as a model statesman providing the best possible example to the leaders of the developing world. According to the president, "What is going on in Iran is about the best thing going on anywhere in the world."[13]

The American-Iranian strategic and economic partnership reached its zenith during the presidency of Richard Nixon. Mohammad Reza Pahlavi and Nixon met for the first time in 1957, when the vice president visited Tehran. A hastily arranged audience designed to be short and formal unexpectedly turned into a conversation that lasted several hours. Both statesmen were clearly impressed by each other—a fact that helped a lot in upgrading the American-Iranian relations during the years of Nixon's presidency. The readiness of the shah to coordinate the foreign-policy strategy of Iran with American interests added more motivation to the American policymakers in rendering more assistance and support to his country.

The End of the Regime of the Shah

The smooth relationship of Shah Reza Pahlavi with the administrations of Presidents Nixon and Ford expired with the coming to power of President Carter. To put it mildly, the shah was not happy with the outcome of the American presidential elections of 1976. Shortly before his death, Mohammad Reza Pahlavi sadly reminisced about the events that had brought tragedy not only to his personal fate, but to the fate of his country as well: "I didn't know it then and perhaps I didn't want to know, but it is clear to me now that the Americans wanted me out. Clearly this is what the human rights advocates in the State Department wanted."[14]

There can be little doubt that, being a deeply religious person, the president was sincere in his search for a moral foundation for the American foreign policy. President Carter thought that the conduct of foreign policy based on the requirements of human rights should be able to undermine the dictatorial regimes within the Soviet sphere of influence while at the same time encouraging the democratic forces of the countries ruled by autocratic pro-American regimes to raise their voice for change.

It would be useful to take a look at the circumstances that brought Jimmy Carter to the presidency of the United States. The whirlwind of negativity toward the Vietnam War and the criticism of the administrations of Presidents Johnson and Nixon were the main factors behind the stunning victory of James Earl Carter in the 1976 election. His lack of experience and knowledge in the field of foreign policy, perceived by many Americans as an arena covered with dirt, suddenly became a huge plus for the soft, well-spoken candidate. Later, however, this became a weak spot for the president, and nowhere else was this deficiency more clear than during the Iranian crisis.

Realizing both his lack of international experience and familiarity with developing situations in many important areas of the world, President Carter hoped to compensate these deficiencies by relying on the advice of competent and experienced associates. Consequently, he offered the position of secretary of state to Cyrus Vance, while Zbigniew Brzezinski became his national security adviser. Unfortunately for the president, there was a rivalry between the two men. In an interview given within the frame of the "Carter Presidency Project" developed by a group of scholars from several prestigious American universities, Carter presents a completely different picture:

> Long before I ever was elected president I recognized Zbig's strengths and some of his possible weaknesses. Zbig put together a constant barrage of new ideas and suggestions and plans, and 90 percent of them in that totality would have to be rejected. Sometimes maybe 50 percent of them, I'm just estimating, would have some essence or benefit that if modified were good and some of them had to be rejected outright.[15]

Unlike the situation involving "Zbig's" dynamism, which evidently was too much for his boss, Jimmy Carter had just the opposite problem with

Secretary Vance: "Now, CY was not a shrinking violet or anything, but when we had a controversial policy to be presented to the public, CY didn't want to do it."[16]

Carter did not reach into his pocket for words when the interviewers asked him about the activities of William Sullivan, the American ambassador to Iran, during the crucial period preceding the outbreak of the Iranian drama: "I should have fired him. . . . In fact, I instructed Cy Vance to bring Sullivan out of Iran, and Cy delayed it. He came back again and again as was his manner and tried to convince me that we should send a Deputy Secretary of State in there to run things . . . and to ease Sullivan out after the crisis had passed."[17]

It could be argued that even if we did not have at our disposal any additional documentary evidence with regard to the foreign policy of President Carter's administration, this interview is able to bring about some very serious doubts in the effectiveness of this policy. The picture emerging out of the former president's answer did not provide any reason for optimism. With a national security adviser whose ideas were rejected at a rate of 90 percent, a secretary of state who did not dare back up any statement of the president, and an ambassador to a critically important country who deserved to be fired almost immediately, chances for a successful US foreign policy with regard to Iran were dim.

In all fairness to him, the president had some good ideas. In his search for new ways to conduct the foreign policy of the United States, President Carter created a special section attached to the Department of State, named the Bureau of Human Rights. The bureau was headed by Patricia Derian, who had a remarkable record of being a political activist who worked in Mississippi during the American Civil Rights Movement of the 1960s, which was one of the most dangerous places for any East Coast–based supporter of Dr. Martin Luther King.[18]

Her record in investigating and revealing the crimes of the Argentinean military regime was also impeccable. Consequently, it was logical that from the point of view of Patricia Derian, the rule of the shah also belonged to the category of the political phenomena deserving condemnation for its human rights record. The participant in the American Civil Rights Movement Andrew Young, nominated by President Carter as ambassador of the United States to the United Nations, was completely under the influence of the rhetoric of the Ayatollah Khomeini. Senator Edward Kennedy also added his powerful voice to the motley chorus.

There was no moral or political problem with such an attitude, provided that the critics of the shah's Iran had a little bit more knowledge about the Iranian political forces and the situation in the country during those fateful days and months. Because of the absence of such knowledge or, even worse, because of the impact of Khomeini's propaganda, the attitude of President Carter's human rights lobby and its influence over the administration's decision making had an extremely negative impact on the future developments in Iran. It was understandable, for instance, that Andrew Young had a negative view of the shah's regime, but it was unforgivable of him to compare Khomeini to a saint.

What the American human rights defenders were not able to see was that all measures born out of their good intentions were in reality removing the obstacles to the establishment of an Islamo-totalitarian dictatorship—a far worse violator of the human rights than the regime of the shah. The main recommendations of the human rights defenders were the release of the political prisoners and the termination of the government efforts designed to prevent the mass demonstrations shaking the Iranian cities.

The release of many hard-core Islamists from the Iranian jails and the lack of any attempt to block even the most violent antigovernment actions, marked the paralysis of the protective mechanisms of the shah's regime and pushed huge crowds of new demonstrators onto the streets. No one, not in Iran or abroad, expressed any indignation over one of the most obnoxious crimes committed by the Islamo-totalitarians, who on August 19, 1978, set on fire a large movie theater in the city of Abadan after blocking its exits; more than four hundred people perished in the flames.[19]

It was the enormous ambition of the shah to modernize Iran in an unprecedented short period of time that brought about a tremendous amount of pressure on the Iranian society. Because of the personal nature of the authoritarian regime ruling the country, an almost inevitable conflict erupted between its main symbol, the monarchy, and the representatives of almost all political forces of the Iranian society, which for different reasons hated the authoritarian regime of the shah. For the communists, he was too reactionary and too pro-American. For the liberals, he was too dictatorial. And for the Islamists, he was too secular. At the same time, each one of the hidden components of the Iranian political scene had its own considerations and strategy with regard to the future of Iran. The communists, for instance, planned to follow Ayatollah Khomeini only up to the point when the Islamic upsurge would be able to topple the regime of the shah. In the chaos that followed, they hoped to establish their control over the machinery of power.

A former member of the Tudeh Party made the following comment: "Considering the fact that we were able to preserve our organization and activities even under the persecution of the regime of the Shah, we believed that we could have attracted people's support in free and fair elections.... We never expected that the real purpose of Khomeini was to establish a theocratic and Fascist dictatorship that was a hundred times worse than the regime of the Shah."[20]

The political enemies of the shah belonged to three different categories: the adherents of the National Front, Marxist-Leninist-Maoist groups, and hard-core Islamists. One could hardly imagine a political spectrum so bitterly divided between the representatives of different ideologies as the political lava brewing under the seemingly unshakable grounds of the oil-rich and heavily armed Iran of the shah.

The constitutionalists (another name for the membership of the National Front) consisted primarily of well-educated intellectuals who supported the main core of Mosaddagh's ideas, such as free press, the application of the rules of the first Iranian Constitution circa 1906, and the transformation of the monarchy from political into representative institution.

The second category of enemies of the imperial regime included the remnants of the once large and influential Communist Party (Tudeh) and tiny splinter groups that had fallen under Chinese rather than Soviet influence. The process of the natural selection transformed the left flank of the clandestine political life of Iran into the best-organized component of it, but at the same time, it was the smallest.

Separated from everyone else, there was an organization called the People's Mujahedin of Iran who were dedicated enemies of the shah, but at the same time, they hated the Islamic alternative to the imperial regime as well. Later they fought the theocratic and totalitarian dictatorship, the establishment of which they were trying to prevent. The Islamists were the most numerous groups among Pahlavi's enemies, but at the same time the most chaotic ones.[21] They became a united force only after the process of their unification, which was launched and directed by Khomeini.

The powerful eruption of the long-dormant Iranian volcano of discontent had been activated by the willpower and the incredible mastery of deceit demonstrated by Ayatollah Ruhollah Khomeini. A Muslim cleric who had taught Islamic philosophy at the religious schools in Nadjaf and Qum for decades, Khomeini achieved national prominence in the beginning of the 1960s when he ferociously opposed the very concept of the White Revolution promulgated by the shah. The main reason for the cleric's hatred for the monarch was his opposition to agrarian reform and, in particular, its efforts to promulgate equal rights for the Iranian women. From the point of view of Khomeini and his associates, the agrarian reform was affecting the economic interests of the clergy, given that its representatives were among the wealthiest landowners in the country. At the same time, the emancipation of the Iranian women was perceived as an assault on the Islamic rules involving the relationship between genders.

There were some additional reasons for the extreme hostility of Khomeini toward the monarch, such as the secular character of his rule, his relations with the United States, and also the fact that Iran was one of the very few Muslim countries that was maintaining any kind of relationship with Israel.

The fact that the Ayatollah was brave enough to openly express his opposition to the shah's rule brought him national prominence, a short detention, and forcible exile to Iraq. Let's concentrate for a while on the intriguing period in Khomeini's life that was solemnly presented to the erstwhile world by his propagandists as an imprisonment by the despotic regime of the shah. The truth was much different and so shocking that Khomeini preferred to leave it to sink into oblivion. In reality, the future absolutist dictator of Iran never set foot in jail because he had been incarcerated in a villa belonging to SAVAK, the shah's notorious secret police. It was a luxurious facility designed to host the foreign guests of Reza Pahlavi![22]

There was much more to the story though. It turned out that once a week the brave cleric had an almost ritualistic lunch with General Hasan Pakravan—the head of SAVAK between 1961 and 1965. The general was a highly educated professional military officer and diplomat who impressed Khomeini to the point of making him declare that he "counts the hours remaining to their next lunch."[23]

In all fairness to Khomeini, the general had been equally impressed with him, who he found to be "an ambitious and forceful individual." On the other hand, however, the general was deeply shocked by the unbelievable ignorance of Khomeini, who had tried to convince him that the United States had been involved in anti-Iranian activities for 25,000 years![24] The saddest part of the story in this strange relationship took place in the aftermath of Khomeini's ascension to power when General Pakravan was arrested. When his worried wife tried to visit him, she was assured that the general was just a "guest of the Ayatollah." Some days later, however, General Hasan Pakravan was murdered.

Coming back to the earlier part of Khomeini's story, after his comfortable stay at SAVAK's villa, he was sent into exile in Iraq, where he unleashed an energetic propaganda campaign designed to undermine the shah's regime. Instead of ordering the kidnapping or just the murder of the dangerous opponent, the all-powerful monarch of Iran made a request to the Iraqi government to force the unwanted cleric to leave the country. The Iraqi regime was happy to oblige, and the heroic visitor of the SAVAK villa found himself in a much more modest house in France.

The French period of Ayatollah Khomeini's life proved wrong the classical rule according to which emigration gradually breaks the connection between the emigrant and the country from which he came. Although physically absent from Iran while living in a modest house located in a small French village rented for him by a group of expatriate Iranian sympathizers, the Ayatollah was shaking the very foundation of the regime of the shah. The entirely negative image of Muhammad Reza Pahlavi created by the world media was in sharp contrast to its insatiable curiosity toward the personality of Khomeini and an open sympathy for him. It was the Western media and primarily the French and British TV stations and newspapers that transformed the unknown Iranian cleric into a household name all over the world. The tapes containing his fiery philippics against the Iranian ruler became the most popular contraband in Iran.

The precipitous rise of the circulation of those tapes gradually transformed Khomeini into a master over the minds and emotions of the majority of the Iranians. Looking back at this incredible success story, one is amazed by the striking similarity between Khomeini's uses of a strategy leading him to the ultimate dictatorship over Iran that was well familiar to every communist leader.

It could be successfully argued within the framework of comparative analysis that on his road to the fulfillment of his inflated political ambitions, Khomeini did everything to assume the power over Iran, while the Shah did not do anything to preserve it. In addition to the impact of his crumbling authority, the Iranian monarch had to fight another battle from which there was no victorious exit. One of the most closely guarded secrets of the shah was the deadly cancer that had started growing inside his body and was discovered by a team of French doctors in 1974. He kept the terrible secret even from his wife. It was one of the numerous mistakes committed by the discreet and sensitive monarch. The announcement of such a dramatic event would have produced a wave of mass compassion for him *before* the development of the revolutionary situation in the country during the period of 1977–1978.

A consistent and well-executed American strategy designed to support the shah could have played a decisive role in preventing the bloodshed and tragedies that followed. There was no such strategy though. Zbigniew Brzezinski, for instance, was calling for firmness, while the State Department's Bureau of Human Rights was trying to convince the shah to speed up the democratic reforms in Iran by allowing the Islamo-totalitarians to destroy the Iranian state structures bit by bit. During those decisive days, the only message that Ambassador Sullivan delivered to the depressed Iranian ruler was the standard phrase that he did not have any instructions from Washington. At the same time, he ranted about the shah to his protector, Cyrus Vance, presenting the Iranian monarch as the initiator of repressive measures against the antigovernment demonstrations that shook the Iranian capital. Those reports were in full keeping with the agenda of the human rights lobby that was an inseparable component of President Carter's administration.

Meanwhile, from his comfortable French exile Ayatollah Khomeini continued to send his incendiary messages to the Iranian people. As far as his real intentions were concerned, the messenger was very careful to hide them so skillfully that no one was able to discover them until it was already too late.

Three months before his triumphal return to Tehran, or to be more precise, on October 25, 1978, Khomeini made the following statement: "Islamic clerics will help lead the revolution but then they will step aside to let others to rule."[25] Less than a year later, however, on August 18, 1979, Khomeini said something very different: "Those who pretend that religious dignitaries should not rule, poison the atmosphere and combat against the Iranian interests."[26] While in exile, the future leader promised his numerous followers that, "Criticism of the Islamic Government will not be tolerated."[27] Again, less than a year later, the subjects of the dictator heard the following: "I repeat for the last time: abstain from holding meetings, from blaspheming, from public protests. Otherwise I will break your teeth."[28]

In the immediate aftermath of his return, the Ayatollah momentarily unleashed a campaign of terror against former government officials and military officers, who were murdered by the hundreds without any judicial procedure or after a totalitarian imitation of such a procedure. As always the case with any totalitarian practice, after the elimination of the enemies, the terror is directed against the former allies whose usefulness had already expired. The organizations and the publications of the idealistic students who had played such an important role in bringing down the shah's regime and who were naïve enough to believe the cleric's promises that the Islamists would leave the structures of power no later than six months after the revolution were mercilessly crushed. The nationalists so actively courted before had their hour of bitterness when Khomeini informed them that, "We do not worship Iran, we worship Allah for patriotism is another name for paganism. I say let this land Iran burn. I say let this land go up in smoke, provided Islam emerges triumphant in the rest of the world."[29]

Many Iranian nationalists who did not get this message the way Khomeini meant it also landed in the overcrowded prisons. All components of the modernization that had been under way during the rule of the shah were eliminated. Case in point, for instance, was the closure of the pregnancy prevention clinics in the rural areas designed to restrict the practice of young female children becoming mothers at a very early age.

The legislature protecting the women from discrimination, abuse, and mistreatment was completely eliminated. The Iranian women were transformed from modernity back to the middle ages. A movie titled *The Stoning of Soraya M*, based on a terrifying true story, shot abroad by émigré Iranian intellectuals and artists, reveals the restoration of the most barbaric acts directed against women after the downfall of the shah's regime.

The Islamo-totalitarian state created by Khomeini and his henchmen eliminated the rights the non-Muslim religious minorities enjoyed under the shah. Senior government posts were reserved exclusively for Muslims. The religious schools established by the representatives of non-Muslim denominations were required to have Muslim principals. Conversion to Islam was encouraged by entitling converts to inherit the entire share of their parents' estate if the rest of the successors had remained non-Muslim.

It would be interesting to reminisce about how all of those dramatic events affected the superpowers, which during the triumph of Khomeini and the Soviet invasion of Afghanistan that took place a year later entered the last decade of their seemingly endless Cold War.

Unlike its American counterpart, the Soviet leadership was able to spot the danger of radical Islam that had inspired Khomeini's takeover of Iran. Their primary concern was that the impact the events that had shaken Iran may have had on the Muslim population of the Central Asian republics of the Soviet Union. There could be little doubt that the Kremlin's decision to invade Afghanistan had a very important Iran-related component. The Soviet-era documents quoted in the prologue of this book do not leave any doubt that at least to a certain degree this decision was dictated by the fear that the Iranian crisis could trigger an expansion of radical Islam along the borders of the Soviet Union. An additional consideration was the fear of some form of an American intervention in the region of the Persian Gulf. The fall of the regime of the shah created a dangerous vacuum that Saddam Hussein tried to fill at the price of an eight-year-long war and about a million human lives lost in the effort. Only the downfall of Soviet totalitarianism saved the United States from even heavier complications.

Being a deeply religious man who had so much genuine concern about human rights and the morality in politics, President Carter nevertheless, together with his closest associates and with the entire human rights–related spectrum of his administration, committed a deeply immoral act by abandoning a loyal American ally at a most critical moment of his life. Most probably, under the influence of the concept that the shah's regime was doomed and under the spell of the illusion that there would be a chance for Washington to reach some kind of understanding with the victorious Ayatollah, the American policy changed overnight. The message the shah found so confused and inconsistent all of a sudden became crystal clear: the Americans wanted him out. When the shah followed this "advice," his tragedy not only did not end, but as a matter of fact, its saddest part had just begun.

Out of fear of Khomeini's revenge, the Carter administration refused to accept the Iranian monarch on American soil. In order to not repeat the entire saga of the sincere friend and ally of the United States in all of its humiliating and morally reprehensible details, it would be enough to explore its most important dimension. It was only the noble act of President Anwar Sadat of Egypt, who out of gratitude for the Iranian generosity in the past, granted asylum to the stateless refugee that prevented the plot of kidnapping the shah from his uncertain refuge in Panama.

In sadistic expectation of their new triumph, the Islamo-totalitarians had already prepared a cage in which the shah was supposed to be paraded through the streets of Tehran before an act of terrifying public torture was supposed to be performed on him, followed by his execution. This horror for the Iranian ruler and this eternal disgrace for Carter's administration was prevented only by the generous gesture of the president of Egypt, Anwar Sadat, who only a year later died under a stream of jihadist bullets.

On the eve of his death, the shah wrote: "My heart bled at what I saw happening in my country. Every day reports had come of murder, bloodshed, and summary executions. . . . All these horrors were part of Khomeini's systemic destruction of the social fabric I had woven for my nation. . . . And not a word of protest from American human rights advocates who had been so vocal in denouncing my 'tyrannical' regime."[30]

There is every reason to believe that the future historians of radical Islam will be amazed by the fact that the most important sequence of the Iranian Revolution has remained misunderstood for such a long time. Its most important outcome expressed itself in the fact that for the first time the ideology of radical Islam had found a host state that has at its disposal billions of oil-related dollars pouring into jihadist coffers. This huge financing enabled them to possess a large army and a repressive apparatus, in comparison with which the Shah's SAVAK looks like a Boy Scout association.

The present rulers of Iran are following the road traced by Khomeini. Every step on this road is loaded with incredible dangers for the rest of the world. The global threat stems from the terrifying reality when humanity is facing a country busy developing an arsenal of atomic weapons. The magnitude of the danger is determined by the fact that Iran is ruled by a fanatical elite, many members of which possess the mentality of the suicidal murderers who are ready to blow themselves up to achieve paradise for themselves while offering hell to everyone else.

Notes

1. Dr. Sam Rihani, "The Experts," www.globalcomplexity.org/The%20'Experts'I.htm.
2. Quoted from "Mohammad Mosaddagh Hero File," www.moreorless.au.com/heroes/Mosaddagh.html.
3. Amin Saikal, *The Rise and the Fall of the Shah* (Princeton, NJ: Princeton University Press, 1980).
4. Mark J. Gasiorowski and Malcolm Byrn, "Mohammed Mosaddagh and the 1953 Coup in Iran," *International Journal of Middle Eastern Studies*, August 1987, 112–116; "Secret History: The CIA in Iran," www.nytimes.com/library/world/Mideast/041600Iran-cia-chapter2.html.

5. Initial Operational Plan for TPAJAX as cabled from Nicosia to Headquarters on June 1, 1953, www.gwu.edu/-nsarchiv/NSAEBB/NSAEBB28/appendix%20A.pdf.

6. Ardehir Zahedi, "Secret History: The CIA and Iran. What Really Happened?" *New York Times*, May 22, 2000.

7. Quoted from "Mohammad Mosaddagh Hero File," www.moreorless.au.com/heroes/Mosaddagh.

8. Dr. Sam Rihani, "The Experts," www.globalcomplexity.org/The%20'Experts'I.htm.

9. Stephen Kintzer, *All the Shah's Men: An American Coup and the Roots of Middle East Terror* (Hoboken, NJ: John Wiley and Sons, 2003); and for a diametrically opposite view, Mark Gasiorowski and Malcolm Byrn. See more details about the situation in Iran on the eve of the coup d'état, Ervand Abrahamian, *Iran between Two Revolutions* (Princeton, NJ: Princeton University Press, 1982).

10. AbrahamianOp.Cit.

11. Mike Evans, *Atomic Iran—Countdown to Armageddon: How the West Can Be Saved* (Phoenix, AZ: Time Worthy Books, 2009), 120.

12. Svetlana Savranskaya and Vladislav Zubok, "The Cold War in the Caucasus," *Cold War International History Bulletin*, Issue 14/15.

13. Evans, *Atomic Iran—Countdown to Armageddon: How the West Can Be Saved*, 125.

14. Slater Bachtavar, "Jimmy Carter's Human Rights Disaster in Iran," *Americanthinker.com*, August 26, 2007.

15. Carter Presidency Report, final edited transcript, interview with Jimmy Carter, November 29, 1982, Plains, GA, www.c-span.org/apa/carter_jimmy-1982-pdf.

16. Ibid.

17. Ibid.

18. See her very informative article, Patricia Derian, "The Carter Administration and Human Rights," http://74.6.116.140/search/srpcashe?ei=UTF-8&p=The+Human+Rights+issue+during+Ca.

19. Daniel L Byman, "The Rise of Low-Tech Terrorism," *Washington Post*, May 6, 2007.

20. Interview with "Shirley," which is the first American name of a former female activist of the Iranian Communist underground, San Diego, 2007.

21. Martin Kramer, "Fundamentalist Iran at Large: The Drive for Power," *Middle East Quarterly* (June 1996), www.meforum.org/artricle/304.

22. Harvard Iranian Oral History Project, "Fatemeh Pakravan Transcripts," www.fas.harvard.edu/-johp/pakravan.html.

23. Ibid.

24. Ibid.

25. Elmer Swenson, "What Happens When Islamists Take Power? The Case of Iran," http://gemsofislamism.tripod.com/Khomeini_promises_kept.html.

26. Ibid.

27. Ibid.

28. Ibid.

29. Ibid.

30. Mohamed Reza Pahlavi, *Answer to History* (New York: Stein and Day, 1980).

8

America and the Jihadist
Axis of Evil

The Saudi-Wahhabi Factor

In a larger sense, the Saudi-Wahhabi factor exemplifies the Sunni dimension of the jihadist axis of evil. The calamity of 9/11 and the fact that to this very day Saudi Arabia is the main financier of religious schools promoting jihad have transformed the American-Saudi relations into one of the most hotly debated and disputed areas of American foreign policy. Ever since the meeting between FDR and King Saud, the relationship between the United States and the Desert Kingdom was equally important for both countries, although for different reasons. From an American point of view, the oil wealth of Saudi Arabia and its strategic location provides a sufficiently strong reason for a very special relationship between Washington and Riyadh.

The attitude of the Saudi monarchy toward the United States is also marked by a touch of uniqueness that defies any simplistic explanations. At least ideologically, the absolutist kingdom is an enemy of the United States. It was on the future territory of the Desert Kingdom where the most extreme version of radical Islam, Wahhabism, was born. A very important, although often ignored development, was the connection between the predecessors of the current ruling dynasty, who became not just followers but also defenders and protectors of Wahhabism.

On the other hand, however, precisely because of the religious ideology of country, the Saudi monarchy has an even more dedicated and extremely dangerous enemy in the also theocratic but Shia-inspired Iran. This situation could explain the billions of dollars Saudi Arabia poured into Saddam Hussein's coffers during the Iran-Iraq War. The same circumstance has determined and continues to determine the pro-American aspect of Saudi politics, which sounds like a paradox but is nevertheless a reality. The most important contribution of the

Desert Kingdom to the partnership with the United States is in the area of the economy. To understand the nature of this contribution, though, we have to clear up some misunderstandings first.

Under the influence of the negative aspects of the Saudi society and politics, many authors tend to offer a very simplistic explanation of the economic strategy of Saudi Arabia. Even such an outstanding expert on the problems of radical Islam as Mark Stein does not offer a correct explanation of the fate of the billions of dollars that the United States poured into the Saudi economy. According to him, "Two trillion dollars poured into the house of Saud's treasury, and what did they do with it? Diversify the economy? Launch new industries? Open up the tourism sector? Not a thing. The country remained the same desert, literally and psychologically, it was a quarter of a century earlier. . . . So where did all that money go?"[1]

Mark Stein continues his Saudi-related story with an absolutely correct description of the kingdom's financing of the Wahhabism mosques and schools throughout the Muslim world and, consequently, pouring oil on the fires of Islamic fanaticism worldwide. There is, however, an important point missing from this presentation. It is true that billions of dollars have been spent so far in support of the cause of the Islamists. What is also true, however, is the fact that, contrary to Stein's explanations, billions of Saudi oil dollars have found their way back to the country where they were printed and thus tremendously helped the American economy.

Stein is also very wrong when claiming that Saudi Arabia was a hopelessly underdeveloped desert area that has remained intact for ages. As a matter of fact, many billions of dollars have been spent on the creation of modern port facilities and transportation systems as well as huge skyscrapers that dot the desert landscape. Part of those billions come back to the United States in the form of Saudi payments for the huge American imports of all kinds of sophisticated weaponry, equipment, food, and a myriad of other items. The volume of the trade exchange between both countries has risen from $41.9 billion in 2006 to $51.6 billion in 2009.[2]

An even more important factor that is playing a particularly meaningful role not only in the sphere of bilateral relations but also in the stability of the American financial system is the magnitude of the Saudi investments in the US economy. Not too many Americans are familiar with the impressive statistics that indicate that 60 percent of the colossal investments of the kingdom made possible by the huge profits from the sale of oil come back to the United States.

When Colonel Bernard Dunn, a former US Defense and Army attaché to Saudi Arabia and an outstanding expert on the Arab world, was asked whether there was any additional reason for the United States to be interested in maintaining some kind of special relationship with the Desert Kingdom, he provided the following answer:

> Whether Saudi Arabia possessed any oil or not, whether it possessed an important position in the Arab world and the Islamic world or not, it occupies a piece of geography that is important to us because it is the hinge between east and west.
>
> First of all the kingdom has coastlines on two very important bodies of water: the Red Sea and the Arabic Gulf. It also provides easy access to and from the Mediterranean, South Asia and the Horn of Africa. . . . From the geographic standpoint Saudi Arabia occupies a position that cannot be wished away. We must deal with it, particularly from a military viewpoint. We must deal with it because of its geography.[3]

Looking at the same problem from a Saudi prospective, the inevitable conclusion would be that in its relations with the United States, the Saudi monarchy is influenced by precisely the same considerations of strategy and economy.

While the economic motivation of Riyadh with regard to the United States is obvious and self-explanatory, the strategic considerations of the Saudi monarchy deserve a little more scrutiny. The recent developments have transformed the United States into not just a Saudi trade partner and ally but also into the only guarantor for the very existence of the Saudi monarchy and quite possibly the country as well. The shocking level of vulnerability of one of the richest countries in the world and its complete dependence on American protection, to a large degree, has been determined by the Iranian Revolution. The theocratic Iran would invade Saudi Arabia in an instant if not for the United States.

At first glance, the magnitude of the communality of the American and Saudi interests should provide a smooth relationship between Washington and Riyadh, but in practice, the reality is very different. Both of the countries have to undertake a major effort to keep the image of the other one acceptable to its own citizens. For the majority of Americans, Saudi Arabia is a hidden enemy that supplied most of the members of the 9/11 team of suicidal murderers, and it provides funding to the religious madrassas that graduate fanatics and jihadists.

On the Saudi side of the equation, there is a growing anti-Americanism that is particularly strong among the younger generation, which reached a level that forced the government to terminate the direct American military presence on Saudi soil. On the surface, though, both countries are optimistic about the nature and future of their relationship. General Colin L. Powell, in his capacity as secretary of state, assured a journalist who asked him whether the Saudis should be considered friends or foes:

> The Saudis are friends. We have been friends with the Saudis for many years, and we want to remain friends with the Saudis.
> Now, there are certain politics they have that we are not happy with. I mean, they have a different form of government. They have a different culture, a different society than ours—things they do that would not be acceptable to us. . . . Frankly, we need their partnership. We need their friendship.[4]

As with so many diplomatic statements, the comment of Secretary Powell does not address the core of the matter. The main reason for the appearance of an intense tension in the once smooth American-Saudi relationship is not the difference between the American and the Saudi political systems, tradition, and culture. There was a time when the United States had a cordial relationship with Riyadh even when slavery was completely legal in the kingdom until its formal abolishment in 1962.

What brings the tension is the paradox of having Wahhabism, which is indisputably the most dangerous version of radical Islam, propagated and popularized by the government of one of the closest American allies in the Middle East. Even more, Wahhabism is spread by a country whose very existence depends on the protection of the United States. As with almost any paradox, this one also has its explanation.

It is Wahhabism that inspires the entire Sunni branch of jihad. The term comes from the personality and ideas of Muhammad ibn Abd al-Wahhab, who was born in 1703 in arguably the most inhospitable environment the world has to offer—the interior part of the Arabian Peninsula. Having traveled widely with different caravans by practicing the only profession the area where he grew up offered—a cross between a nonwealthy merchant and a security man—the deeply religious youngster acquired enough knowledge and inspiration to allow him to start preaching his own version of Islam.[5]

Al-Wahhab could be considered a precursor of the present-day radical Islamists and Jihadists because of the main core of his teachings: the appeal for the full restoration of the political and judicial realities that existed during the life of Prophet Mohammed. As with the case of every brand of an extremist ideology, Wahhabism breaks some of the major rules of Islam, although the purpose of al-Wahhab had been to "purify" the Muslim religion. The most serious of those breaks was the belief that Wahhabis are in their "right" to murder every Muslim who is not ready to accept their version of Islam. In other words, the *other* Muslims represent a target for elimination to the same degree as the Christians and Jews. During the times of Prophet Mohammed, the concept that a group of Muslims would accept the murder of all Muslims who did not agree with them would have been considered outright heresy, and the proponents of it would have been subjected to a most severe punishment.

Particularly vicious was the Wahhabite hatred for the Shia branch of Islam. In 1801, for instance, the Saudi-Wahhabi troops took one of holiest Shia cities, Kerbala (located in present-day Iraq), killing in the process over 4,000 residents of the city, totally looting all of their properties, and burning all Shia books, including priceless medieval copies of the Koran.[6]

It was WWI that made possible the Al Saud clan's dream to create its own state able to control the Muslim holy sites of Mecca and Medina and to benefit financially from the endless river of pilgrims visiting them. The first major conflict of the twentieth century provided the leaders of the Saudi clan with their first experience in the area of international relations. After getting in touch with some British politicians and extracting their promise that the Arab possessions of the Ottoman Empire would obtain independence after the war, the future King Saud promised his cooperation to London. A historic fact that does not look well on the Saudi-Wahhabi resume was the Saudi alliance with a Christian state (Great Britain) against a Muslim one (the Ottoman Empire). With this consideration in mind, this shocking fact is never mentioned in jihadist propaganda.

As it turned out, after the war the British made the same promise to the leaders of the Jewish community of the future British Palestine. At the same time, having received from the Turks the title of Emir of Riyadh, the leader of the clan, Ibn Saud, started playing the British and Turks against each other. After the defeat of the Turks and in the aftermath of the dissolution of the Ottoman Empire, Great Britain became the only power with whom the Saudis maintained a somewhat friendly relationship. This Anglo-Saudi "cooperation" continued all the way through the twentieth century and in some important aspects continues to this day.

Historically, Wahhabism proved itself to be extremely narrow-minded and bestially cruel toward the Muslims who did not share its credo. When during the 1920s the troops of Ibn Saud entered the sacred cities of Mecca and Medina, one of the first actions of the conquerors was the destruction of the cemetery that was a burying place for the four imams revered by the Shia.[7] There was a lot of looting and pillage throughout the cities, and in addition to that, some priceless medieval copies of the Koran were set on fire by the Wahhabi clerics who were upset by their suspected Shia identity.

In general, Wahhabism has proved that from the beginning its ideology has been marked by a complete lack of tolerance for other people's beliefs and also a complete lack of respect for human life. There also was not the slightest respect for women's rights. What the Wahhabis had introduced as a moral code regulating the duties and behavior of the female members of society had reduced them to a status that could be described only as an institutionalized form of home-based slavery.[8] The Al Saud–Wahhabi alliance acquired formal status in the aftermath of the establishment of the Kingdom of Saudi Arabia in 1932. The Wahhabi clerics not only gained complete control over the religious and educational institutions of the newborn country, but they had been given the authority to enforce the strictest interpretation of sharia law.

The world did not know anything about Wahhabism and, frankly speaking, did not care about the internal problems of the new, remote, and very poor in those distant pre–oil days of the kingdom. The sectarian rigidness of Wahhabism remained confined within the borders of Saudi Arabia for the first three decades after the birth of the kingdom.

What was even more dangerous for the ruling Saudi elite was the widening gap between the Wahhabi clergy and the king's court. The reason for the gap was the role the monarchy played in the process of the modernization of the country. To develop new facilities and expand oil exports, the country needed transportation facilities and modern ports. In short, for the monarchy, the modernization was a necessity, while for the powerful clergy, it contained the temptation of a Western lifestyle that threatened to water down the purity of strict Wahhabism. The other reason for the worries of the Saudi rulers was the erosion of their prestige among the younger generation, which because of the high birthrate constituted the majority of the population of the country.

As if all those problems were not enough, the very end of the 1970s brought about the Iranian Revolution. This monumental event became the reason for serious concern among both components of the Saudi elite. The king's court was deeply worried by the new makeup of Iran's government that had unified the Iranian people on the basis of its devotion to the theocratic regime of Ayatollah Khomeini. For the Wahhabi clerics of Saudi Arabia, the most disturbing dimension of the Iranian developments was the powerful revival of the much-hated Shia version of Islam that had become the ideology of the main rival of the Desert Kingdom.

From the prospective of the Saudis and Wahhabis, there were two positive developments that happened at the end of the 1970s and beginning of the 1980s. The first was the Soviet invasion of Afghanistan, which was briefly followed by the second, the outbreak of the Iran-Iraq War. The spontaneous resistance of the Afghan population against the Soviet occupation was perceived in Riyadh as a God-given opportunity to shift the people's attention from the numerous and growing internal problems.

The Wahhabi clergy was also more than happy about the assistance generously rendered to their fellow Muslims fighting a godless invader. This support primarily materialized as very substantial financial assistance to the cause of the Afghan mujahideen delivered through the channels of Pakistani intelligence. A highly unusual strategic triangle suddenly came into the picture that connected the main supporters of the mujahideen's guerilla struggle: the United States, Saudi Arabia, and Pakistan. This support came very much on time for the Saudi elite because of the unique opportunity to connect the dots between the different aspects of its complicated policy. The best comparison of the actions of the Saudi policymakers would be to present them as a downhill spiral slalom, where the skier tries to avoid the dangers offered at every turn while snaking his way around the American protectors, the attitudes of the majority of the Saudis, and the most ardent Wahhabi followers.

In some miraculous way, the Soviet-related period of the Afghan War smoothed all differences, contradictions, and dilemmas for Riyadh. The life-and-death fight that had erupted in the gloomy mountains of Afghanistan turned out to be the only factor that was able to provide communality of interest between the United States, Pakistan, both components of the Saudi political elite, and its most radical Islamic enemies.

Another important factor that enabled the temporary coexistence of contradictory interests that lasted for a decade was the Iran-Iraq War. From an American point of view, an Iranian victory would have brought the nightmarish prospective of the rapid radicalization and complete destabilization of one of the most strategically important regions in the world.

The same development would have been outright catastrophic for both the Saudi monarchy and the Wahhabi clergy because the triumph of the Shia-dominated Iran could have been fatal for the monarchy and it would have inflicted a terrible blow on the authority and power of the Wahhabi branch of Islam. Consequently, when the Saudi government opened its coffers to provide billions of dollars to Saddam Hussein, its actions were warmly supported, even by the most radical enemies of the monarchy.

This situation, however, did not last for long. When Gorbachev decided to put an end to the hopeless and unpopular war in Afghanistan and Khomeini and Saddam Hussein finally managed to understand that there could be no final victory for either of them, the unstable coalition of unlikely partners started quickly falling apart.

Regardless of ominous signs and explicit warnings concerning the true nature of the Taliban component of the Afghan resistance, American policymakers suddenly lost any interest in the future of the country they had pledged to liberate from Soviet occupation. Osama bin Laden and his followers also quite suddenly turned anti-American. The crisis that erupted over the Iraqi occupation of Kuwait brought about the double rupture of bin Laden's relationships with both of his temporary allies: the United States and Saudi Arabia. The al-Qaeda leader terminated his relations with Riyadh because of the rejection of his advice not to accept any American military assistance. Instead, bin Laden had promoted the idea to help the Saudi army with his body of "foreign fighters" who had been hardened by their participation in the anti-Soviet guerilla war.

As far as the break with the United States was concerned, bin Laden's euphoria and paranoia in the mid-1990s had reached a level that prompted the jihadist leader to declare war on the world's only remaining superpower.[9] Regardless of its pretentious title (or maybe because of it), bin Laden's declaration of war on the United States left the impression of a rather clumsy composition filled with a lot of hatred but little logic. According to jihadist number one, "The blood of Muslims no longer has a price . . . Tajikistan, Burma, Kashmir, Assam, the Philippines, Ogaden, Somalia, Eritrea, Chechnya, and Bosnia-Herzegovina, where the Muslims have been the victims of atrocious acts of butchery."[10] In none of those places was there any American participation in the murder of their Muslim residents. In fact, as far as Bosnia-Herzegovina was concerned, there were Americans who did their best to prevent the suffering of the Muslim population.

Undisturbed by such "insignificant details," bin Laden continued his harangue by accusing the devilish Americans of an even more serious crime: "The most recent calamity to have struck Muslims is the occupation of the land of the two sanctuaries, the hearth of the abode of Islam and the cradle of prophesy, since the death of the Prophet and the source of the divine message—the site of the holy Kasbah, to which all Muslims pray. And who is occupying it—the armies of the American Christians and their allies."[11]

This "argument" by bin Laden was so outrageous that it sounded outright stupid. To start with, there *never* were any American forces stationed in Mecca or Medina; the American military presence on the territory of Saudi Arabia was located hundreds of miles away from both cities. Saudi Arabia was not in a position to defend itself against any Iraqi or Iranian assault. Consequently, the American military presence on Saudi territory not only did not violate the status of both revered cities but provided security the kingdom so badly needed.

An interesting question is, what was bin Laden's attitude toward the Saudi monarchy? According to some American experts, bin Laden was remarkably mild in his critique of the rulers of his native country. In other words, being satisfied with the Saudi financial support rendered to him "under the table," bin Laden was mounting his jihad against the Christian and democratic world without harboring much hostility toward the house of the Saudis. In the view of Stephen Schwarz, satisfied with the financial contribution of the monarchy to al-Qaeda, all bin Laden expected from the Saudi rulers was the termination of their connection with America while continuing the tacit support for the cause of jihad.

It could be argued, though, that there was more complexity in bin Laden's attitude with regard to Saudi Arabia. If we accept that there is a positive component of this attitude, it is expressed *solely* toward the Wahhabi dimension of the Saudi structure of power.

As far as the monarchy was concerned, in the eyes of bin Laden, it was a corrupt and nepotistic institution unable to protect and promote the Wahhabi agenda.

What very often remains overlooked is the Saudi-related dimension of 9/11. The inclusion of fifteen Saudi citizens in the team of suicidal murderers was far from incidental. The overrepresentation of Saudis in the performance of the major terrorist assault against the United States, the magnitude of which raised it to the level of an act of war, could be perceived as prompted by bin Laden's desire to break the American-Saudi alliance by creating an entirely negative image of Saudi Arabia in the eyes of American public opinion.

The jihadist leader had the choice to select individuals from all Muslim countries. If bin Laden wanted to send the message that the carnage in New York City was the Muslim world taking revenge on the United States, he could have selected a motley crew of suicidal murderers from Pakistan, Egypt, Yemen, or Bosnia to inflict the strike. Given that his main additional consideration was most probably to break the relationship between the United States and Saudi Arabia, the jihadist leader selected a team composed almost entirely of Saudis.

The biggest terrorist act in the history of the United States that took the lives of more Americans than Pearl Harbor and the indisputable connection of citizens from the Desert Kingdom prompted a closer look by American authorities into the negative side of the Saudi legacy. The intensive follow-up of the Saudi link to 9/11 that started in the fall of 2001 confirmed some earlier warnings that had previously been systematically ignored. The attention of the American intelligence and security agencies concentrated on the areas of Saudi-related activities that had become a threat to the United States.

Some serious problem areas that were connected with the Saudi foundations involved not only the financing of the jihadist terrorist network but also with the increase of its ranks from the graduates of numerous Wahhabi schools and Islamic "cultural" centers. During the 1990s, for instance, when the Balkan wars erupted and reached a level that prompted the American intervention that took place under the indifferent gaze of Europe, Washington and Riyadh seemingly again acted together. In the beginning, the American and Saudi action in the volatile area of the Balkans looked quite harmonious when the Americans were bombing the Serbians out of Kosovo while the Saudis helped the Muslim victims of the ethnic cleansing that took place in Bosnia and Kosovo. King Fahd, for instance, personally dispatched two planes to Albania carrying 120 tons of tents, blankets, and food supplies. Some supplies were also provided to the refugee centers in Macedonia, which were designed to help the Albanian refugees.

On the other hand, however, the Saudi foundations and "missionaries" were busy conducting activities that were definitely not in keeping with the official humanitarian purpose guiding the actions of their country. Recently, Jakub Selimovski, who is in charge of the religious education offered to the Muslim population of Macedonia, has made the following observation: "Wahhabism in Macedonia, the Balkans and in Europe has become more aggressive in the last ten years."[12] Speaking of the Saudi "missionaries," Selimovski added, "They are in Bosnia, here, Kosovo, Serbia, Croatia and lately they have appeared in Bulgaria."[13] The Saudi foundations have unleashed strenuous activity in Bulgaria where they have spent a large amount of money. Over 150 mosques and so-called teaching centers are spreading Wahhabism among the substantially large Muslim community of the country. The former chief mufti of Bulgaria, Nedim Gendzhev, described very well the Wahhabi design for the Balkans as an attempt to create "a fundamentalist triangle" formed by Bosnia, Macedonia, and Bulgaria's Western Rhodope Mountains.[14]

Unfortunately, the geometric expression of the Wahhabite penetration of the Balkans is much larger than the triangle described by Gendzhev because in the long run it includes the territories of Serbia, Croatia, and Bulgaria in addition to the already Muslim-populated Kosovo and Albania, the residents of which are supposed to be "only" radicalized. It is true that in 2003 the Bulgarian authorities closed down a number of Islamic centers because of Wahhabite activities and "to prevent terrorists getting a foothold in Bulgaria."[15] Evidently those measures turned out to be inadequate because the activity of several Saudi- or Gulenist-funded schools, which graduated 3,000 students in the course of the last twenty years, continues to this very day.[16]

Given that oil and dollar streams were flowing smoothly between Washington and Riyadh, no American policymaker paid too much attention to the jihadist-related "educational" activities not only in Europe but in the United States as well. This situation changed overnight in a most drastic way in the immediate aftermath of 9/11. There were some very important, and to a degree, contradictory Saudi-related components of the tragedy. There could be little doubt that regardless of the intentions and considerations of the Saudi rulers, their contribution to the development of the Wahhabi terrorist network played a very important role.

Before 9/11, for instance, the "zakat," or donation, in keeping with the requirements of Islam, could be performed just by placing a check or cash into the boxes attached to every mosque of the kingdom. Consequently, there was limitless opportunity to transfer unlimited amounts of money to the terrorists by their strongest supporters—the members of the Wahhabi clergy. Many Saudi sympathizers of al-Qaeda were also members of the boards of the numerous Saudi educational and health care institutions. Equally shocking (if not even more damaging) is the continuing Saudi financing of educational and religious activities and institutions that contribute in a most substantial way for the popularization of the ideology that inspires the terrorists.

In other words, there is a large-scale Saudi role in enrolling new recruits in the growing army of jihadists all over the world. Some of the numbers involved in the process of those activities are very impressive indeed; the Saudi subsidies made possible the establishment of 1,500 mosques, 202 colleges, and some 2,000 schools for Muslim children "in the non-Islamic countries in Europe, North and South America, Australia and Asia."[17]

Under quick and rising American pressure, the Saudi authorities banned the direct collection of money by the dubious foundations, extended their delayed and reluctant cooperation to the United States, and conducted an investigation into the international transfers of money from and into the kingdom. An investigation of the content of the schoolbooks taught at the schools sponsored and financed by the Saudis revealed a shocking situation that far exceeded the worst American expectations. The investigation performed by the Center for Religious Freedom of Freedom House and Institute for Gulf Affairs outlined the main areas of American concern involving the image of the non-Wahhabi religions and groups presented to the students by the Saudi-sponsored schools. According to the findings of the Center,

> Regarding Sunni, Shiite, Sufi and other non-Wahhabi or non-Salafi Muslims, the textbooks condemn the majority of Sunni Muslims around the world as "bad successors" of "bad predecessors."
>
> Condemn and denigrate Shiite and Sufi Muslims' beliefs and practices as heretical, and call them "polytheists."
>
> Denounce Muslims who do not interpret the Koran "literally."
>
> Regarding Christians, Jews, Polytheists (including Muslims who are not followers of Wahhabism) and other infidels, the books: Command Muslims to "hate" Christians, Jews, Polytheists and

other "unbelievers," including non-Wahhabi Muslims though, incongruously, not to treat them "unjustly."

Teach that the Crusades never ended, and identify the American Universities in Beirut and Cairo, other Western and Christian social service providers, media outlets, centers for academic studies of Orientalism, and campaign for women's rights as part of the modern phase of the Crusades.

Teach that "the Jews and the Christians are enemies of the (Muslim) believers and "the clash" between the two realms "continues until the day of Resurrection."

Instructs students not to "greet," "befriend," "imitate," "show loyalty to," "be courteous to," or "respect" non-believers.

Define Jihad to include "wrestling with the infidels by calling them to the faith and battling against them and asserting that the spread of Islam through jihad is a "religious obligation."

Regarding Anti-Semitism, they: Instruct that "the struggle between Muslims and Jews 'will continue' until the hour (of judgment)" and that "Muslims will triumph because they are right" and "he who is right is always victorious."

Cite a selective teaching of violence against Jews, while in the same lesson, ignoring the passages of the Koran and hadiths (narratives of the life of the Prophet) that counsel tolerance.

Teach the Protocols of the Elders of Zion as historical fact and relate modern events to it.

Discuss Jews in violent terms, blaming them for virtually all the "subversion" and wars."[18]

The American side evidently did not push too hard, and the Saudi reaction was one of denial and delay, because it took almost four years after 9/11 for the expression of a very serious American concern about the content of those books.

The years that have passed by since the calamity of 9/11 did not change the dynamics of the paradoxes and the contradictions marking the American-Saudi relations. It is beyond any doubt that today, even more than ten years after the calamity of 9/11, the Saudi rulers are firmly convinced that because of the location of their country, its oil wealth, and its mammoth investments in the US economy, the United States had to accept all the negatives marking the bilateral relations. At the same time, it is also abundantly clear that without terminating the spread of the poisonous hatred toward every human being who dares to think differently from the Wahhabi prescriptions, there could not be and would not be any victory over the jihadist enemies of freedom, culture, and tolerance.

Starting with the American-Saudi relations, for decades the relationship between Washington and Riyadh resembled the uneasy existence of Siamese twins who do not like each other. The glue that keeps America tied to the withering body of the corrupted Saudi monarchy is composed of oil, strategic location, and a Saudi investment on American soil that in the foreseeable future could easily reach $500 billion. Because of the increasing danger of Islamo-totalitarianism, the American policymakers inevitably need to detach their country from the dangerous embrace of Wahhabism, even at the price of losing all existing benefits stemming from the Siamese-like relationship with the Desert Kingdom.

In other words, the time is coming when America has to stop turning a blind eye to the Wahhabi poison distributed around the world. A rupture of the relationship with Saudi Arabia (in the case the monarchy will not take any practical measures against Wahhabism in keeping with the provisions of a critically important US ultimatum that one day should be presented by all means) will extract its inevitable toll on the American financial and strategic interests. However, the price that the United States and the world will pay for the continuation of the jihadist activities of the Saudi "foundations" will be much higher.

The Pakistani Factor Related to the Anti-American Jihad

It may sound paradoxical, but for the Cold War era American policymakers, the Muslim identity of Pakistan was irrelevant.[19] What mattered to them was the country's choice to be on the American side during the Cold War. From the Pakistani prospective, this choice was determined by the long and seemingly endless conflict with neighboring India over the Muslim-populated Indian region of Kashmir. Being smaller and weaker than its powerful rival, Pakistan needed protection from every state able and ready to render it. Because of the hostility between China and India, Pakistan developed good relations with China, which later prompted additional American interest when President Nixon started his ping-pong-like games with Chairman Mao.

Meanwhile, with its strong Muslim identity that was the main reason for the appearance of the country on the map of the world, Pakistan attracted the attention of numerous Wahhabi foundations from Saudi Arabia. The military rulers of Pakistan, on the other hand, saw the Saudi-sponsored Islamic "reeducation" of the young generation of their deeply divided country as an effective instrument that provided both cohesion and control.

It was this connection that determined the Pakistani-related dimension of the anti-Christian, anti-Semitic, antidemocratic, and anti-American jihad. Going back into the recent past, however, it was the enforced Islamization of the country that instead of cohesion brought about its breakup. An unintended and highly undesirable development for the Pakistani rulers was the ferocious resistance of the population of eastern Pakistan against the assault on its culture, tradition, and, above all, on its Bengali national identity. It was amid the agony and bloodshed of this confrontation that a new country was born—Bangladesh.

During the theoretically impossible time when the Soviet occupation of Afghanistan gave birth to an absurd coalition that had united many present-day enemies, Pakistan became one of the closest allies of the United States through its support rendered to the Afghan resistance. Things changed abruptly in the aftermath of the Soviet withdrawal from Afghanistan. Against the background of the American indifference, in cahoots with Saudi Arabia, Pakistan made an important contribution to the victory of the Taliban. Pakistan also became the only country in the world that extended its recognition to the barbaric Taliban regime and established diplomatic relations with Kabul. The events of 9/11 produced a new switch in Pakistani politics: the military government of the country took the American side in Washington's action against its Taliban allies. At the same time, however, Pakistan was one of the most anti-American countries in the world, if not *the* most anti-American.

The future trends in the development of Pakistani public opinion are destined to play a crucial role in the war against Islamo-totalitarianism. An Islamic takeover of Islamabad would create a powerful base for the jihadists who would have at their disposal a country possessing an atomic arsenal. Even without such a calamity occurring, which fortunately, at least for the time being, is highly unlikely, Pakistan represents a big danger to the United States with its scores of angry and disgruntled youngsters who blame America for every problem in the world. Considering the fact that almost a quarter of a million Pakistanis living in the United States visit their country of birth each year, it would be quite a challenge for law-enforcement agencies to discover the potential stream of suicidal murderers swimming amid the current of this mighty river of people who travel between both countries.

In different times and places, I had the opportunity to talk to Pakistanis from different walks of life: a teacher, an engineer, a taxi driver, and a couple of students. All of them were unanimous in their condemnation of American politics with regard to their country. At the same time, however, none of them expressed any desire to live under the Islamist dictatorship. Where the equation between the Pakistani jihadist recruits and their compatriots who have a high appreciation for freedom will lead Pakistan represents one of the most important questions one could possibly ask.

The Shia and Iranian Dimensions of Anti-American Jihad

There was a time when some American policymakers connected their hopes for an improvement of the US position in the Middle East with the Iran-Iraq War. It seemed to them that the conflict took away some of the intensity of Sunni and Shia fanatics on both sides of the religious fault line dividing the Muslim world who wanted to burn Western civilization at stake. During the 1980s, it was Iran that constituted the main danger for the United States' strategic interests in the area. Consequently, America, together with Saudi Arabia, supported the Iraqi military effort.

This support was so important that President Reagan had the future secretary of defense during the Iraqi war, Donald Rumsfeld, dispatched to Baghdad, where he conferred with Saddam Hussein. Much later, in one of his interviews, Rumsfeld provided the following explanation for his mission:

> President Reagan asked me to take a leave of absence from my company and serve as a temporary special envoy. . . . And among other things, we believed it would be helpful if Saddam Hussein's Iraq would behave in a way in that region that would be helpful to our goals with respect to Syria and the terrorist threat that existed. And we decided it was worth having me go in and meet with him. In that visit, I cautioned him about the use of chemical weapons, as a matter of fact, and discussed a host of other things.[20]

Two decades later, Iraq replaced Iran as the main American enemy.

In the aftermath of the Iraqi war, however, with its atomic ambitions, the anti-Semitic harangues of its president, and the unmistakable ambitions for regional domination, Iran again became the main source of danger for American interests. There are two very important questions involving the current shape of the conflict between the Shia and Sunni branches of the Muslim religion, and what is its influence over the war between the United States and the Islamo-totalitarian forces? The answer to the first question is far from easy. The problem starts with the fact that at the terrorist level, so to speak, the Shia and Sunni Islamists were not (and are not) involved in any theological discussions.

Instead, their attention is focused on pure "practicalities," such as what kind of explosive they are about to use.

Outside of the frame of terrorist "cooperation," the contradiction between the representatives of the main branches of Islam continues to exist. The Iranian Revolution brought about a substantial rise in the self-esteem of the Shia communities that had been accustomed to living for centuries as suppressed minorities throughout the Arab world. At the same time, in Iraq, the only Arab country where they are a majority, the Shia had been brutally suppressed by the Sunni-based dictatorship of Saddam Hussein. The important revival of Shia was due not only to the revolutionary fervor inflamed by the hysterics of the anti-American crowds in Teheran, but also by the skillful strategy of Khomeini with regard to the Arab world in general and to the Israeli-Palestinian conflict in particular.

During the Iranian war against Iraq, the Khomeinists created Hezbollah and Hamas to make their appearance in the Palestinian territories. The purpose of Teheran's strategy was to create Arab (which means Sunni) political, military, and social structures to challenge Israel in southern Lebanon and also to establish domination over the Palestinian movement. Evidently such domination had been considered a particularly precious asset by the theocratic and totalitarian regime ruling Iran. Considering the popularity of the Palestinian cause and the intensity of the anti-Israeli and anti-American emotions running high throughout the Muslim world, such a domination provided unprecedented opportunities for Teheran to establish a sphere of Shia influence within the basically Sunni Muslim world.[21]

The tough stand of Hezbollah during the campaign of 2006 and of Hamas during the battle for Gaza earned them immense popularity in the Sunni part of the Muslim world. The portraits of Sheik Nasralla, the leader of Hezbollah, dotted the walls of many Muslim houses in Lebanon. And as far as Hamas was concerned, it won the competition with the secular Fatah during the elections conducted in Gaza.

Serving the interests of Teheran provided both organizations with instructions, financing, and weapons, and their leadership managed to build up a very effective structure that operated at three levels. While some of their members were busy creating a smoothly functioning infrastructure to offer health and educational services, a second component trained for terrorist or military action. Finally, there was a third component responsible for financing the activities of Hezbollah and Hamas.

Last but not least, both organizations developed their American connections. Hamas was particularly successful in entrenching itself on American soil.[22] This entrenchment reached a level that allowed the members of Hamas cells to offer training in terrorist activities performed on American soil![23] However, there is more to it: the instructor who taught the trade of making and planting car bombs to twenty-five young Palestinians in the outskirts of Chicago turned out to be a Libyan American and a former marine who was married to an American woman.[24]

It would be reasonable to assume that today Hamas is even better entrenched on American soil than ever before. The question is, why did the strengthening of the American security agencies in the aftermath of 9/11 and the elimination of the barrier that in the past separated the findings of the CIA and FBI not bring about the discovery and dismantling of the Hamas cells on American soil? The answer is that, unlike the other jihadist sympathizers in America, the Hamas cells have been ordered to organize and wait.

The latest developments in the region, such as the intensification of the American military effort in Afghanistan and the progress of the Iranian atomic project, have prompted some very important changes that went under the radar of the American media. To start, for the first time since the establishment of the state of Israel, the strategic interests and priorities of the United States and Israel do not match each other. To make a complex issue simple and understandable, let's start with a very basic fact: at this juncture in history, the main enemy of the United States is the Wahhabi terrorist ideology that inspires both al-Qaeda and the Taliban. The main battlefield of this war is Afghanistan. At the same time, the main enemies of Israel are Iran and its Arab proxies, Hezbollah and Hamas.

At least on its surface the situation gets even more paradoxical if we look at its additional dimensions. The strategic interests of the United States and Iran currently coincide as far as the Afghan war is concerned. It is abundantly clear why al-Qaeda and the Taliban are ferocious enemies of the United States. What we need to remember, however, is that they are enemies of Iran as well. For the Wahhabi-inspired Sunni fanatics, all Shia are heretics, and Iran is the center and major force behind the heresy. The Farsi-speaking component of the Afghan population sympathizes with Iran, and, for this reason, the Taliban guerilla detachments have slaughtered thousands of Shia Afghans.[25]

Theoretically, an Iranian contribution to the American military effort in Afghanistan would have posed a tremendous problem to the Taliban. On the other side of the strange realignment, as far as the strategic interests were concerned, Saudi Arabia, the birthplace of Wahhabism and its main supporter, was as much worried by the prospective appearance of an atomic Iran as Israel. If at a certain point Israel decides to inflict a preliminary strike against the Iranian nuclear facilities (but let's hope that it will not happen), the emotions in Riyadh will match the ones reigning supreme in Tel Aviv.

Of course, no one in his right mind expects to see the Iranian mullahs changing their spots and sending candy to the GIs in Afghanistan or the sudden birth of a Saudi-Israeli axis. Nevertheless, the appearance of different geopolitical realities imposes a lot of tension between old friends and opens the opportunities for a new look at the old rivals. The option involving the establishment of an American-Iranian strategic alliance has been explored in depth by only one American author Robert Baer.[26] The essence of Baer's concept involves the changing dynamics in the Middle East. According to him, because of the growing influence of Iran, it would be advantageous for the United States to abandon most of the existing stereotypes and to establish closer relations with an emerging powerful player rather than to get involved in a conflict.

There is one troubling aspect, however, to an otherwise well-written book. The author operates with the terms "Iran" and "the Iranians" as if Iran is populated by some kind of unique population that shares the same attitude. Examples are abundant, such as "Iran is not fighting a crusade" or "It (Iran) does not want to convert us to Islam."[27] Particularly troubling is the following statement by Baer: "Iran is not a totalitarian state run by Islamo-Fascists."[28]

Starting with the last thought, Baer is wrong—beyond any shadow of doubt, Iran is a totalitarian state, and it is run by Islamo-Fascists.[29] When he talks about "the Iranians," it is absolutely necessary for him to make sure which "Iranians" he is talking about. There are those who were murdered on the streets of Teheran while expressing their discontent with rigged elections and those who were murdering them. Besides, isn't Baer afraid that if the United States gets too close to the Islamo-totalitarians currently ruling Iran, the story with the extremely unfavorable consequences that stemmed from the complete and unconditional American support for the shah could be repeated after the fall of the present regime? Or, maybe, he thinks that it will last forever?

If this is the case, we have to underline the only positive Iranian development from the point of view of the United States: America benefited tremendously from the fact that in the course of the last thirty years, the Iranian Islamo-totalitarians managed to completely repel the young generation of the country that represents by far the largest group in the population. Having said that, I agree with Baer that some kind of cooperation, with possible Russian support in the future, could be developed, even with the present Iranian regime. The question is whether it possible for Iran to replace Saudi Arabia as an American ally in the Middle East. I personally do not share Baer's optimism in this regard—at least as long as the mullahs hold the power in Tehran.

At this point of time, however, the Shia-based and Shia-related danger for the United States could materialize in the case of direct or indirect American involvement in conflict with Iran. Under this scenario, the sleeping cells on American soil will be activated. The only solution to the complex problem could be found only within the framework of a well-planned and masterfully executed strategy, which at the time being does not exist.

Notes

1. Mark Steyn, "America Alone—The End of the World as We Know It." (Washington DC: Regnery Publishing House, 2008), 71–72.
2. The Royal Embassy of Saudi Arabia, Washington DC, www.saudiembassy. net/print/latest/_news/news10809003.aspx.
3. Interview with Colonel Dunn, www.saudi-american-forum.org/articles/2003/030313p-saudi-dunn.html.
4. Secretary Colin Powell, "Comments on US-Saudi Relationship," www.saudi-us-relations.org/newletter2004/saudi-relations-41.html.
5. Stephen Schwarz, *The Two Faces of Islam: The House of Saud from Tradition to Terror* (New York: Doubleday, 2002).
6. Ibid., 92–93.
7. Ibid.
8. Ibid.
9. Ibid., 106.
10. "Declaration of Jihad against the Americans Occupying the Land of the Two Holy Sanctuaries," http://middleeast.about.com/od/terrorism/a/bin-laden-jihad.html.
11. Ibid.
12. The Associated Press, Konstantin Testorides, "Radical Islam on Rise in the Balkans," www.google.com/hostednews/ap/article/ALegM5j1EtCda2eWk9xiv4J7EFWuwnZ.
13. Ibid.
14. Ibid.
15. Ibid.
16. Ibid.

17. Schwarz, *The Two Faces of Islam: The House of Saud from Tradition to Terror*, 184.

18. Center for Religious Freedom of Freedom House and Institute for Gulf Affairs. Saudi Arabia's Curriculum of Intolerance. With Excerpts from Saudi Ministry of Education Textbooks for Islamic Studies, Freedom House, Washington DC, 2006, 13–14.

19. Schwarz, *The Two Faces of Islam: The House of Saud from Tradition to Terror*, 184.

20. Center for Religious Freedom of Freedom House and Institute for Gulf Affairs. Saudi Arabia's Curriculum of Intolerance. With Excerpts from Saudi Ministry of Education Textbooks for Islamic Studies, Freedom House, Washington DC, 2006, 13–14.

21. Stephen Philip Cohen, *The Idea of Pakistan* (Washington DC: Brookings Institution, 2004).

22. "Rumsfeld's Plans to Propose NATO Rapid Reaction Force," www.usembassy. it/file2002_09/alia/a2092001.html.

23. The best description of the changing dynamics of the Shia-Sunni conflict can be found in Vali Nasr, *The Shia Revival: How Conflicts within Islam Will Shape the Future* (New York: W.W. Norton and Co., 2006).

24. Steven Emerson, *American Jihad: The Terrorists Living among Us* (New York: The Free Press, 2002), 79–108.

25. Ibid.

26. Ibid.

27. Nasr, *The Shia Revival: How Conflicts within Islam Will Shape the Future*, 157–158.

28. Robert Baer, *The Devil We Know* (New York: The Three Rivers Press, 2009).

29. Ibid., 75–76.

9

The Jihadist Penetration of America

During a visit to the United States, the charismatic leader of the Dutch nationalists, Geert Wilders, was asked how he would compare the advancement of radical Islam in Europe and the United States. He pointed to the clock and said that if the European clock shows midnight sharp, the reading on the American clock is quarter to midnight.

Here is the description of the way the former jihadist Kamal Saleem chose to demonstrate to what extent the United States is blind to the threat of Islamic terrorism: "I want to show you America on 9/11." He then went downstage and lay down on the plank floor, suit and all, and pretended to be sleeping. Sitting up, he said, "I want to show you America today after 9/11," at which point he pretended to hit the snooze button, then went back to sleep. His message was clear: America had to be awoken to the danger of Islamic terror.[1]

The Denial

It will not be necessary, in keeping with Saleem's example, to get down on the floor to accept his concept. Undoubtedly, the most shocking truth concerning the biggest threat the United States has ever encountered is that millions of Americans do not realize either the nature or the scope of the threat hanging over their country. This situation reveals another shocking reality—that at this very important juncture in its history America is tragically unprepared for the most serious conflict already ravaging its own territory.

The first shocking component of a potentially very tragic situation involves the ignorance about the nature of the enemy. The people have become so accustomed to the term "War on Terror," which has been so popular since 9/11, that they do not pay any attention to its absurdity. Is it necessary to convince each other that "terror" could define only the *method* used by the enemy, but by no means the *enemy* itself?

171

The denial of the Islamo-totalitarian danger and the fear of using the very name of the enemy begins with the highest level of the American government. Starting with the president, Obama prefers to use the term "extremists" when he wants to attach some name to those who are planning and causing deadly explosions and who are dreaming to replace the political system of the United States with an absolute dictatorship of their own. Granted, President Obama is right to use the term extremists when it is applied to individuals capable of performing a mass murder of completely innocent people.

At the same time, however, it is abundantly clear that, besides being extremists, the mass murderers are in possession of a belief system capable of inspiring them to sacrifice their own lives while taking away the lives of other human beings. Obviously the belief system of the "extremists" that provides a permanent inspiration to its adherents to commit murders all the way from the distant Indonesian island of Bali to a remote military base in Texas deserves to be mentioned by name. What would have been the effect of the wartime strategy of FDR if he had chosen to call the followers of Adolf Hitler "extremists" while carefully avoiding the term "Nazi"?

It was President Obama who, in June 2009, sent a very important message to the Muslim world with a speech delivered at Cairo University. Unfortunately, the message was based on a deeply wrong premise: according to Obama, mentioning the real name of the American enemy will offend the Muslims. With this consideration in mind, the new president of the United States never used the absolutely necessary term "radical Islam," nor "Islamic fundamentalism," "Islamo-Fascism," or "jihadism." Instead, except for a brief mention of the "extremists" who committed the monstrous crime on 9/11, Obama preferred to ignore the Islamo-totalitarian assault on the world. He preferred to philosophize in the most general terms about the history of the conflicts between the West and Islam. Here is a piece of his rhetoric: "The relationship between Islam and the West includes centuries of coexistence and cooperation, but also conflict and religious wars. More recently, tension has been fed by colonialism that denied rights and opportunities to many Muslims."[2]

As a matter of fact, much more recently than colonialism, it is radical Islam that has denied rights and opportunities to every human being who does not share the jihadist ambition to move mankind back into the seventh century. The historical excursion undertaken in Cairo by President Obama was highly selective. Having decided to enter the

172

annals of the past, Obama should have mentioned the invasions of Europe organized by the Arab caliphate as early as the eighth century and the centuries-long expansion of the Ottoman Empire into Europe that was terminated only in 1683 at the gates of Vienna.

Speaking of the "denied rights and opportunities" to the Muslims, maybe a very good example the president could (and should) have offered to his audience would have been the current Islamic discrimination against women. By the way, the president touched this sensitive issue, but in a rather peculiar way, by saying, "It is important for Western countries to avoid impeding Muslim citizens from practicing religion as they see fit—for instance, by dictating what clothes a Muslim woman should wear."[3] This remarkable thought leaves enough room for the question, what about the rights of the women living in the Muslim countries to decide what clothes to wear?

The Cairo speech by President Obama is one of the best examples of the confusion and lack of preparedness on the part of not just the current administration but also of a large number of Americans to face the reality of an impending life-and-death confrontation with radical Islam. In addition, this battle could last for generations and can be avoided only at the price of a total American capitulation in front of the Islamo-totalitarianism.

One must be blind, stupid, or hypocritical to deny one of the most visible links in this world—the one between radical Islam and the political terrorism shaking the very foundations of the Western world. The denial of even the most obvious dimensions of the mortal danger hanging over the United States, however, is not a prerogative of the president. It marks the terminology of his administration, which got the message that terms such as "radical Islam," "Muslim fundamentalism," and "Islamo-Fascism" are strictly forbidden. Sometimes the degree of this denial reaches outright comic undertones.

On May 13, 2010, an unusual exchange took place at the hearing of the House Judiciary Committee in connection with the recent incidents involving radical Islam–related crimes and attempts to commit crimes, such as the Christmas Day and Times Square bombers and the Fort Hood murderer:

> Rep. Lamar Smith (R-Tex): "Do you feel that these individuals might have been incited to take the actions that they did because of radical Islam?"
>
> Attorney General Eric Holder: "There are a variety of reasons why I think people have taken these actions."

Smith: "Okay, but radical Islam could have been one of the reasons?"

Holder: "There are a variety of reasons why people—"

Smith: "But was radical Islam one of them?"

Holder: "There are a variety of reasons why people do these things. Some of them are potentially religious based."[4]

So, some of the crimes could be "religious based" but not committed by radical Islamists. What Attorney General Holder does not suspect is that his remarkable answers most certainly have been carefully analyzed by the Jihadists.

The attitude of denial so well demonstrated by Holder was born out of a culture of denial. The majority of American journalists, in addition to most of the academia in the area of the humanities and social sciences, are under the ideological influence of multiculturalism. For the numerous adherents of this attitude, American patriotism (by the way, the strongest dam against the rising waters of radical Islam) is an old-fashioned emotion exploited by the government circles that serves the interests of the big multinational corporations. As far as the Christian religion is concerned, similarly to their European colleagues, the multiculturalists are convinced that America and Europe are already living in a post-Christian world.

Another huge social anomaly marking the American conflict with totalitarian Islam is the drastically uneven distribution of its burden over the members of American society. The first dimension of this impact involves the complete absence of the sons and the daughters of the political and social elite of the United States from even the idea of service in the armed forces of the country. In this respect, there is a shocking difference between the United States and Great Britain. During WWI, 80 percent of the graduates of Oxford and Cambridge perished in the trenches. The war-related genetic loss suffered by the British landed aristocracy that was supplying the country with leaders ever since the times of the Glorious Revolution was so big that as a group this aristocracy never reappeared on the British political scene. This noble and rough British tradition continued all the way to the times of the present Afghan War where Prince Harry served in a regular unit, sharing all the inconveniencies and risks with the other soldiers. During the same time, *none* of the members of Congress who in 2003 sent other people's sons and daughters under the fire of the jihadist RPG missiles of the Iraqi War had a child serving in the armed forces of the United States.

What aggravated the picture even more was the bias of the media that did not inform the rest of the world of the amazing accomplishment of the American armed forces on Iraqi soil. Within the framework of an unexpected and unpredictable situation and under the worst possible conditions determined by the wrong planning of the war, the soldiers of America and their leaders managed to achieve a degree of stabilization of the country that very few people were expecting during the period of 2003–2007. In addition, while not fighting the enemy, the GIs were busy building schools, water supplies, and providing electricity. It was also the American occupation that enabled fair elections that could mark the beginning of a new phase in the long and tortuous history of Iraq.

The American media did not discharge its moral responsibilities toward those warriors and their stunning accomplishments under incredible odds. During a trip to Europe, I had real difficulty dispersing the completely wrong but firm belief of the majority of people I talked to that the Americans are using the oil deposits of Iraq for free! At the same time, the *New York Times* had devoted 150 materials relating to Abu Ghraib scandal. What is really hard to explain is the lack of understanding demonstrated by some of the most-qualified American journalists of the simplest fact that the kind of coverage addressing only the negative aspects of the American military effort in Iraq and Afghanistan elevates the level of anti-Americanism and, consequently, facilitates the jihadist war against the United States.

As far as the answer to the question, what is the name of the enemy? The answer is amazingly simple: it is the dangerously growing contingent of jihadists inspired by the ideology of radical Islam. Whenever the Wahhabis and the Khomeinists claim that they represent the one and only true Islam, they are lying. Neither Prophet Mohammed nor any of the first caliphs of the medieval Muslim caliphate called "the righteous ones" would have ordered the beheading of an eleven-year-old boy, which jihadists did in Iraq because the boy informed a group of American soldiers where an RPG device had been buried. None of them would have approved the terrifying murder of another boy who was seven years old when he was beheaded by the Afghan Talibs. The political system the jihadists are trying to impose on the United States is *not* the one that existed in the medieval Arabian Peninsula during the period of early Islam. What is beyond any shadow of doubt, however, is that the system the victorious jihadists would install would be a *totalitarian* one.

If at least some present-day Americans are moderately curious about their possible future, let's try to take a glimpse of it from a couple of important angles. The degree of Islamic control destined to be imposed upon mankind once the global Islamo-totalitarian dream is transformed into reality is best described by the first modern-era theocratic Islamic dictator, Ayatollah Khomeini. In one of his lectures delivered at the religious school in Nadjaf, Khomeini made abundantly clear the degree of control of the future global Islamic government over its subjects:

> Islam and divine governments . . . have a commandment for every-body, everywhere, at any place, in any condition. If a person were to commit an immoral dirty deed right next to his house, Islamic governments have business with him. . . . Islam has rules for every person, even before birth, before his marriage, until his marriages, pregnancy, birth, until upbringing of the child, the education of the adult, until puberty, youth, until old age, until death, into the grave, and beyond the grave.[5]

Those remarkable thoughts shared by Khomeini with his students in Nadjaf on September 28, 1977, should give cold feet to any American complaining of the tyranny of big government. Why then do so many of those complainers not see the danger emanating from those who are trying to install a *really big* government on American soil?

If some individual had the shy hope that the Islamic government would be not so rough on the ways the subjects of the global caliph-ate would be enjoying their time off, this person is deadly wrong. Evidently, the all-powerful dictator Khomeini did not leave any room for similar illusions:

> Allah didn't create man so that he could have fun. The aim of creation was for mankind to be put to the test through hardship and prayer. An Islamic regime must be serious in every field. There are no jokes in Islam. There is no humor in Islam. There is no fun in Islam. There can be no fun and joy in whatever is serious. Islam does not allow swim-ming in the sea and is opposed to radio and television serials. Islam however allows marksmanship, horseback riding and competition.[6]

If we decide to reminisce a little bit deeper over those thoughts, we will make a stunning discovery. It is quite obvious that in his attempt to regulate the lives of all the residents of the world, Khomeini was looking at himself as a prophetic figure. The last thing that could have been on the mind of Prophet Mohammed in the process of creating a new faith in the rough desert environment of the Arabian Peninsula would have been the ban on "swimming in the sea." For Khomeini, however, who for some reason did not like swimming, he presented it as an un-Islamic activity.[7] Everything would have been perfect with this bold but strange statement provided that it had been presented as an activity not in keeping with the requirements of *radical* Islam.

The other part of the Ayatollah's statement is even stranger—how on earth the Iranian cleric and dictator could have known the attitude of Prophet Mohammed with regard to television! Again, this statement represents a replacement of the term "radical Islam" with the term "Islam." In short, the Khomeinism that still inspires part of the followers of the Shia branch of jihadism is based upon the ideology of a particularly narrow-minded and fanatical fundamentalism.

In the eyes of bin Laden and his al-Qaeda associates the Khomeinists were heretics because of their Shia identity. Nevertheless, the theoretically opposed ideologies share the same goal. Their vision of the future of the world represents precisely the same kind of theocratic totalitarian utopia that inspired Khomeini. Regardless of another important difference determined by the status of Khomeinist Iran, where jihadism is in possession of the instrumentality of a state organization while al-Qaeda is a stateless structure, the main goal of both branches remains the same: the destruction of the United States and the establishment of the global Islamic caliphate.

The radical Islamists from both persuasions are in the habit of constantly repeating that their jihad against Western civilization is the realization of the main goal of the Muslim religion. The terroristic "theoreticians," however, prefer to forget two pieces of a rather inconvenient truth. To start, one of the absolutely uncontested and uncontestable dimensions of the Muslim faith is the categorical ban on suicide, which is considered one of the heaviest crimes a Muslim could ever commit and is punishable by eternity in hell. The jihadists have changed this order into a brand-new rule: according to them, suicide is not only acceptable but a highly rewarding act, provided that the person committing it manages to take out the lives of one or more of the "infidels." Where did the jihadists borrow this approach? When not engaged in an outright lie, they are remarkably silent on the subject.

Another important difference between the legacy of Islam and the fundamentalist's murderers is that under early Islam the Christians and the Jews had been given the status of a protected minority. The fact that present-day Islamo-totalitarians are justifying the murder of innocent civilians, including children, and the magnitude of their hatred

177

for Christians and Jews, makes inevitable the conclusion that once in power they will perform genocide of unseen proportions.[8]

Naturally, the United States is the main enemy of the jihadists. There are two reasons for that. In theory, the Americans (all of them!) are to blame for all calamities that have befallen every Muslim country involved in any kind of conflict. At a strategic level, the most promising approach from the jihadist point of view is the isolation and defeat of the strongest country of the much-hated Christian and democratic world. I will never forget the comment made by a Pakistani sympathizer of the jihadists: "Once American chip goes down, the rest will be a piece of cake—Europe, Africa and South America will fall as over ripened fruits into Islam's basket." He did not provide any answer, however, to my question of whether China is also about to fall without any resistance into the Islamist basket.

The Islamic Strategy of War on the United States

It would be a rather difficult task to determine *when* precisely the decision of the jihadists to unleash a war on the United States took place. What is certain, however, is that upon meeting on the battlefields of Afghanistan in the mid-1980s and forging their partnership to the point of being able to organize some terrorist acts during the early 1990s, bin Laden and Ayman al-Zawahiri got busy preparing the ground for future terrorist activities against the United States. At the end of 1994 and in early 1995, three consecutive mini-summits took place in Tehran, Khartoum, and some place in Cyprus. One of the participants was Imad Fadhia al-Mughniyah, a Hezbollah character wanted by the US authorities for murdering an American passenger on a commercial airliner and dumping the body on the Beirut airport tarmac.[9] Another Islamist who attended the meetings and whose participation would have very important consequences was Fathi Shiqaqi, a Palestinian leader who at the end of the 1970s, while studying in Egypt, created an organization named the Palestinian Islamic Jihad.[10]

The participation of Shiqaqi in the meetings organized by the number two al-Qaeda leader, al-Zawahiri, had a very important consequence along two different but equally meaningful lines. The first was to speed up the Islamization of a growing part of the Palestinian nationalists. The second was the acceptance of the indiscriminate terror against Israeli citizens, regardless of their status, age, or gender, by the use of suicidal murderers as the main form of their struggle. The fact that several months later, in October of 1995, Shiqaqi was gunned down, probably by the agents of the Israeli Mossad, on the streets of Nicosia (Cyprus), did not change the steady trend leading to the Islamization and radicalization of a substantial part of the Palestinian youth. This process was in full keeping with the al-Qaeda strategy because a potential peaceful solution of the Israeli-Palestinian conflict would have been a catastrophe for al-Qaeda, which could only thrive within an atmosphere of hatred.

It was Zawahiri who provided the next important objectives of radical Islam with regard to the United States and Europe. What the Egyptian jihadist offered was a speed up of the actions of the Islamic networks in London and in the Brooklyn area of New York, the activation of the Islamic network in the Balkans, and increased support to the armed Islamist groups in Somalia and Ethiopia.[11]

In 1996, al-Zawahiri visited the United States. He was successful in collecting a large amount of money for "the widows and orphans" of Afghanistan. The success of the theoretically risky endeavor was a clear-cut indication that al-Zawahiri counted on the support of an already existing Islamic network on American soil. Upon the return of Osama bin Laden and al-Zawahiri to Afghanistan in 1996, they devoted particular attention to the development of the Islamist strategy toward the United States. The fanatical pair had already produced a large volume of documentation, including a formal declaration of war on the United States. A short excerpt from the declaration is more than enough to create some idea about the jihadist concepts and morality: "The ruling to kill Americans and their allies—civilian and military—is an individual duty for every Muslim who can do it in any country in which it is possible to do it, in order to liberate al-Agsa mosque from their grip, and in order for their armies to move out of all the lands of Islam, defeated and unable to threaten any Muslim."[12]

In one of his rare interviews, bin Laden provided the following answer to the easily predictable question of why he thinks that his organization will be able to defeat such a powerful country as the United States: "This battle is not between the Al-Qaeda and the U.S. This is a battle of Muslims against the global crusaders. . . . God, who provided us with his support and kept us steadfast until the Soviet Union was defeated, is able to provide us once more with his support to defeat America on the same land and with the same people."[13]

Needless to say, a society controlled by the jihadists will be an antidemocratic one as far as the political system based on a radical Islamist ideology is concerned. This society would be transformed into an outright barbarian community given that every creative effort in the area of literature, music, and art would labeled "anti-Islamic." The future Islamo-totalitarian world will undoubtedly be fiercely anti-Semitic as well, and its masters will perform a complete destruction of the Jewish community. An Islamo-totalitarian system will share another very important feature of the "classical" totalitarian system of the Stalinist-Hitlerist kind—the aggressive impulse pushing the rulers to unleash new wars leading to new conquests. In short, an Islamo-totalitarian world would combine the worst features of the well-familiar government structures established by Stalin and Hitler.

The Islamist strategy with regard to the United States has the same features described in the document captured in the Swiss villa more than two decades ago. In short, at the earliest stages of their assault on the West, the Islamo-totalitarians have based their entire strategy on the opportunities offered by the Western world to the well-organized and well-financed activities designed to bring down democracy. What should not be forgotten is that the transformation of Western democratic ideas into a functioning state organization took place in a completely different social and political condition. One of the most tragic aspects of the successful jihadist assault is connected with the gradual but systemic restriction of the power of government's agencies to control and monitor the behavior of the citizens.

In other words, the expansion of the rights of the citizens and the restrictions imposed upon the function of the agencies protecting the law and order, typical for every democratic country, turned out to be extremely beneficial to the jihadists. That is why it became possible for the Somali followers of Osama bin Laden to look for new recruits directly in the state of Minnesota and for radical Islamists to establish their training camps in Oregon. Isn't this the biggest paradox so blatantly ignored by the mainstream American media? It manifests itself in the sad reality that it is so much easier to recruit future murderers in Minnesota and Oregon rather than in Jordan, Egypt, Morocco, or Saudi Arabia.

It would be correct to accept the thesis that all methods used by jihadists in Europe are also used in the United States. This similarity is determined by the situations existing on both sides of the Big Pond, such as the triumph of multiculturalism and political correctness. Consequently, a common dimension of the jihadist approach is the use of all opportunities offered by Western democracy in the area of immigration, social assistance, education, and the protection of minority rights, to name a few, to promote the agenda of radical Islam. Besides, the open and hidden proponents of radical Islam are assuming the role of the defenders and protectors of the Muslim community against "racist" and "anti-Muslim" publications and statements.

Inevitably, there are some important differences determined by the specifics of the barriers built on the road of the Islamo-totalitarian expansion by the American tradition and mentality. The first among those obstacles is symbolized by the fact that in the United States the religious factor plays a more important social role than in Europe. Being a nation of immigrants, one of the most essential components of the American tradition found its expression in a much stronger connection between the different churches and their constituents. In other words, the fact that no Christian church has ever been part of the privileged elite in the United States, as was the case in Europe, elevates the social significance of religion.

At the same time, there are two other factors that facilitate the jihadist strategy with regard to the United States. The first one is the deep division currently existing within the framework of American society: the nation has been never been so polarized as the way it is now. On the other hand, there is a strong contradiction between the fact that the majority of Americans hold more or less conservative views as opposed to the fact that the ratio between the progressives and conservatives within the teaching staff of American colleges and universities is nine to one. Consequently, there is a serious divide between the attitudes of the majority of the country and its intellectual elite raised in the politically correct and multicultural atmosphere reigning supreme at the American institutions of higher learning. And there is something else: the limitless supply of Saudi petrodollars financing the jihadist activities on American soil.

In one of the best movie documentaries ever made about the nature and threat of radical Islam, *The Road to Nine Eleven*, Dr. Bernard Lewis makes a succinct analogy in the process of describing the role of the Wahhabi propaganda financed by the stream of oil-related Saudi dollars. Dr. Lewis appeals to the viewers to imagine a situation where the Ku Klux Klan, supported by all the money that Texas oil could generate, launched a global campaign to finance schools and colleges to spread the Klan's ideology.

One of the most important goals of the jihadist action on American soil is to spread an Islamo-totalitarian ideology based upon the most rigid and sectarian branches of the Muslim religion under the guise of the one and only truthful Islam. Their primary and most important target is the American Muslim community.

The Islamization of the American Muslim Community

Similar to the situation with Europe, no one knows how many Muslims are living in the United States. The assessments range from 2.5 million all the way to 7 million.[14] The increase of the Muslim population of the country has been because of the influx of immigrants, primarily from the Arab regions of the Middle East, Iran, and representatives of the Muslim communities of the Indian subcontinent. There are groups from virtually all areas and nationalities of the Muslim world, such as Somalis, Turks, Balkan Muslims, and residents of the Muslim states of Central Asia.

There can be little doubt that because of its extreme diversity the Muslim community of the United States is maybe the most complex subject area for sociological and psychological analysis. In general, unlike the situation in Europe, many American Muslims are very well integrated into the mainstream American society. If we take, for example, the Arab community, about 70 percent of the Arab Americans belong to the middle class. Research conducted in Chicago has established that 16 percent of the community members are medical doctors, 33 percent are engineers, and 84 percent had at least a bachelor's degree. Only 2 percent of the Muslim residents had less than a high school education.[15] Those numbers provide enough reason to qualify the just quoted achievements as some of the most impressive success stories involving the pursuit of the American dream.

However, there are some groups within the Muslim community who have a much lower success rate. Many of the Somali residents of the United States concentrated in the area of Minneapolis–St. Paul, for instance, are on welfare. The most probable reason for such an anomaly is the failed state organization of their native country, which for a long time has proven its lack of ability to provide even the most basic educational services to its people.

At the same time, the shock of 9/11 created a feeling of alienation between a substantial part of the Muslim community and the rest of their fellow Americans. There are many Muslims who are convinced that their community is a target of suspicion and discrimination in the aftermath of the mammoth crime committed by the suicidal murderers on 9/11. By the way, according to the Pew report of 2009, almost 60 percent of the non-Muslim Americans think that the Muslims are the subject of discrimination.[16] What is even more interesting is that, according to the polls, the majority of the American Muslims are also concerned about the rise of the Islamic fundamentalism around the world.[17]

Unfortunately, there is a clearly visible negative trend that undermines the connection between the Muslims and the rest of their compatriots. It is not an easy task to determine the exact response of the American Muslim community to the jihadist propaganda and recruitment. In some important aspects, the Muslim community in the United States is so diverse that we have to take into account this diversity before any attempt to analyze the attitude of this community toward American democracy and the Islamist jihad against America.

First of all, let's make one point abundantly clear: there is no such thing as a collective position of the American Muslims. Let's not forget about the existence of a part of the American Muslim community whose mentality and attitudes are still under the radar of the media and research. This segment of the American Muslim world is, figuratively speaking, miles apart from the sophisticated and successful professionals with Arab, Turkish, or Iranian backgrounds who are part of the American middle and upper-middle class. The above-mentioned parallel Muslim universe, whose numbers are growing, is composed of people who came to America long ago but uncannily, like their European counterparts, have preserved the mentality and the traditions of the countries and regions from which they arrived.

The specifics of this world are revealed in a very candid and amazingly illuminative way in a book entitled *Caged in America* that undeservedly is not well-known to the American readers.[18] The author of the book, Jasmine Sharif, is a young and charming Yemeni woman who was forced to escape not only from an abusive husband but also from her own family. The Yemeni neighborhood in Dearborn, Michigan, where she was born and raised, lives its own life completely detached from American culture and laws. Jasmine had been pushed against her will into a set of prearranged marriages. The first one took place when she was only fourteen. The marriage that turned out to be successful was brought to an end by her parents, who forced her to accept their decision to terminate it.

The description of the neighborhood where Jasmine was born and raised leaves the impression of a place that hides an institutionalized domestic slavery for women, who are subjected to constant sexual and physical abuse, and also an amazingly high level of alcoholism, despite the strict rules of the Muslim religion in this regard. The book also contains a remarkable gallery of violent male characters who belong to different national groups. Although the book is not political, and given that Jasmine is a deeply religious person, she provides an amazingly powerful description of the gloomy reality that continues its hidden existence parallel but outside of the frame of the American society.

One could easily spot some of the male members of the mini-world described by Jasmine, who having lost the positive features of traditional society have never managed to acquire anything from the world of personal freedom, the opportunities of the free enterprise system, or from the culture and values of American democracy. One of those characters openly expressed his desire to see "all Americans killed," which prompted Jasmine to question why the bloodthirsty individual came to America when he did not like anything about the country. Such individuals constitute a substantial component of the growing group that is culturally and psychologically predisposed to accept the hateful message of the Islamo-totalitarians. The only factor that unifies this component of the active or potential jihadists with their educated and sophisticated partners in hatred or crime is the equal degree of alienation from any aspect of Western culture and civilization.

One of the most important areas of the jihadist penetration of the United States is the education of the Muslims. What makes possible the growth of the radicalism and the impact of the jihadist message is the genuine concern of many American Muslims who want their children to be well educated and well prepared for a successful professional career, but who at the same time want their children to preserve their national and religious identity.[19]

Professor Hussam S. Timani has performed exhaustive research on the Islamic schools in the United States that produced some amazing results. Many Americans are wrong in believing that the meaningful aspect of the mentality and activities of the Muslim organizations in the United States is their concern with the negative attitudes toward the Muslims. Let's make an important division at this juncture: there are many American Muslims who are afraid that the continuation of the Islamist jihad against their country will bring about Islamophobia and, potentially, repression against their community. At the same time, however, major organizations allegedly created to defend the interests of the Muslim community and to promote dialogue with the rest of the population of the country are secretly following a completely different agenda. The most shocking example in this respect is offered by some actions of the largest Muslim organization, the Council on American-Islamic Relations (CAIR).[20]

The attitude of the leaders of CAIR does not help the cause their organization could have defended so effectively by protecting the rights of the Muslims whenever those rights have been violated and, at the same time, establishing a dialogue with the rest of America. The purpose of this dialogue should be the powerful expression of the opinion of the majority of the Muslims who are an inseparable component of American society. We are living in rough and demanding times when, regardless of his or her belief system, anyone who has appreciation for the freedoms and opportunities offered by the United States to all of its residents and citizens has to take a stand against the Islamo-totalitarian assault on the American social and political system. A powerful voice raised on behalf of the huge majority of Muslims who do not have anything to do with the jihadists would have eliminated *all* problems the Muslims are facing. Let's be very clear on a meaningful issue: many of the negative feelings toward the Muslims and their religion stem from the fact that such a voice has never been heard. The the rest of America is right to ask, given that the aforementioned majority consists of good and law-abiding individuals, why is it so silent about the most important danger their country is facing?

The refusal of CAIR to provide the answer to this question is the main factor contributing to the emergence of negative emotions toward Islam and Muslims. It is a regrettable but nevertheless true fact that the basic messages of CAIR are deeply wrong. Let's take a quick look at them. The first one is the spread of a subculture of victimization that presents a distorted picture of the lives of American Muslims and their religion being constantly attacked by hateful Americans. This false victimization is bringing about alienation that opens the door for the acceptance of the jihadist message by some Muslims, while at the same time creating the image that all Muslims are opposed to American society and politics.

The second main point constantly reinforced by CAIR is the thesis that every religion produces its fundamentalists. The continuation of this logic must lead us to the conclusion that Islam is not an exception. It would be useless to convince ourselves that this message is also wrong. It is true, of course, that every religion has its extremists. No other religion, however, is used by theocratic, totalitarian, and terrorist organizations as an instrument to recruit new terrorists ready to be a part of the Islamo-Fascist quest for world domination. Besides, one

185

could ask a very simple question: how many people have been blown to pieces or beheaded by Christian or Jewish fundamentalists during the last ten years?

One of the most damaging consequences of CAIR's practice is the attitude of the leadership of the organization, according to which everyone who is against the jihadists is a Muslim hater by definition. The other dimension of the same practice is that for CAIR every jihadist captured or arrested by the authorities is an innocent victim of American Islamophobia.

One example in this aspect is particularly shocking. Several years ago, an American Muslim convert by the name of Randall "Ismail" Royer who started working for CAIR and traveled to Pakistan on his own to receive military training at one of the camps run by the jihadist organization Lashkar-e-Taiba. By the way, Lashkar was (and still is) closely connected with al-Qaeda and was responsible for the mass murder that took place in the Indian city of Mumbai in 2008. Upon his return, Royer became a ringleader of a group called the Virginia Jihad Network.[21] The group's plans were quite ambitious and ranged from a plot for a chemical attack on the FBI building in Washington to the idea to assassinate the former president of the United States George W. Bush. CAIR not only never condemned the actions and plans of the jihadist cell that started growing in close proximity to the nation's capital, but they did not spare either effort or money to buy the best possible defense for the detained jihadists. The question is how CAIR has the nerve to accuse Americans who do not trust its activities of Islamophobia.

Meanwhile, the jihadists are taking advantage of the most positive features of Muslim tradition, such as the hospitality and the readiness to help a coregionalist in need to ingrain them in the American Muslim community. Their purpose in this regard is very simple: they want all other Americans to see a jihadist every time they are looking at a Muslim.

Besides the Muslims, the second extremely important American target group for the Islamo-totalitarians is the black community in general and black inmates in particular. The conversion of black inmates incarcerated in American prisons acquired an intensity never seen before. Again there is a Saudi-Wahhabi touch in this potentially extremely dangerous endeavor. The financing of the mechanism enabling the large-scale conversion of black inmates to Islam is provided by the National Islamic Prison Foundation. Again using the largely open doors American democracy offers, even to its most dangerous enemies, the jihadists are very often the ones serving the spiritual needs of the Muslim prisoners.

Warith Den Umar, a retired prison chaplain who for twenty years ministered to thousands of inmates and recruited and trained dozens of chaplains, did not mince words while offering his views on Islam and the mass murder committed on 9/11. According to him, the suicidal murderers should be considered martyrs and honored as such.[22] The imam also predicted that the natural candidates who will volunteer to take part in the attack that one day will be launched against America for its "crimes" against Muslims will be black former inmates who converted to Islam while in prison.

The biography of the evidently unpatriotic cleric is quite impressive. Born Wallace Gene Marks, the future imam, according to his own words, "went to jail too many times to count." At the end of the 1960s, the young criminal went to New York City, where he became one of the members of a group that went into the police files as the Harlem Five. In 1971, the group was tried on conspiracy to murder charges. Four of the Harlem Five were successful in beating the charges by arguing that their talk was just bravado. Marks, however, was sent to jail for illegal possession of weapons. As far as the bravado talk was concerned, Marks and his codefendants were discussing a completely innocent subject. The only action the five men were planning was "taking off pigs (police officers) and spreading guns and weapons to people."

Before beginning his two-year prison term, Marks visited the Nation of Islam leader Louis Farrakhan. The meeting ended with Farrakhan's promise that Allah would extend his protection over the convict. Marks became a Nation of Islam leader in prison, and it was there where he changed his name. Shortly after his release in 1975, Warith Den Umar was put on the State of New York's payroll to become one of the first two Muslim chaplains serving the spiritual needs of Muslim inmates. Since 1978, Imam Umar made the mandatory Muslim pilgrimage to Mecca four times. Those trips were paid for by the Saudi government, which covered the expenses of American prison chaplains among the other categories of Muslim pilgrims coming from the United States.

Not incidentally, given that many Muslim chaplains have been hired by Imam Umar, the prison authorities across the state of New York were shocked to hear the content of the comments made by the Muslim chaplains in the immediate aftermath of 9/11. Many of them hailed the mass murder as positive news involving God's punishment on America.The deliberate neglect of the issue of radical Islam in present-day America aggravates the process of the Islamization of a large number of black prisoners. If this neglect continues, one day Imam Umar may turn out to be right in his prediction of the role the cohort of converted inmates will play in the latter stages of the jihadist war against the United States.

What we followed closely was the start of an intense Islamist effort directed at the conversion of black prisoners into Islam. There are no definite answers to some crucial questions. What happens when the new converts leave the prisons' cells? Who is taking care of them? Who is covering the expenses of the former inmates while they are on their own? Is there any centralized handling of them? Finally, how many former convicts and present converts are waiting for their hour to strike?

There are several very dangerous dimensions that mark the present stage of the Islamic assault on the United States. The most damaging among them is the stark contrast between the tiny minority of Americans whose service, efforts, and sacrifice have created the line of defense against the jihadists and the attitudes of all those who do not feel any reason to be worried. The deliberate blindness of the Obama administration to "the clear and present danger," if we have to repeat Tom Clancy's words, is a huge factor that greatly facilitates the enemy's assault and at the same time undermines the resistance to it. The same effect is produced by the state of denial reigning supreme in most of the media and academia. The fact that the United States is the primary target of the jihadist assault makes the country responsible for the preservation of democracy worldwide.

It is time to end this chapter with a short reflection on Geert Wilders's thought that, unlike Europe, America has a little bit more time to prepare itself for the inevitable confrontation with radical Islam. One of the important aspects of the conflict can be expressed by a really simple definition: the Muslim world needs more secularity, while Western civilization needs more faith. Maybe Wilders's observation was determined by the fact that the United States is a far more religious country than any of its European allies. Consequently, this is the reason why, on the eve of the decisive battle with radical Islam, America has a little bit more time at its disposal. What should not be forgotten, however, is that the clock is ticking.

Notes

1. "Former Jihadists Speak Out," in www.aina.org/news/20070427103413.htm.
2. "President Obama's Speech in Cairo," in www.usatoday.com/news/world/2009–06–04-Obama-text_N.htm.
3. "Lamar Smith Wants Eric Holder to Say Radical Islam." www.huffingtonpostcom/2010/05/14/lamar-smith-reallywants_N_576764html.
4. Ibid.
5. "Political Thought and Legacy of Khomeini," http://en.wikipedia.org/wiki.
6. Ibid.
7. See the very informative article of Jonathan D. Halevi, "Al-Qaeda's Intellectual Legacy: New Radical Islamic Thinking Justifying the Genocide of Infidels," *Jerusalem Viewpoints*, no. 508 (December 2003).
8. Nimrod Raphael, "Ayman Muhammad Rabi Al Zawahiri: The Making of an Arch-Terrorist," *Terrorism and Political Violence* 14, no. 4 (Winter 2002), 13.
9. Ibid.
10. Ibid.
11. "Declaration of Jihad against the Americans Occupying the Land of the Two Holy Sanctuaries," http://middleeast.about.com/od/terrorism/a/bin-laden-jihad.html.
12. *CNN.com*, transcript of Bin Laden's interview, February 5, 2002.
13. "Islam in the United States," http://en.wikipedia.org/wiki/Islam_in_the_United_States.
14. Ibid.
15. Ibid.
16. Jasmine Sharif, *Caged in America* (San Diego: Pen & Publish Inc., 2009).
17. Timani, "Islamic Schools in America: Islam's Vehicle to the Future?," www.forumonpublic policy.com/archive06/timanipdf.
18. Jihad Watch, www.jihadwatch.org/2004/01/virginia-jihad-activist-pleads-guilty.html.
19. "Black America, Prisons and Radical Islam," *A Report of the Center for Islamic Pluralism*, Washington DC, London, September 2008.
20. Ibid.
21. Ibid.
22. Ibid.

10

The American-Russian Divide after the Breakup of the Soviet Union

An interesting and somewhat provocative question is the following: was the present-day American-Russian confrontation inevitable? The shortest correct answer to this question is a negative one: because of the influence of factors such as the disappearance of the American enemy from the Cold War era, the downfall of Russian and Eastern European communism, and the gradual buildup of a new political system in Russia, at least theoretically, have opened unprecedented opportunities for a radical change in the area of American-Russian relations. It would be natural to assume that the exploration of the seemingly unreal possibility for an American-Russian alliance involves the analysis of the factors that stimulate or block it. The very start of such analysis would reveal the existence of a powerful negative factor that eliminates even the thought for joint American-Russian action against the jihadist assault on the world. What we are talking about is the failure of the majority of the population of both countries to realize the nature and the magnitude of the danger threatening the very existence of America and Russia alike.

The time factor also has a very negative impact on the possibility for an American-Russian alliance. If we use again Geert Wilders's time-related allegory, if the clock shows midnight in Western Europe and quarter to midnight in the United States, the time in Moscow would be five minutes past midnight. First of all, the Russian clock is ticking quicker because of the demographic catastrophe that ravages the country. Second, the elimination of the legacy and influence of the almost hysterical Russian anti-Americanism and the less powerful but strong enough negative American attitude toward Russia would require new thinking and a search for new approaches on the part of American and Russian policymakers. What should not be ignored or forgotten, however, is that an American-Russian alliance against totalitarian Islam would be possible only in case that the ship of Russian politics does not drift into deeper anti-American currents or, even worse, into some variety of bottomless neo-totalitarian waters.

The Breakup of the Soviet Union, or Who Won the Cold War?

Too many important features of recent Russian developments have shaken the world, and any attempt to guess what the future holds makes their analysis mandatory. To address those features, I have elected to offer my own comments of the observations and opinions of Dr. Stephen F. Cohen. The reason for my choice is very simple: my analysis of the same subject areas tends to differ in almost any meaningful way from Dr. Cohen's. Stephen F. Cohen is a professor of Russian studies and history at New York University and professor of politics emeritus at Princeton University. Undoubtedly, he is one of the leading American experts on Russian, Soviet, and post-Soviet history. Dr. Cohen is the author of numerous books—my favorite among them being his marvelous biography of the predecessor of Mikhail Gorbachev, Nikolai Bukharin, who was murdered by Joseph Stalin, of course.

At the same time, however, I am in a complete disagreement with the explanations provided by Dr. Cohen's interpretations of the most important events in the history of Russia during the last twenty years presented in the interview he gave to the *Columbia Journal of International Affairs* and in one of his articles.[1] This is the reason why, by dissecting point by point Dr. Cohen's main arguments, I hope to be able to present an alternative view on the recent history of Russia.

The most important area of my disagreement with Dr. Cohen was created by his interpretation of the American role in the downfall of Soviet communism and the following breakup of the Soviet Union. According to the aforementioned interpretation, it turned out that the different presidents of the United States have announced the end of the Cold War so often that in the final account in his vain hope to defeat the young but dangerous Democratic opponent, William Jefferson Clinton, President George H. W. Bush declared American victory over the Soviet Union in the Cold War. This theory is so interesting, even fascinating, that it deserves more than a superficial glance.

According to Dr. Cohen,

> Historically, it is very clear how and when it ended. President Reagan declared when he left office in January 1989, "the Cold War is over." That was almost three years before the end of the Soviet Union itself, and he credited himself and Gorbachev. The first President Bush and the Soviet President Gorbachev then declared, at Malta in 1989 and later, that the Cold War had ended and that they were wrapping it up. In 1990–1991, this seemed to be true: Russia essentially sided with the United States in the first Gulf War against Saddam Hussein, and Bush didn't intervene in Eastern Europe when the Berlin Wall came down in 1989. Gorbachev accepted the reunification of Germany. It appeared that the former Cold War rivals were now cooperating in solving major problems, from the Persian Gulf to Berlin.
>
> Then the Soviet Union disappeared, and suddenly Washington essentially proclaimed, "We won the Cold War by defeating the Soviet Union." It was a completely different and untrue narrative. The first person to trot out this nonsense was the first President Bush, who feared losing re-election to Clinton in 1992 and wanted to claim victory for himself in the Cold War.[2]

Dr. Cohen obviously believes that this long explanation covers the details of the end of the Cold War. There is just one major inconvenience, however. If the illustrious professor accepts the premise that one of the only two world superpowers cannot just disappear like snow during a springtime meltdown, then evidently some factor is behind this disappearance, isn't it?

Unlike Dr. Cohen, I think that there was such a factor. It was the foreign policy strategy applied by President Ronald Reagan during the period 1981–1988 with regard to the Soviet Union that inflicted the last deadly blow upon the Soviet economy, the collapse of which precipitated the downfall of the Soviet totalitarian model and the breakup of the Soviet Union. Honesty forces me to admit that this opinion of mine had been formed under the influence of an interpretation I heard back in my native country of Bulgaria as early as 1986 or 1987.

I cannot precisely recall the year, but I very clearly recall the man. I met him at a small bus stop in the depth of the Bulgarian countryside, where I was trying to locate my students sent there to collect the yield of the completely neglected collectivized fields. He was old but still a strong individual, powerfully built close to the ground. His eyes were inflamed, his hands were roughened by manual labor to a degree I have very rarely seen in my life, and his face was covered with snow white two-day-old stubble.

Highly unusually, even for the latest phase of Bulgarian totalitarianism, the old man did not mind discussing politics with a stranger. His formal education had expired somewhere in the lower classes of high school, which he had been forced to leave after his father's death. At the time of our conversation, I was an associate professor of history and political science, which meant that it was me who had to explain politics to the old man rather than the other way around.

When the old but sturdy farmer heard what I was doing for a living, he asked me point blank, how long will communism last? At that time, I was firmly convinced that the Soviet Union, Bulgarian totalitarianism, and the Berlin Wall, of course, would continue their existence after my death, and I told him so. The old man did not accept my pessimistic prognosis. With an iron certainty, he told me,

> Professor (regardless of my objections he continued to upgrade my status), you are wrong! President Reagan (he badly mispronounced his name) had found the right way how to deal with the bastards. By putting more money into the war in Afghanistan (he mispronounced that name as well) and by making America more powerful by giving more money to the military guys, he is forcing the Russians to do the same. There is something else though: the Americans have money and the Russians don't. Remember my words, Professor, the Soviet Union is finished!

With an almost unhidden touch of irony, I asked the old man from where he had obtained such interesting information. His answer was totally unexpected. It turned out that the farmer had followed how much the prices of everything had gone up in Bulgaria since the start of Reagan's presidency, and he deduced that the same development had taken place in the Soviet Union. He reached the conclusion that President Regan had found the best way to strangle the communist system.

Most probably the man died long ago, and this book is the most appropriate place to make public my recognition of the fact that I was on the wrong side of the long-gone debate with him. Yes, the man who did not graduate from high school because he had to replace his deceased father in the fields; the man with the inflamed eyes, rough hands, and two-day-old stubble; the man who mispronounced the names of President Reagan and the country of Afghanistan had an intuitive but much better and deeper understanding of the very mechanism of international politics than me. I often think of what kind of comment Dr. Cohen would have made on the prediction of the Old Bulgarian farmer. Or, given that he was not a Princeton graduate, his opinion would not count?

Speaking of President Reagan's contribution to the end of Soviet and Eastern European totalitarianism, the first issue that comes to mind is to prove it. To start, Ronald Reagan was a deeply religious man and a firm believer in the principles upon which the American political and social system were based. Small wonder then that the Soviet Union was for him an epitome of everything he hated. For the new president of the United States, the communist experiment represented "a sad, bizarre chapter in human history whose last pages are not even written."[3] At the same time, Reagan was an enemy of the policy of so-called detente established by Nixon and Kissinger that had remained unchanged during the mandates of Presidents Ford and Carter. To be more precise, what President Reagan did not like was not the detente itself but rather the Soviet misuse of the term because, according to him, in the eyes of the Kremlin-based rulers, the detente was just "the freedom to pursue whatever policies of subversion, aggression and expansionism they wanted anywhere in the world."[4]

When on June 6, 1982, in the course of his address delivered to the British House of Commons, Reagan expressed the opinion that it was already time for communism to end up in the "garbage can of history," he was completely sincere. So was he while calling the Soviet Union "an empire of evil." Back in 1981, not so much intellectually but rather intuitively, the new president of the United States grasped the reality that all deficiencies of the American approaches applied until that moment with regard to the Soviet Union did not work. As a result of this discovery, Ronald Reagan developed a strategy of his own. The main purpose of the American foreign policy toward the Soviet Union and its Eastern European dependencies became the promotion of long-term changes within the Soviet Union and Eastern Europe.

On one hand, President Reagan was applying a crushing pressure on the fragile Soviet economy by the intensification of military expenditures, which rose from $134 billion in 1980 to $253 billion in 1989.[5] This measure pushed the Soviet defense spending from 22 percent to 27 percent of GDP, while it froze the production of civilian goods at 1980 levels.[6] The massive military aid package rendered by the United States to the Afghan mujahideen and to the Nicaraguan Contras was also depleting even more the inadequate Soviet resources. At the same time, however, Ronald Reagan was ready to talk to the Soviet leaders with regard to finding some ways to avoid a nuclear confrontation between both countries and to reduce huge American and Russian atomic and missile arsenals.

Such a complicated phenomenon as the disappearance from the world scene of a superpower does not allow simplistic explanations involving the strategy or the willpower of one single individual. Without any doubt, huge credit must be given to the Soviet leader Michael Gorbachev for his ability to avoid the nightmarish "Yugoslavian" scenarios during the period of his reforms that against all of his expectations had proven to be deadly for the system he had tried to save. President Reagan would say later that the larger part of the credit for the successful American-Soviet dialogue during the period 1985–1988 must go to Gorbachev.

There can be no objections whatsoever to Dr. Stephen Cohen's opinion that the activities of Mikhail Gorbachev and his associates represented an attempt to "modernize the Soviet Union by dismantling the Stalinist system with the consent of the people and, for the first time, with democracy as the driving force of the modernization process."[7]

Thoughts on the Reforms and the Reformers throughout the History of Russia

From the topic of modernization, Cohen's analysis takes a turn toward the modernizers in Russian history. He defines the "leap" model of reforms imposed from above as a nondemocratic by its nature and quotes the names of Peter the Great and Joseph Stalin as examples. The alternative model had been symbolized by Emperor Alexander II who terminated the factual slave status of the Russian peasants and initiated an array of democratic reforms. To the image of this outstanding reformer, Stephen Cohen added Lenin on the grounds that he had introduced the New Economic Policy (NEP).

The inclusion of Emperor Alexander II and Lenin into the same category did not work for me. They were very different human beings, and, far more importantly, they played completely different roles in the history of Russia. The first one had been called "the Liberator" by his people, while the second one was the founder of the first totalitarian state in world history. Beyond any doubt, Lenin introduced greater changes in Russian history that anyone else. The question is what kind of reforms were they? Did they make Russia freer and more prosperous or just pave the way to the establishment of the murderous Stalinist tyranny?

What is really hard to understand is how Professor Cohen could have named Lenin as a reformer while bypassing such a remarkable statesman as Peter Stolypin, whose reforms had all the potential to transform Russia into a modern and democratic state. By the way, the effectiveness of the Stolypin reforms reached a magnitude that sank Lenin into a deep pessimism about the diminishing chances for the dreamed revolution to occur. It was the murder of Stolypin that brought back Lenin's hopes.

For Alexander Yakovlev, the man whom Gorbachev called "the Philosopher of the Perestroika," Lenin was the organizer of "the October Counterrevolution" that developed in the aftermath of the Bolshevik coup, as opposed to the one and only democratic revolution that took place in February of 1917.[8]

The next area of my strong disagreement with Professor Cohen involves his assessment of the downfall of Soviet totalitarianism and the breakup of the Soviet Union. Let's focus our attention on his following statement:

> For most Western commentators the Soviet breakup was an unambiguously positive turning point in Russian and world history. And it quickly became the defining moment in a new American triumphalism narrative, the hope that Mikhail Gorbachev's pro-Soviet democratic and market reforms of 1985–1991 would succeed was forgotten. Soviet history was now presented as "Russia's seven decades as a rigid and ruthless police state."[9]

This quote leaves the unmistakable impression that the author was unhappy with the downfall of Soviet totalitarianism. By the way, the professor does not use this term, which does not mean that it is not applicable to the Soviet realities. The same quote brings about an uneasy question: how many *more* million people was the Stalinist totalitarianism supposed to kill to justify, in the eyes of Dr. Cohen, the assessment that the Soviet Union was "a rigid and ruthless police state"?

As far as the analysis of the Soviet political system is concerned, I have always wondered why, while trying to describe and explain the complexities of the Soviet history, many American scholars and educators have ignored the opinions of the most accomplished representatives of Russian intelligentsia. Don't they think that the systemic neglect of what the most brilliant minds of the country ruled by the right-wing, communist, or Islamic totalitarianism have to say about the tyranny suffocating their countries makes them ignorant about the realities they

197

are trying to explain? Also, don't they think that such neglect reflects at least a certain amount of intellectual arrogance?

During the first years of Gorbachev's rule, a limited number of trusted advisers and associates of the leader received unlimited access to the most secret archives of the Soviet Union. We owe to the devotion and integrity of Alexander Yakovlev the emergence of a remarkable collection of words and thoughts of the most distinguished representatives of the Russian intelligentsia that the Stalinists had condemned to life without parole in the vaults of their secret archives. For instance, as early as 1934, a group of Soviet writers composed a letter to their foreign colleagues attending the First Congress of the Soviet Writers. A small excerpt from this letter speaks for itself: "Back in your countries you have created different committees designed to save the victims of fascism, you are organizing as well congresses condemning the militarism and the wars, and libraries containing the books burnt by Hitler. . . . Why however are we not able to see any activity of yours designed to save the victims of *our Soviet Fascism* (italics mine), promoted by Stalin?"[10]

It was also during 1934 that the founder of modern physiology, the Nobel Prize–winner Ivan Petrovich Pavlov, sent a letter to the Soviet leadership that contained the following lines: "In vain you believe in the world revolution. . . . What you are sowing is not a revolution but fascism."[11] Knowing Joseph Stalin, maybe the death of Pavlov in 1935 was not accidental.

According to one of the most formidable Soviet scholars and Nobel Prize winners Lev Davidovich Landau, "the system that has been formed after October 1917 was a Fascist one."[12] As far as Lenin was concerned, Landau did not mince his words: "It is beyond any doubt that Lenin was the first fascist."[13]

The words of those remarkable men provide enough reason for the rejection of Cohen's thesis where Lenin is qualified as a reformer and Stalin as a statesman who had successfully performed a revolution from above. There is more to it. It is already time the thoughts and feelings of the leading Russian intellectuals finally find their way into American colleges, universities, and schoolbooks.

The fact that Lenin introduced the New Economic Policy (NEP), which was no more than a maneuver enforced upon the Bolsheviks by the calamity of the civil war and the complete devastation of every sphere of the social and economic life of the country, does not make him a reformer of the rank of Alexander II, who was murdered, by the way, by revolutionary socialists who were Lenin's predecessors.

According to Stephen Cohen, "Joseph Stalin overthrew NEP in 1929 for an economic leap he later termed, rightly in my view, 'Revolution from Above.'"[14] In my opinion, however, this term is deeply wrong. The correct description of the actions of Joseph Stalin would be "*Counterrevolution* (italics mine) from Above." The main ingredient of the social aspect of this counterrevolution was the complete reversal of the reforms of Emperor Alexander II by the restoration of the slave status of the peasants, depriving them of ownership of the land and herding them onto the much-hated and miserable collective farms. In addition, by not issuing them so-called internal passports, the supreme master of the Soviet Union made the escape of the hungry residents of the collective farms even more difficult than any attempt by black slaves to leave the plantations of the Deep South.

Even more, in June of 1940, Joseph Stalin managed to impose slave status upon the labor force in the city areas as well. According to the Stalinist rules, no worker had the right to leave his working place, while at the same time the state had acquired "the right" to send him wherever it considered necessary. There was more to it: even the slightest delay by the worker to report to his working place, for instance, because of a transportation bottleneck, became a crime punishable by sending the unfortunate worker to some deadly gulag camp. It was an "accomplishment" that even the cruelest Russian czars had been unable to match. But in all fairness to them, they had never tried.

There were many similarities between Michael Gorbachev and Boris Yeltsin.[15] Both of them shared a modest social background in addition to the fierce ambition to make a career by using the powerful elevator of party membership. Both of them were strong and sincere believers in the communist ideology. During the last stages of their respective careers, when Gorbachev was the supreme party leader and Yeltsin was the head of Moscow's party organization, both of them developed worldviews of their own. As far as their mentality and actions were concerned, however, both statesmen differed as night and day.

They were very different, even by their appearances. When he wanted to, Gorbachev looked like a mild intellectual, while Yeltsin looked like a foreman from a construction site. Gorbachev had a facial expression that was subject to change, depending on the message its owner wanted to present to the outside world, while Yeltsin belonged to a type very rare among politicians that could be described as "what you look is what you get." Boris Yeltsin also bore a physical resemblance to Emperor Alexander III, who ruled Russia between 1881 and 1894.

Both statesmen emanated the familiar and much-exploited image of a powerful and tenacious Russian bear intensely staring at the world from behind the bars of the cage separating the endless vistas of the largest country in the world from the rest of it. While Gorbachev had managed to make his way to the top of the Soviet nomenclature by hiding his true thoughts and feelings behind the aforementioned facial mask, I believe that what protected Yeltsin during the long and dangerous road to the totalitarian heights was his look of an occasionally heavy-drinking construction foreman.

Speaking of this look, it had not just been produced by the acting talent of an apparatchik trying to present himself as "a man of the people." As it turned out, Boris Yeltsin was a graduate of Ural Polytechnic Institute, majoring in construction, who during his first year of work was successful in mastering twelve construction skills, such as stonemason, carpenter, glazier, and so on. Why had the young man volunteered for qualifications no one had required from him? Well, simply because he was immediately offered a foreman's position at the site of his first job—an offer he would only accept after mastering all the skills of the people whose supervisor he was about to be.

When the era of reforms finally arrived in Russia, Gorbachev had rejected the murderous practice of Stalinism but not the totalitarian ideology of Leninism, while Yeltsin had rejected both. Gorbachev had the illusion that a totalitarian system could be made more human, while Yeltsin felt that the old structure had to be completely removed and replaced by a brand-new one. And when it came to their ability to act under pressure and danger, the difference between both Russian statesmen was staggering as well. To make the long story of the August 1991 putsch short, even a person with a very fertile imagination would not be able to picture Gorbachev addressing a riotous crowd while standing on a tank the way Yeltsin did.

Dr. Stephen Cohen was right, at least in the first part of his following observation: "After the Soviet Union ended in 1991, Yeltsin continued Gorbachev's democratization in some respects but his policies resulted in the beginning of Russia's de-democratization, which in the United States is usually, and incorrectly, attributed to his successor, Putin."[16]

It is an indisputable fact that, similarly to Gorbachev, Yeltsin also was influenced by the mentality of the Soviet nomenclature.[17] There were many moments when he displayed autocratic features in his leadership. There were as well many mistakes he committed, the most serious one being the privatization of the economy. At the same time, there was much more freedom of the press and of the political life in Russia under

Yeltsin than under Putin. Yeltsin was able to tolerate even the most vicious verbal attacks of his opponents—a quality Putin does not have.

The fact that all "republics" of the Soviet Union followed the precedent provided by Lithuania that had chosen the path of the independence, had proven Yeltsin to be right, and Gorbachev wrong. It was the main reason why the political career of Gorbachev ended with the dissolution of the Soviet Union, while Boris Yeltsin became the first president of new Russia.

Unlike the case with Gorbachev, Yeltsin's agenda had been firmly set: the gradual transformation of Russia into a democratic state by establishing close relations with the West in general and with the United States in particular. At the same time, Boris Yeltsin left such a complicated legacy that only future historians will be able to decipher and evaluate it. On one hand, he was undoubtedly a democrat who sincerely wanted to see Russia as a free and prosperous country. On the other hand, however, on many occasions, Yeltsin displayed an autocratic style in the process of transforming his ideas into reality.

An important feature separating Yeltsin from Gorbachev is that the first president of Russia thrived under pressure, but he was often sloppy about following a daily routine. Gorbachev was able to handle the rigors of an intense schedule, but his willpower was often inadequate when facing a critical situation. Too many of Boris Yeltsin's decisions were wrong. The biggest failures occurred in the process of the privatization of the Russian economy, and, as a result, the social fabrics of Russian society were torn apart during the First Chechen War.

On the other hand, Boris Yeltsin was successful in preventing the very real danger of possible installment of neo-fascist dictatorship born out from a combination of the inveterate Communists led by Zyuganov and the motley crowd attracted by the neo-Fascist and anti-Semitic harangues of Jirinovsky. Basic democratic freedoms were preserved, freedom of speech and the press became a reality, and the archives of the seventy-year-old totalitarian regime were opened. But Boris Yeltsin's ambitious program to not just terminate Russia's isolation but to make the country a part of the emerging democratic global community did not become a reality. It was not his fault, however.

The Popular Appeal of Russian Anti-Americanism

The intensity and popular appeal of anti-Americanism in contemporary Russia represent the most serious obstacle for the establishment of an American-Russian alliance. There can be little doubt that the level of anti-Americanism in Russia is high and growing. One of the seemingly paradoxical facts involving this issue is the contradiction between the largely positive image of America during the times of Soviet totalitarianism and the intensely negative image of the United States decades after the fall of communism. A closer following of the dynamics of the Russian attitudes toward the United States will reveal that it was the presidency of Boris Yeltsin that provided the starting point for the development of postcommunist Russian anti-Americanism.

To start, the economic measures designed to introduce the basic components of a free-market economy in Russia not only did not produce the expected effect but deepened the social crisis in the country. In addition, the hastily performed privatization on the eve of the presidential elections in 1996 brought drastic social inequities by creating a small group of super-rich oligarchs for whom the laws did not apply as opposed to the impoverished majority of the population. The reason for this damaging hurry-up was that Yeltsin's team was in desperate need of money for a very challenging 1996 election campaign.

The social background of postcommunist Russian anti-Americanism was created by the confusion of some key political and economic terms that had acquired completely different meanings within the context of the Russian realities. For the average Russian citizen, for instance, one of the most beautiful and dreamed about words, "democracy," at the end of the 1990s had acquired the meaning of a combination of chaos, demagoguery, and corruption. The term "free market," on the other hand, meant cutthroat Darwinian-style competition where the most arrogant and best-connected criminals played the role of the new capitalistic elite. The influx of too many American components of the Western lifestyle, such as fast-food chains, a huge variety of different products, and Hollywood movies, did not help in improving the American image in the eyes of the Russians.

From a political point of view, the first new Russian negativities with regard to the United States involved the different attitudes of both countries toward the crisis ravaging the former Yugoslavia, particularly the NATO bombing of Serbia in the aftermath of the ethnic cleansing performed by Milosevic's regime against the Albanian population of Kosovo. The historical and cultural tradition connecting the Russians and Serbs as opposed to the bombings managed to alienate even Boris Yeltsin from his previous pro-American stand.

Considering all those developments, one can only be amazed that as late as 2002 slightly more than half of the participants in one of the polls expressed a very or somewhat favorable view of the United States. The situation abruptly changed in the aftermath of the Iraq War. According to the data from a poll conducted by the most prestigious Russian polling organization—the Russian initials are FOM (Public Opinion Foundation)—only 3.6 percent of the participants gave a "certainly yes" answer to the question "Is the US a friendly country?" The answer "certainly not" was provided by 18.3 percent of the participants. Of those who provided a more definite answer, on average 40 percent of the respondents liked the United States while 60 percent did not.

There is a touch of complexity, though, provided by the answers given by respondents to the question "In your opinion, today, which society is more just and fair—Russian or Western?" Only 6.8 percent of the respondents expressed the most categorical opinion that Russian society is fairer to its citizens. All in all, 23.4 percent of the respondents believed in the moral advantage of Russian society over the Western one, while the opposite opinion had been expressed by 47.4 percent of them.[18]

The distribution of those answers along the lines of the age of the participants provided enough serious reasons for pessimism to anyone who is interested in the development of better relations between the United States and Russia. As the polls showed, the representatives of the younger generation of Russians were more hostile to the United States than the older respondents. The reason is that in the last ten years in particular, the undoubtedly much freer Russian media, compared to its Soviet-era predecessors, has been demonstrating the same amount of hostility toward the United States. A very important component of this hostility is the staggering ignorance of the average Russian with regard to many essential features of American considerations and actions. In strange contradiction to the Soviet era, when the same average Russian knew much more about the United States than the average American knew about Russia, today the previous interest has been replaced by indifference and an arrogance born out of ignorance.

As a matter of fact, the ignorance in question is a deliberate one. I have explored thousands of e-mail comments by Russian readers on articles offered to their attention by a site exploring the content of media outlets that analyze international politics. My conclusion is that too many Russian consumers of information that was hidden from them during the totalitarian times are approaching the news and comments of the international media with an already existing attitude that cannot be changed, even by the most convincing facts that contradict it.

A large numbers of Russians, for instance, sincerely believe that American occupational authorities are in complete control of the Iraqi oil deposits and that the United States is profiting from the sales of Iraqi oil. Very few Russians know that the armed forces of the United States have invested a lot of time, effort, and financial resources in the development of infrastructure or in the creation of water and electricity-producing facilities or that they are developing educational services and facilities in Iraq and Afghanistan.

Many Russian consumers of the international news are also familiar with the fact that while under the Taliban regime the production of opium had been forbidden, but now, with the presence of a large American force in the country, the poppy-growing business is thriving. This correct fact, however, leads many users of the site in question to a wrong conclusion, the essence of which is easy to predict: they are firmly convinced that the CIA and the American armed forces have turned a blind eye to this issue and, according to some comments, even profited from it. Some of the comments are filled with a satisfaction for having discovered one of the darkest American secrets: that is why the poppy-growing business started to thrive again.

It does not matter to those readers that many experts and journalists have provided details of a completely different picture. It was the Taliban that encouraged and protected the production of the poisonous and murderous plants they banned while in power. The change of heart, so to speak, took place because it helped to finance their guerilla war against the United States and their allies to the tune of $400 million per year, which they collect from the poppy growers in the rural areas they dominate.[19]

I have been tempted as well to make a comparative analysis of the comments of the Russian Internet users to the American-related articles, and vice versa, the American reaction to Russian-related subjects. The most revealing difference was that I did not find *one single* American comment containing an offensive name for Russians. But the Russian comments are filled with offensive language that very often contains unprintable words designed to replace the word "American."

At the same time, the attitude of the average Russian toward the regime established in Russia during the presidency of Vladimir Putin and preserved under his premiership and the presidency of Dmitri Medvedev, at least for a long period of time, was extremely positive.

The mixture offered by this regime that appealed so much to the majority of Russian people represents a cocktail of authoritarianism and better living for many Russians. In a way, "the Putinism" reminds one of the "Goulash" brands of socialism practiced by the " mild" Hungarian dictator ,Yanosh Kadar, who managed to compensate the lack of freedom with a higher standard of living compared to the rest of the totalitarian countries of Eastern Europe.

There are serious differences between both models, to be sure. On one hand, the current political system of Russia is early capitalistic, partially authoritarian, but at the same time contains at least some components of a representative democracy. The large popularity of Putin is connected with the fact that his regime was successful in putting an end to the misery and uncertainties of the Yeltsin era and provided at least a substantial part of the city dwellers, including the new middle class created against the background of the increased oil revenues, with the opportunity to have plenty of food, normal services, limitless access to the Western sources of information (including the Internet options), and, very importantly, the opportunity to travel and vacation abroad.

While the demographic meltdown continues to reduce the number of Slavic and Russian components in the population, life in the rural areas remains the same for the elderly people who primarily remained there, and there is a significant number of city residents who could be considered poor. There is another dark side to Russia's current situation that involves a huge danger lurking beneath the glitz of Moscow and Saint Petersburg, but for the time being it remains invisible for many Russians, who are still enjoying the best lives they have ever had since the coming of the Bolsheviks to power a century ago.

The Strange Geopolitics of Russian Anti-Americanism

Before talking about contemporary Russian geopolitics, it is necessary to make one point abundantly clear: the current political system of Russia is still in its formative years. For the time being, it looks like a corporation run by former KGB officers who are encouraging and controlling the capitalistic development of the country. Unlike China, the main Russian decision makers have accepted the introduction of some important democratic components. In a way, Russia is currently situated on a highly unusual no man's land between freedom and non-freedom, between capitalism and some form of socialism, and, finally, between democracy and some form of neo-totalitarianism. As far as the current foreign policy of Russia is concerned, its anti-American aspect is expressed in Moscow's readiness to establish and develop closer relations with every country that fully or partially shares the Putin regime's attitude toward the United States.

As a result of the contradictions between Russia and the United States, such as the eastward expansion of NATO and the issues of Kosovo, Ukraine, and Georgia, just to name a few, the Russian leadership decided to answer American actions with similar moves in different areas. Case in point, the creation of an independent Albanian-dominated state in Kosovo was countered by Russian support for separatist forces in American-friendly Georgia. According to Father Jakov Krotov, who is one of the best Russian religious and political writers,

> The Russian militarism behaves like an adolescent who during a game of chess is repeating the moves of his adversary with the hope to reach at least a draw at the end of the game. The question is: if he manages to take out several of his enemies' pawns, can we say that he will win the game? No, he won't. The experienced chess player will easily outsmart an adversary who is confronting him with symmetrical moves.[20]

Russia's Western European strategy proposes to take advantage of every sign of tension or misunderstanding between Washington and its NATO partners. Eastern Europe continues to be regarded in Moscow as an area of legitimate Russian interests. Unfortunately, there is no leading principle based on the premise to locate the main danger threatening the very existence of the country and the Russian nation and what could have been the most beneficial partnership in the long run. True, there is an ongoing attempt for the creation of a geopolitical concept that could serve as a basis for the practical realization of the most important goals. Unfortunately, the current Russian flirtation with geopolitics is producing a completely wrong picture that within a short period of time could inflict irreparable damage to the national interests of Russia.

The leading geo-politician of the current Russian regime is Alexander Dugin. Born into the family of a high-ranking Soviet intelligence officer, Dugin started his studies at the Moscow Aviation Institute but later became a journalist. In 1988, in the middle of Gorbachev's perestroika, Dugin joined the ultra-nationalist group Pamiat. While many of the educated Russians at that time were dreaming about democratic Russia, which according them was due to emerge from the rubbles of communism, the future geopolitician of Putin's Russia had sunk into a completely different reverie. In short, during that time, Dugin was nothing short of a totalitarian in general and an ardent Nazi sympathizer in particular.

In 1997, the future leading foreign policy strategist of Russia wrote an article under the title "Fascism—Borderless and Red." According to the enthusiastic author, "The excesses of this ideology in Germany are a matter exclusively of the Germans, while Russian fascism is a combination of natural conservatism with a passionate desire for true changes."[21] Dugin expressed his particular admiration for the "Scientific Department of SS" and for one of the architects of the Holocaust, Reinhardt Heidrich.[22]

In the admiring eyes of Alexander Dugin, the accomplished SS murderer was the role model for all those who, like Dugin, see world politics as an eternal struggle between the Eurasianists (the residents of the European and Asian landmass) and the Atlantists who encompass the population of the countries connected with the legacy of "maritime oriented civilizations." According to Dugin, the conflict between the representatives of both categories ravages Russia as well. To not insult the intelligence of the readers, I will not go any deeper inside the murky waters of Dugin's conspiracy theories and theosophical revelations. It is enough to say that, according to the famous Russian strategist, Nikita Khrushchev was an agent of the Atlantists.

It would be much more interesting to turn to Dugin's concepts involving radical Islam. According to him, there is no threat whatsoever emanating from radical Islam. He believes everything is amazingly simple:

> With the existence of the Islamist or fundamentalist danger the leaders of NATO are justifying the existence of the alliance. The same argument is one of the most important ones within the political and strategic relations of the West with Russia. What West wants from Russia is to play the role of a barrier in front of this invented evil. This concept is just a smoke curtain behind which the West is conducting its real and much more sophisticated strategic operations that have for [their] purpose . . . the conflict between potential allies within the camp of the rivals in order to eliminate them one by one.[23]

Let's try to summarize this stunning concept: according to Dugin, there is no danger whatsoever emanating from radical Islam, and the purpose of the evil West is just to eliminate the opportunity for the establishment of a close relationship between Russia and the Muslim world. The premise involving an evil Western conspiracy against Russia is deeply wrong, of course, but Dugin is entitled to his opinion.

The issue is very different, however, when he is trying to conduct a political analysis of the problems of the Islamic world. According to the man whom many observers are convinced has the ear of Putin himself, "Saudi based Wahhabism extremism in combination with the totalitarian rule of the oil sheikhs, is an absolute ally of the Atlantic West, and is also the most reliable bastion of the United States in the countries of the Middle East and in the Islamic world."[24]

If we follow Dugin's questionable logic, the calamity of 9/11 was caused by the representatives of "the bastion of the United States in the Middle East." The Russian expert has expressed his theory about the Shia version of radical Islam along the following lines:

> From a geopolitical point of view we have every reason to consider the pro-Iranian, Shia-Soufist trends within contemporary Islam as "Eurasian" and "continental." As a rule they have a common denominator—a radical negative attitude toward the West and the Atlantism, sacred hatred toward technocratic, materialistic and the atheistic civilizations of the rich North, considered to be The Great Satan.[25]

Undoubtedly, there is some truth in the aforementioned statement, but an extremely important component of the pro-Iranian Shia version of radical Islam is missing. Dugin failed to analyze the anti-Christian aspect of the ideology that inspires the Iranian theocratic totalitarians. Besides that, the Russian theoretician considers the different versions of the Arab socialism propagated by the Ba'ath parties of Iraq and Syria, for instance, as a third separate variety of Islam. This is simply nonsense. Everyone with even the most superficial knowledge and understanding of Islam-related problems knows very well that the parties and movements inspired by the Ba'athist ideology were secular.

Strictly secular was the regime of President Nasser of Egypt as well, wrongly considered by Dugin as an example of the fourth separate branch of Islam. So was the political system of Turkey based upon the very secular doctrine of Kemalism and consequently there is no way to be defined as "educational Islam," the way Alexander Dugin does that.[26] It is absurd, of course, to divide Islam into "pro-Eurasian" and "pro-Atlantist" branches. The purpose of this book, however, is not to analyze the wrong image Dugin has about Islam. My purpose was to point out the danger for Russia in case his geopolitical prescriptions are transformed into a political strategy, regardless of their absurdity.

What is at the core of Dugin's geopolitical dreams is the assumption that the United States of America is the eternal enemy of Russia. Realizing the economic and military potential of America, he recommends the re-creation of the main line of the Nazi axis, Berlin and Tokyo, with the addition of Russia and Iran into this coalition. The primary purpose of the Russian foreign policy should become the restoration not just of the Soviet Union but also the reenactment of the relationship that existed between the Soviet Union and its Eastern European dependencies. The "Eurasian" coalition of Alexander Dugin proposes to reach some kind of agreement with certain branches of Islam that will help the "Eurasians" in their conflict with the "Atlantists."

Judging by some recent actions of Russian diplomacy, Dugin's advice has not remained unheard. The practical realization of the occasionally confusing and almost always confused geopolitical concepts of Alexander Dugin does not appear to be a complicated matter. A strategy designed to deepen the rift between Eurasian Europe and the Atlantist America, in addition to the improvement of the relations of Russia with every regime that is hostile to the United States, from Iran all the way to Venezuela, looks quite appealing to some Russian policymakers. But they had better think twice because this policy will bring a real catastrophe to their country.

A thoughtful Russian leadership would have several very serious reasons for pessimism given that too many of Dugin's geopolitical prescriptions are transformed into permanent and consistent foreign-policy actions. To start, and illogically at first sight, every important success achieved through following the anti-American strategy so intensely recommended by Dugin will bring about very serious negative consequences for Russia.

Let's follow the scenario where the growing unpopularity of the Afghan War produces a Vietnam-style American withdrawal from Afghanistan. Considering that radical Islam already has some positions in the former Muslim republics of the Soviet Union, with Taliban support the jihadists will establish themselves along the almost 2,000-mile border between Russia and its Central Asian Muslim neighbors.

Dugin's dream about an anti-American axis of Moscow-Tehran will remain unrealized. Because of his lack of understanding of radical Islam, Dugin is not able to master the simplest truth that no non-Muslim country has any chance of receiving the support of the mullahs. Such an axis will become a possibility only in case of the Islamization of Russia. To grasp all the implications of this consideration, I strongly recommend that Dugin gets acquainted with the entire background of the letter that Ayatollah Khomeini wrote to Gorbachev. It was the first personal message sent by the misanthropic cleric to a foreign country's head of state. On January 3, 1988, Ayatollah Abdullah Jvadi Amoli landed with his precious cargo at Moscow's airport. What he was carrying was a very special message from his supreme leader that ended with these words: "I claim that the Islamic Republic of Iran, as greatest base for Islam, can help you to solve the problem of religiosity and anyway we believe in having relationship and respect it."[27]

This part of the letter written by the totalitarian and theocratic ruler of Iran inevitably leads to an interesting conclusion: the Iranian leader was not interested in either economic or political relations with the important neighboring country. The *only* reason for Khomeini's letter was the prospect for a possible Islamization of Russia. One is tempted to ask Dugin what the source is for his certitude that the present rulers of Iran will be interested in establishing not just trade and economic relations with Russia but becoming a Russian ally? Does he seriously believe that in case of an American withdrawal from the Middle East under the aforementioned scenario that instead of encouraging the spread of the Shia version of Islam in the vacuum created in Central Asia, Tehran will stay idle because of its "alliance" with Moscow? Besides, if Russia openly sides with Tehran, wouldn't it damage its connections with the members of the European Union and with the Arab world that are not enchanted with the prospects of an atomic Iran?

In the case of a reappearance of a new version of American isolationism, the massive and increasing stream of "guest workers," consisting primarily of young people from Central Asian countries, to the main metropolitan areas of Russia considered against the background of the long and easily penetrable border area between the countries they have come from could provide a perfect opportunity for jihadists to hit straight in the heart of the country.

The process involving the growing Islamization of Turkey would intensify its pace, which inevitably will have powerful influence over the jihadist activities in the area of Caucasus. A circumstance that by no means should be forgotten is that the disproportion between the birthrate of the Muslim and Slavic components of the population of Russia in near future will produce a fifty-fifty ratio between the Muslim and Slavic recruits of the Russian Army.

On the other hand, regardless of the recent acquisition of Crimea, Russia has neither the human nor the material resources to accomplish a new conquest of the Soviet era" republics" ,and the former totalitarian dependencies of Eastern Europe in keeping with the visions of Alexander Dugin. This is the reason why President Putin is afraid of an all -out conflict with the West. The depopulation of the Russian Far East that borders some of the most overpopulated areas of China also does not leave much room for expansionist excursions throughout Eastern Europe along the lines of the invasions in Hungary in 1956 and Czechoslovakia circa 1968.

Such conquest will not take place, and it would be so much better if all Russian policymakers gave up forever the dangerous pipe dream of their most prominent geo-politician. There is another "soft" version of the appearance of a Russian-led group of Eastern European states that in a way will be considered a new version of the Russian Empire. What we are talking about is the creation of some kind of close economic and political connections between Russia and Eastern Europe. Such an idea has been raised by the chairman of the Russian Duma's committee on the issues of economy and the enterprise, Evgeny Fedorov. I think that under certain set of circumstances such a union could make its appearance. The most probable contributing factors for that would be a termination of the active role the United States is playing in the world and the intensification of the Islamization of Western Europe.

Notes

1. "Rethinking Russia: US-Russian Relations in an Age of American Triumphalism," interview with Stephen F. Cohen, *Columbia Journal of International Affairs* 63, no. 2, (Spring/Summer 2010), 191–205.
2. Ibid.
3. "The Collapse of the Soviet Union and Ronald Reagan," http://wais.stanford.edu/History/history_ussrandreagan.htm.
4. Ibid.
5. Ibid.
6. Cohen, "Rethinking Russia: US-Russian Relations in an Age of American Triumphalism."
7. Ibid.
8. Alexander Yakovlev, *The Twilight* (Sofia, Bulgaria: Hristo Botev Publishing House, 2005), 131.
9. Stephen Cohen, "The Breakup of the Soviet Union Ended Russia's March to Democracy," *The Guardian*, December 13, 2006.
10. Yakovlev, *The Twilight*, 133.
11. Ibid., 134.

12. Ibid.
13. Ibid.
14. Cohen, "Rethinking Russia: US-Russian Relations in an Age of American Triumphalism."
15. Yakovlev, *The Twilight*, 503–563.
16. Cohen, "Rethinking Russia: US-Russian Relations in an Age of American Triumphalism."
17. A substantial part of the comparative analysis of both leaders was based on the following books: Mikhail Gorbachev, *Life and Reforms*, 2 vols. (Moscow: Novosti, 1995) and *On My Country and the World* (New York: Columbia University Press, 2000).

    Boris Yeltsin, *Against the Grains: An Autobiography* (New York Simon and Schuster, 1990) and *The Struggle for Russia* (Times Books, 1994). An excellent biography of Yeltsin is Timothy Colton, *Yeltsin: A Life* (Basic Books, 2008).
18. Sergei Guriev, Maxim Trudolyubov, and Aleh Tsyvinski, "Russian Attitudes toward the West," *Centre for Economic and Financial Research at New Economic School*, Working Paper No. 135, December 2008, 6.
19. Ahmed Rashid, *Descent into Chaos: The United States and the Failure of Nation Building in Pakistan, Afghanistan and Central Asia* (New York: Viking, 2010), 117–138.
20. Jakov Krotov, "The Asymmetry of Peace," www.librev.com/component/content/article/328.
21. Andreas Umland, "Will United Russia Become a Fascist Party?" *Turkish Daily News*, Tuesday, April 16, 2008.
22. A. Dugin, "Islam against Islam," www.arctogaia.com/public/dug7.htm.
23. Ibid.
24. Ibid.
25. Ibid.
26. Ibid.
27. "Imam Khomeini's Letter to Gorbachev," www.tebyan.net/Islam_Features/Prophet/Articles/2005/1/2/26776.html.

Epilogue

The most serious obstacle blocking the creation of an effective security system to protect the world from the assault of radical Islam is the lack of realization of the nature and magnitude of the Islamo-totalitarian threat. As far as the United States and Russia, unlike the case with the Nazi danger, neither the ideology nor the actions of the Islamo-totalitarian forces have been addressed by the leading policymakers of either country in the depth that the dangerous phenomenon deserves.

Starting with the American side of the equation, the danger stemming from the ideology and strategy of radical Islam was not able to reach a level where it became an issue addressed by the contenders for the presidency during the 2008 elections. The junior senator from Illinois, Barack Obama, became the president of the United States without making clear his position on the challenges of radical Islam. Beyond any doubt, Barack Obama is an immensely talented orator and natural-born campaigner that arguably made him one of the very best in the history of the United States. Yet he never mentioned radical Islam.

It is reasonable to imagine how the idea of offering a brand-new American approach looked tempting to the new president. The purpose of President Obama's huge propaganda campaign at the beginning of his term was designed to produce a radical change in the world's perception of the United States. Developed against the background of the public relations calamity marking the presidency of his predecessor, George W. Bush, President Obama's campaign turned out to be a stunning success. As a result, the image of the United States dramatically improved throughout most of the world. The people were delighted to see a seemingly sophisticated, young, and dynamic leader promising peace instead of war, mutual respect instead of conflict, and negotiations instead of confrontations.

In some regions, the popularity of the United States and particularly the appeal of its new president skyrocketed. The most positive reaction to his personality and ideas came from Germany.

Evidently, it is too early to try to pass any final judgment on Obama's presidency. At the same time, the concept and the execution of his foreign policy in general and his attitude with regard to the Muslim world and radical Islam in particular offer enough room for analysis.

From the very beginning, however, we have to separate the term "Muslim religion" from "radical Islam" because the second term does not exist for the president. He cannot, or does not want to, comprehend the link between the Muslim religion and the political movement of radical Islam. It is because of this denial that the Islamo-totalitarian challenge the world is facing represents the main problem for the Obama administration.

The essence of the problem is the ban imposed on the usage of the term "radical Islam" at every level within the government and the military bureaucracy. It is an imposed taboo for which no one can offer an explanation. In all fairness, not many individuals have expressed a curiosity about that taboo. Feeling the magnitude of the public indifference with regard to the danger emanating from radical Islam, Obama administration never developed a strategy designed to counter the threat emanating from Jihadism. The big question of course is why?

At least theoretically, the immense and growing Muslim world occupies an important place within the planning and execution of American foreign policy under President Obama. Unfortunately, this approach is based on a deeply wrong premise that there is no connection whatsoever between the religion of Islam and its contemporary political dimension that provides the ground for the ideology, organization, and strategy of the jihadists.

In one of his unjustifiably ignored statements involving Islam, Obama expressed the opinion that there is no more beautiful sound on earth than the call for the early morning prayer that comes at dawn from every mosque in the world. At the same time, the president is convinced that there is no connection whatsoever between the Muslim religion and the political dimensions of Islam. His answer to the question "Who are the enemies?" in the War on Terror is rather simple; it turns out that America is fighting a war against "extremists."

Consequently, given that the main enemy of the United States remains deliberately unidentified at the whim of the president, the country has never developed an effective strategy with regard to radical Islam. The reason that such a disastrous blindness is able to exist and to persist at the very top of the American political pyramid is crystal clear; the jihadist-related danger does not exist either for

President Obama or for his carefully selected associates such as his secretaries of state Hillary Clinton and John Kerry or his attorney general, Eric Holder.

Some people are raising objections to the logic of this analysis along the lines of the argument that the war the current administration is waging in Afghanistan shows how seriously the president is looking at the conflict with radical Islam. The representatives of the same category point out that the murder of some prominent jihadists (including bin Laden) in Pakistan, Afghanistan, and Yemen, conveniently forgetting the much larger number of innocent civilians that the military bureaucracy coin "collateral damage," is important proof of the anti-jihadist activities of the administration.

President Obama personally expressed a positive opinion of his own actions when he assured Americans of the groundbreaking importance of the assassination of Osama bin Laden. In all fairness to Obama, he mentioned the opportunity for organizations sharing the ideology of al-Qaeda to continue their terrorist activities. What the president failed to say during his press conference in August of 2013, in an "update" of his earlier statements, was that the Islamo-totalitarian forces were not only eliminated or broken down after the assassination of their iconic leader but, rather, have stepped up their activities worldwide.

The main mistake made by the politically correct supporters of President Obama involves the fact that they are confusing the meaning of the terms "strategy" and "tactics." Yes, it is true that the president is the supreme commander of the American military forces fighting the jihadists. Yes, a lot of credit must go to Obama for approving the high-risk operation that claimed the life of Osama bin Laden. In the great picture of the American conflict with radical Islam, however, those achievements look more like improvised tactical responses to a powerful strategic challenge. Neither the magnitude nor the nature of the Obama administration's response is able to match that challenge.

The beginning of 2011 brought about the most serious challenge to President Obama in the Middle East. The so-called Arab Spring was greeted with wild enthusiasm by a large segment of the American media. To say the least, the whirlwind of optimistic expectations for the future of the most important country of the Arab world turned out to be groundless.

The gigantic explosion of public outcry over the autocratic rule of President Mubarak, instead of bringing about more freedom, led to the consolidation and expansion of the influence of the Muslim Brotherhood. It was a time when American diplomacy needed to have a firmly established step-by-step strategy. In the absence of such an approach, the uncontrollable situation continued to escalate.

The first problem appeared in the early part of 2011 when mass demonstrations broke out. As always, the lack of strategy produced not previously agreed upon nor well-coordinated actions supported by clear-cut statements. The biggest confusion erupted when the White House and the Department of State had to decide whether to support or to abandon President Mubarak—the man who had strictly discharged all of his responsibilities by maintaining peace with Israel and protecting American interests.

The decision of the Obama administration to throw President Mubarak under the bus was a fatal mistake. In addition, American diplomacy did not have any constructive approach to support the aspirations of the Egyptian people for democracy. During a decisive moment in the history of Egypt, Secretary of State Hillary Clinton declared that the United States considered the Muslim Brotherhood a legitimate participant in the political process. This downright stupid decision was completely opposed to the interests of the United States, Israel, and the people of Egypt.

Let's follow the mechanism of this fateful decision at close range. The Department of State announcement came in July of 2011, when Secretary Clinton's Department of State issued a declaration recognizing the rights of the Muslim Brotherhood as a completely legitimate political organization. In addition, the Department of State expressed its readiness to establish political contacts with the Brotherhood whenever necessary for the advancement of the democratic process.

Theoretically speaking, Secretary Clinton had every right to establish a closer cooperation with the best-organized political force of Egypt regardless of all bans and restrictions imposed upon the Brotherhood by the authoritarian regime of President Mubarak. It sounds quite convincing. Unfortunately, Clinton's decision to show US friendship to the Muslim Brotherhood constitutes one of the most serious mistakes (among the many) committed by Secretary Clinton.

Well before July 2011, when the pro-Brotherhood decision had been made by the Department of State, an important statement by the organization should have attracted the attention of the American policymakers. It was in May 2011 (two months *before* the decision was approved by Secretary Clinton), when the leadership of the Brotherhood made an important decision: "neither a Copt nor a woman could be President of Egypt."[1]

All the Department of State had to do was issue a declaration making it abundantly clear that the United States would respect the right of the people of Egypt to choose a government of its liking. At the same time, however, the same statement should have left no doubt that Washington would not offer any form of assistance to a tyrannical government that is ready to violate the human rights and political freedom of women and minorities.

If President Obama and Hillary Clinton had done that, the United States would not have had to face the problems they are encountering today, not to mention the high probability that the secular candidate General Ahmed Shafiq could have been the winner of the 2011 elections held in Egypt. Instead, the American recognition of the Muslim Brotherhood was perceived in Egypt as open support from the Obama administration to the Islamists, and that brought the candidate of the Brotherhood, Mohammed Morsi, to power.

Once in power, Morsi's very first step, without too much noise, was to transform into reality his intent to achieve the permanent supremacy of the Brotherhood over Egypt. In the meantime, a new round of conflict broke out in Gaza. The new leader of Egypt tightened the knot of the cord that President Obama had placed around his own wrists by his unconditional support for Morsi. On the one hand, the president of Egypt sent his prime minister, Hesham Qandi, to Gaza right in the middle of the bloody duel between Hamas's missiles and Israeli bombings to unleash a series of highly provocative speeches encouraging the continuation of Hamas's attacks on Israel.

On the other hand, Morsi was playing a game with President Obama that was designed to create the impression that he, the leader of Egypt, was the only politician in the world who could convince Hamas to accept a peaceful alternative to the bloodshed in Gaza. It was Morsi's idea to have Obama send Secretary of State Clinton to Cairo all the way from distant Burma. Upon reaching the Egyptian capital, the jet-lagged secretary of state was happy to hear Morsi's assurances that Hamas was ready to stop shooting missiles into Israel.

The inexperience of the untested American president showed itself in Egypt, where Obama managed to perform an almost impossible achievement by creating the impression among the traditionally anti-American Brotherhood members that he is an enemy of the Islamic world while at the same time, in the eyes of the Egyptian military and civil secularists, that he is a firm supporter of the Muslim Brotherhood. It was this strange phenomenon that produced the recent powerful outbreak of anti-Americanism in Egypt.

Another stunning development that was completely ignored by the American media is the dramatic mismanagement by President Obama and the former secretary of state Clinton of the US policy with regard to Turkey—a very important player in an area where too many strategic interests are involved. Turkey has been a strong American ally ever since the time of the Truman Doctrine, which was adopted back in 1947 to offer US protection at a time when the country was threatened by postwar Stalinist expansionism.

For decades, Turkey was run along the lines of a secular pattern established back in 1923 by the founder of the Turkish Republic, Kemal Ataturk. The creator of contemporary Turkey wanted to see the medieval dream of a global Islamic caliphate replaced by a secular and pro-Western state. The materialization of his vision made the country the only Muslim state that without being fully democratic, if we apply the highest standards, in many respects contained most components of a functioning democracy.

This situation started to change in a rather dramatic way after the election in 2003 that brought to power the Islamist-oriented Party of Justice and Development. The Turkish prime minister, Tayyip Erdogan, the former mayor of Istanbul who was briefly imprisoned for pro-Islamic activity, turned out to be a gifted politician who contributed immensely to the substantial growth of the Turkish economy.

At the same time, Erdogan is a hard-core Islamist and loyal follower of Fethullah Gulen and is involved in the slow-paced, creeping Islamization of Turkey. The most stunning achievement by Erdogan was the success of his strategy to portray an important step toward the transformation of Turkey into an Islamic state as an expansion of Turkish democracy.

The explanation of this strange, at first glance, phenomenon is not complicated at all. It was Kemal Ataturk who attached a prominent political role to the armed forces of the country. In other words, the founding father of the modern and secular Turkey had decided that the army should play the role of guarantor of the secular political system.

Contemporary Turkey possesses a large pool of educated and well-trained professionals. What is certain is that the vast majority of them do not want to live in a country dominated by jihadists. On the other hand, however, they do not want the officer corps of the Turkish Army to have the final say in determining the political future of the county.

Consequently, by creating real hysteria about the real and alleged conspiracies unified under the name "Ergenekon," the Islamists, led by Erdogan, are presenting the imprisonment or forcible retirement of many generals and hundreds of officers as a deed entirely designed to protect the civil freedoms of the country. What definitely does not fit the protection of the civil freedoms in Turkey is the arrest and imprisonment of around eighty Turkish journalists and an unknown number of young students and political activists in the aftermath of the outbreak of protests that recently shook the largest cities of the country.

Similar to the shameful events of 2009, when the United States was one of the very few countries that remained silent while the blood of young protesters was shed on the streets and squares of Tehran, the conspiracy of silence surrounding the Obama-Clinton tandem was and still is in full force. Neither the provocative behavior of Turkey with regard to the relationship with Israel, which had been deliberately damaged by Erdogan, nor the Islamist connection of the Turkish prime minister to Hamas and the Muslim brotherhood in Egypt was able to influence in any way the conduct of the deeply wrong policy of the US administration toward the country. Last but not least, the connection of Erdogan with the Syrian jihadists (who, by the way, are condemned by more than 80 percent of Turks according to recent polls) did not attract the attention of the American media.

Notwithstanding all those factors, President Obama had rated Tayyip Erdogan among his five best friends while the former secretary of state, Hillary Clinton, constantly mentioned Turkey as one of the best allies the United States ever had.

The political philosophy and politics of President Obama do not leave room for any doubt that the current administration does not understand, or pretends not to understand, the nature and the magnitude of the Islamo-totalitarian threat. The feeling of acute danger that would force the president and the team around him to start looking for allies does not exist. If you do not feel that your country is threatened, what would prompt you to start looking for allies?

* * *

If the United States is the "Big Satan" for Islamists, then Russia is the "Little Satan." Out of the same politically correct considerations, so well familiar to President Obama, the Russian autocratic leader Vladimir Putin also prefers not to "rock the Islamic boat" too much. On the other hand, however, he dares to use terms such as "radical Islam" and "jihadism." As far as the Islamo-totalitarian danger hanging over the vastness of Russia is concerned, the country is in more peril than the United States.

Although considered finished, the Chechen conflict is not yet history, and there is an endemic Islamic terrorist activity in the areas of Chechnya and Dagestan. In addition, although the Russian leadership recognized the autonomy of Tatarstan long ago and the area seems to be calm, the problems persist there as well. The dynamics of the Wahhabite penetration and the expansion of the influence of radical Islam among the nationalistic Tartar youth are eliminating any guarantee that this calm will continue in the future.

There is no better expert on this issue than the Muslim theologian Farad Salman, a former mufti of Tatarstan, who is currently the leader of the nongovernment organization Center for Research of the Koran and the Sunni. Fortunately, Farad Salman is not a man who minces his words. Consequently, it would be worthwhile to listen to what he has to say on this issue: "There is no salafist, (radical Islamic) underground in Tatarstan because it is completely integrated with the official religious power."[2]

Internationally, Russia acquired the unique status of an observer during the sessions of the Conference of the Islamic States. This situation created a very dangerous illusion in the minds of some Russian policymakers. The essence of this illusion comes down to the idea that good relations with the Muslim states, particularly with Turkey and Iran, will in the long run help to solve the jihadist-related problems of Russia. Another aspect of the same illusion is that such a relationship will weaken the American influence in the Middle East and the Caucasus.

The previously mentioned Alexander Dugin, who has both a passion for geopolitics and a certain influence in political circles, has gone a step further by suggesting a direct alliance between Russia and Iran. Dugin sees in the face of the mullahs very effective allies in his anti-American crusade. Undoubtedly, such recommendations would have been wholeheartedly supported by Obergruppenfüehrer SS and the Reich protector of the Nazi "Protectorate" of Bohemia and Moravia, Reinhardt Heidrich. Because of his "Euroasianism," the Nazi murderer was one of Dugin's former role models during his younger years. The problem is that I do not think that the ideas of Obergruppenfüehrer SS Heidrich and his Russian student could serve the national interests of Russia. Just the other way around, following those recommendations would constitute a mortal danger for the future of the country.

There are some very strong arguments in favor of such an opinion. To start, Dugin should read very carefully the letter Khomeini sent to Gorbachev twenty years ago. This letter is very important because it marked the beginning of a distinctive Islamo-totalitarian strategy with regard to Russia. The strategy in question is very different from the one applied toward the United States. In the Russian case, the jihadists are trying to win the critically important country to their side. Well, there is one condition for the launching of the Islamo-Russian alliance: Russia must become a Muslim country. What must be remembered is that Khomeini's letter was *only the first step* in suggesting the voluntary Islamization of Russia.

In 2003, when President Vladimir Putin was invited to the tenth session of the Conference of the Islamic States that took place in Kuala Lumpur, the prime minister of Malaysia, Mahathir Mohammed, directly addressed the Russian statesman along these lines:

> The population of the Islamic world is rapidly growing, but it suffers from cultural and intellectual deficiency. What the Islamic world is missing is a developed country capable of assuming the position of leadership. The Islamic world needs a country with a white population and *Russia could become such a country.*
>
> Russia should accept Islam in order to make the entire world start trembling again at the thought of the Russian nuclear arsenal. In those days the West doesn't take this arsenal seriously, being afraid only of the chance that the Muslims could obtain access to this arsenal. In case Russia decides to adopt Islam however, this entire arsenal will become Muslim property, and the main enemy of the Muslim world (Israel) will be wiped out with a couple of strikes. Then the entire world will find itself fallen under the feet of Russia (italics mine).[3]

If we start applying the logic of the Malaysian politician, we could reach the conclusion that the Muslims will be even happier if the United States becomes a Muslim country.

For the time being, there is not a chance for the United States to receive such a generous offer. The issue here is that if Russia follows Mahathir Mohammed's advice, it will not be Russia anymore. I do not believe that the Russian people will accept such an offer. Consequently, the search for a powerful ally facing the same danger sooner or later could logically create the conditions for the emergence of an American-Russian coalition directed against the expansion of radical Islam

What should be added to this point, however, is the undeniable fact that the American-Russian alliance could become a reality only in the realization of the worst-possible scenario (involving, for instance, a steady development that in the long run will bring about an almost complete Islamization of large tracts of Europe). Any development short of that will preserve the seemingly unbreakable ice between America and Russia.

The analysis of the Russian side of the current rift between Moscow and Washington is a relatively easy matter because the Russian political scene is not very complicated as far as foreign policy is concerned. Without any doubt, there are no voices expressing opinions different from the foreign-policy concepts of Putin. The Russian president was the man who had decided to place the United States in the unenviable spot of enemy number one of his country.

True, there was a period of time of relative improvement in bilateral relations during the short time of Medvedev, who warmed the bench of the presidency for Putin for four years. It was not long enough or strong enough to produce a substantial change for the better in the relationship between both countries. With the return of Putin to the presidency in 2012, the cold wind started blowing again over the capitals of both countries.

By the way, it would be incorrect to accuse President Putin of some kind of hysterical and permanent anti-Americanism. What should not be forgotten is that Vladimir Putin was the first foreign statesman who expressed his condolences to President Bush in the immediate aftermath of 9/11. He was also extremely helpful during the initial phase of the Afghan war, which in 2001 ended the domination of the Taliban over the country.

Later, however, things changed for the worse. Because of the Iraq War, the Balkan imbroglio around Kosovo, and the conflict in Georgia, the United States and Russia found themselves on different sides of the political divide in all those areas.

The current political moment, with American-Russian contradictions running so high, seems to be absolutely inappropriate to even mention the possibility for a better option for improvement in the relationship between both countries. Meanwhile, in full keeping with the tough laws of geopolitics, the communality of interests is producing opportunities that exist regardless of the ability of the policymakers to take advantage of them.

Ironically, the opportunities that are waiting to be seen by Washington and Moscow involve two of the areas ravaged by the roughest conflicts where Russia and the United States are heavily involved with the opposing parties. In contrast to the stupid theories of Alexander Dugin, an area of common US and Russian interests covers the embattled land of Afghanistan.

The possible re-Talibanization of Afghanistan in the aftermath of an American withdrawal from the Afghan battlefield in 2014 will have a devastating impact on the global strategic position and prestige of the United States. To start, and looking through the lens of American experts, nothing could prevent the unification of the Pashtu-populated areas of Afghanistan and Pakistan into an extremely large, uncontrolled, and uncontrollable territory offering its hospitality to the Islamic global terrorist network.

Looking at the same picture from Moscow, the most disturbing effect of a potential American defeat in Afghanistan would be the dramatic increase of the flow of narcotics into Russia through the unprotected borders of Afghanistan into Tajikistan and Kirgizstan, and from there into Russia. Even more disturbing for the Russian policymakers would be the spread of the influence of radical Islam throughout Central Asia, which will establish an extremely long, vulnerable, and dangerous southern Russian border.

Consequently, neither the United States nor Russia is interested in the transformation of Afghanistan into an area threatening, in the most serious way, both countries. Will this communality of political and geopolitical interests be able to generate a joint strategy? It remains to be seen, of course.

It was the Syrian conflict, however, that became the most aggravating recent factor that had a tremendous impact on American-Russian relations. The different roads taken by the presidents of both countries with regard to the civil war ravaging Syria led to an even deeper divide between Moscow and Washington.

The early stage of the outbreak of the conflict between President Assad's army and the motley coalition of enemies of his authoritarian regime was marked by the presence of individuals and organizations running across the entire political spectrum. The indignation caused by the corruption and repression practiced by the authoritarian regime of the Assad dynasty in addition to the powerful impact of the so-called Arab Spring contributed to the outbreak of the conflict. Gradually, however, the situation started changing, and with the arrival of thousands of jihadists, the radical Islamists got an upper hand among the enemies of the Assad regime.

The same fact added an even sharper dimension to the conflict because in some strange way it expanded the social base of the Assad regime. The explanation of this strange, at first glance, phenomenon involves the fanaticism of the jihadists. The Alawite component of the Arab population, the Christians, and many Kurds (who, by the way, are burning in nationalist fever instead of a religious one) have been turned into enemies of radical Islam.

If we try to make an honest comparison between the American and Russian attitudes with regard to the Syrian situation, the first huge difference between them is that the Russian politics in the region is based on a strictly followed strategy while the American actions are performed on the spur of the moment. Even the quickest and most superficial look at Russian actions with regard to Syria will convince the observer that those actions are based on logic and a strategy established well in advance.

Starting with the main premise, Russia was and is interested in preserving Syria in its capacity as an old ally since the Soviet times and in addition providing the Russian Navy with its only base in the Mediterranean region. President Putin, however, has a second strategic consideration that is maybe more important than the first one; given the Islamic guerilla campaign in the Caucasus or a terror activity in Moscow, Putin is trying to have at least normal relations with Iran. He needs this normalcy so as not to enlarge Russia's war with radical Islam by adding the Shia-inspired jihadists to the ranks of the Sunni-Wahhabi enemies of his country.

In short, a victory for the jihadists in Syria would substantially deteriorate Russia's strategic position in the eastern Mediterranean and will increase the Islamic guerilla and terror campaign within the borders of Russia. In his capacity as the president of Russia, Vladimir Putin was trying to prevent this from happening, and to reach his goal he selected to embark on the prevention of a jihadist victory in Syria.

The United States, on the other hand, did not have a strategy in the Syrian conflict. The Obama administration gave some indication that the president did not want a victory for the jihadists in Syria. On the other hand, however, the American intelligence operatives, in close cooperation with their Turkish counterparts, working for the pro-Islamist prime minister of Turkey, Erdogan, were involved in the dubious and severely underreported activities in the area of the Turkish-Syrian border. There are persistent rumors involving the delivery of weaponry and supplies to the jihadists.

By the way, Prime Minister Erdogan, the usually brilliant performer, committed a huge mistake by involving himself with the Islamic enemies of his recent friend, President Bashar Assad of Syria. There were three factors he badly miscalculated. The first mistake stemmed from the conviction that Bashar Assad will be the next victim of the Arab Spring. The second failure was caused by his former ally Assad, who wisely withdrew his troops from the Kurdish-populated areas, which caused a confrontation between the Kurds and the jihadists. Finally, Erdogan never imagined how strongly his Syrian strategy would be condemned at home. According to Turkish polls taken in 2012, the disapproval of his actions in Syria reached over 80 percent.

* * *

The relatively stable, although cold and hostile, pattern of American-Russian relations that has emerged as a result of the Syrian crisis suddenly acquired a brand-new and dangerous turn in August of 2013. Secretary of State John Kerry made a strong accusation that Assad's regime had used chemical weapons against his own people. It sounded more like a declaration of war against Syria. This act by the US secretary of state placed President Obama in a rather awkward position. Given the reluctance of the American public to render its support for a new war in the Middle East, the president is supposed to order some kind of punitive action against Syria without declaring war on the country.

On August 27, 2013, the White House issued a declaration that the strikes against Syria will be for the purpose of removing President Assad from power. This presents a reasonable and legitimate question: what then is the purpose of the strikes?

Wasn't Syria punished enough by the brutal war that killed 100,000 people, ravaged the country, and transformed almost one-tenth of its population into a crowd of destitute refugees? If the strikes were designed to be symbolic and bloodless, what was the sense of launching them? What if the regime suffered some kind of breakdown that could precipitate a snowball effect in bringing down all elements of law and order similar to the situation that happened in Libya? Isn't the Obama administration risking far greater negative consequences if the chemical weapons end up in the hands of the jihadists?

The issue has another dimension too. What will happen if Syria and Hezbollah attack Israel? What will the United States do if encountered by a powerful campaign of murders and kidnappings of American citizens all over the world? Wouldn't it have been far better if the president had decided to wait for a few days while the UN inspectors completed their investigation at the sites where the chemical weapons had been used?

Small wonder that, as far as the United States' and Russia's politics during the August 2013 crisis is concerned, both countries are in opposite corners of the Syrian ring. Even a relatively minor step, such as the creation of a joint American and Russian team of experts on chemical weapons was not considered by either side.

The entire hysteria and the readiness of the White House to plunge the United States into an unpredictable and extremely dangerous military adventure have an additional problem; the main enemy of world freedom is radical Islam, whose adherents could extract huge advantages from the Syrian situation. The important development involving Obama's decision to obtain congressional approval before taking any action was an encouraging step. What will be his next action?

When President Obama is ready to listen to the assessment of someone who, unlike him, knows both radical Islam and the Middle East well enough, he should pay some attention to the warning issued by the director of Israeli Military Intelligence (AMAN), Major-General Aviv Kochavi, who in July of 2013 expressed the following opinion: "Syria now attracts thousands of global Jihad activists and Muslim extremists from the region and around the world, who base themselves in the country, not only to bring down Assad, but to promote the vision of a state based on Islamic law."[4]

Particularly useful for the president could be the straight warning issued by General Kochavi: "Before our very eyes, at our very doorstep, a large-scale center of the global jihad is developing, which may affect not only Syria and not just the borders of Israel, but Lebanon, Jordan, Sinai, and can radiate onto the entire region."[5]

Considering the inevitable appearance of "a large-scale center of the global jihad" that in the near future could easily encompass a large tract of the territory of Pakistan and Afghanistan, what is happening today in Syria could tomorrow look to us as a deviation from a much larger and far more dangerous conflict.

* * *

Much more serious deviation from the growing and approaching hurricane of blind, fanatical and cruel Islamic barbarism threatening the very survival of the United States and Russia is the current Ukraine related confrontation between both countries. It is obvious that the main reason for the conflict in Ukraine is President Putin's strategy designed to destabilize every not- NATO affiliated country bordering Russia.

At the same time what is also perfectly clear is the fact that opposite to the opinion expressed by Hillary Clinton, Vladimir Putin is very different kind of politician if compared to Adolph Hitler. It is highly unlikely that Putin will expand Russian aggression. As pointed out, regardless of unprecedented but temporary magnitude of public support the Russian president is currently enjoying in his country, Russia doesn't have either the resources or the desire for an all- out confrontation with the West. Given that not only West needs normal relations with Russia, but Russia also needs normality in its relations with Europe or America. Without underestimating the serious challenge presented by Ukrainian crisis, it is too early to look forward the second edition of the Cold War.

Meanwhile similarly to an incontrollable cancerous growth, radical Islam will continue to metastasize. Then one of the most important questions will be whether the nature and the magnitude of the Islamo-totalitarian danger will be able to force the United States and Russia to change their negative perceptions about each other and the politics toward each other. Or maybe it will be too late.

Notes

1. Khan Web, The Muslim Brotherhood Official English Website, May 11, 2011.
2. "Radical Islam in Tatarstan: Is the Application of Force the only Solution?" Publication of the Institute of Religion and Policy, Moscow, http://i-r-p.ru/page/stream-event/index-26694.html.
3. "An Islamic Russia—Myth or Reality," Caucasian Diary, Georgia, www.inosmi.ru/russia/20100911/162824069-print .html.
4. Robert Spenser, "What Is Wrong with Going into Syria" http://frontpagmag.com/2013/robert-spencer.
5. Ibid.

Index